IMAGES
of America

SULLIVAN COUNTY

On the cover: Cherry Mills was one of two mills located on the Little Loyalsock Creek that was once a stopping place on the Susquehanna and Tioga Turnpike. Built about 1846, the gristmill was located three miles from Dushore (Route 87) and was first owned by a Mr. Coganhogan before the Civil War. He sold out to Benjamin Sylvara, who, after a year, sold the mills to Charles S. Sick in 1866. In turn, Sick sold the operations and property to his brother Joseph. The gristmill was a 20-horsepower operation and sat between the brothers' residences; a sawmill sat farther downstream at the mouth of Lick Creek. After selling the mill, Sick became postmaster at the Cherry Mills post office. Although the land has changed hands several times since and is now a bed-and-breakfast, the name Cherry Mills has remained to this day. (Courtesy of Sullivan County Historical Society and Museum.)

IMAGES
of America

SULLIVAN COUNTY

C. J. Hatch with the Sullivan County
Historical Society and Museum

ARCADIA
PUBLISHING

ISBN 978-0-7385-6231-5

Published by Arcadia Publishing
Charleston, South Carolina

Printed in the United States of America

Library of Congress Control Number: 2008933326

For all general information contact Arcadia Publishing at:
Telephone 843-853-2070
Fax 843-853-0044
E-mail sales@arcadiapublishing.com
For customer service and orders:
Toll-Free 1-888-313-2665

Visit us on the Internet at www.arcadiapublishing.com

Dedicated to local residents of Sullivan County;
to the memory of Vernon and Florence (Fawcett) Hatch;
and Joseph and Flora (Monfee) Gregg.

Contents

Acknowledgments

The Sullivan County Historical Society would like to thank the Pennsylvania Historical and Museum Commission (PHMC) and the Sullivan County commissioners for their support in this project. Their funding helps with projects such as this and other community events.

Many thanks to the following for their memories, insights, and help: Burton Adams, Dale Bedford, Joan Blank, Bonnie Boyles, Ruth Carpenter, Grace and Carl Cott, Gene Day, John Edkin, J. Wilson Ferguson, Winifred Ferguson, Gary Fiester, Warren Fiester, David J. Gephart II, Richard Gleockner, Darwin Hatch, Phil Herman, Richard L. Holcombe, Doris Hugo, Charles Hunter, Robert Jackson, Gwen Klus, Jo and Jerome Lane, Kenneth Lee, Katherine Leljedal, Ferdinand Marek, Lois Morgan Norton, Bill O'Reilly, Jake and Dottie Pardoe, John Peterman, Joan Pond, LaVerne and Janice Rinker, Ruth Rode, Carol Roinick, Joyce Hatch Ross, Joseph and Diane Roupp, Carol St. Clair, Doris Pewterbaugh Shrimp, Nancy Spencer, Doris McCarty Whiteley Stephens, Robert Sweeney, Joe Taber, Mary Tennant, Sondra Burgess Thomas, Irene Tubach, Ann Waldron, Fairy M. Walters, Leslie and Louise Molyneux Woodhead, and anyone whom I unintentionally did not mention. Thanks also go out to others who contributed much to this publication but who wish to remain anonymous.

And a special thank-you to Erin Vosgien and Arcadia Publishing for your time and patience with this project.

The Sullivan County Historical Society and Museum continually strives to preserve this area's history. Origins for the society began in 1932 with incorporation in 1938. Presented here is a small segment of our county's history from both private and public collections. Unless otherwise noted, the images in this volume appear courtesy of the Sullivan County Historical Society and Museum.

INTRODUCTION

From 1792 until 1814, Pennsylvania law decreed that land could be purchased at 6¾¢ an acre with the cost of a warrant and survey added. Even though the law stipulated that only 400 acres could be sold to any one individual, some buyers evaded it by buying under multiple family names. The state did not survey the land first but sold it and then issued warrants for surveying. This is how a few capitalists purchased vast tracts of thousands of acres of land in Pennsylvania, a tiny part of which became Sullivan County.

Sullivan County is in the part of Pennsylvania that Charles II of England granted to William Penn, land that Connecticut had previously claimed. The Decree of Trenton (1782) resolved this dispute and granted Penn heirs all land up to 42 degrees north latitude. Penn divided the area into three counties: Chester, Bucks, and Northumberland, with the first white settler arriving less than 20 years after the Fort Stanwyx treaty (1768). In 1796, Lycoming County was established.

In 1820, George Lewis, Edward J. Eldred, William King, and William Molyneux, with Joseph Priestley Jr. assisting, made an attempt to organize a county. It was to be called Lewis County with Mount Lewis (now Eagles Mere) the county seat. But this did not succeed.

In 1847, Charles C. Sullivan, a senator from the Butler district in western Pennsylvania, took an active part in procuring the passage of a bill erecting parts of Lycoming County into forming Sullivan County. The most prominent argument for the formation of this new county was the long distance to Williamsport, the seat of Lycoming County. After the formation of Sullivan County, disputes arose between landowners in different townships about where to place the county seat. Three different commissions were named to settle these disputes. The first commission chose the Center (Laporte), but a second commission moved the seat to Cherry Hill (near Dushore) in 1849. A third commission returned the location to the Center in 1850. Then the township and borough were named for John Laporte, onetime surveyor general of Pennsylvania. As a means to end the dispute, Michael Meylert donated a portion of his land located in the center of the county and provided funds for building the first courthouse.

Industries such as farming, lumber and logging, coal mining, and tanneries attracted European immigrants. For instance, the Susquehanna and Tioga Turnpike was mostly built by Germans; the canal building of the 1830s across Pennsylvania was completed mostly by Irish; and coal mining was done by eastern Europeans; however, English colonists constituted the major population in Sullivan County. The turnpike, Wallis Path, and the Genesee Road (old Towanda Path) were the three main roads cut through the county.

Sullivan County is located between the divide of the North Branch and West Branch of the Susquehanna River, covering 434 square miles or 277,760 acres, and lies between 41 and

42 degrees north latitude and is one-half degree from the longitude of Washington, D.C. The headwaters of the Big Loyalsock are at the boundaries of Sullivan and Wyoming Counties with the Little Loyalsock beginning in Cherry Township. Both creeks come together at the Forks (Forksville) and lose the designations of "big" and "little"; from there down to its confluence with the Susquehanna River, the creek is simply called the Loyalsock Creek. The name Loyalsock was derived from the Lenape Indian word *la-wi-sa-quik*, meaning "the middle creek" between the Muncy and Lycoming Creeks.

The headwaters of the Muncy and Fishing Creeks are in the southern part of the county. Muncy Creek empties into the West Branch at Muncy, and Fishing Creek empties into the North Branch near Bloomsburg. Pleasant Stream (Fox Township) empties into Lycoming Creek above Williamsport. The Mehoopany Creek cuts through the north part of Colley Township.

In the early part of the 1790s, much of the land comprising the county was part of a 200,000-acre tract purchased by the Asylum Land Company, a venture to bring in French royalists who escaped the French Revolution. This tract covered what are now Sullivan, Bradford, Luzerne, and Lycoming Counties. This swath consisted of 100,000 acres located along the Loyalsock Creek. Land agent Charles Felix Rui Boulogne explored this area until his death by drowning in the Loyalsock at what is now present-day Hillsgrove. The Asylum Land Company endeavor failed after the French Revolution ended and most of the royalists returned to their home country.

Samuel Wallis of Muncy (Lycoming County) and Joseph Priestley, the discoverer of oxygen, purchased much of the land that later formed the county. The purchase was made from the commonwealth that had purchased the land from the Penn family. After Priestley's death, his son Joseph Priestley Jr. and John Vaughn purchased more land from Wallis. William Molyneux, Powell Bird, and John Warren were part of Priestley's surveying party in 1794 and founded the Millview settlement upstream of the Forks of the Little Loyalsock. In the same year, Charles Walstoncraft bought the rest of Wallis's land and sold 10,217 acres in what is now Shrewsbury Township to Lewis, a speculator from New York City.

Western Sullivan County was settled mostly by the English, Germans, and Irish. Methodist missionaries visited this area as early as 1798. A Friends meetinghouse was erected at Eldredsville in 1805. Mainly Lutheran and Roman Catholic organizations were formed in the eastern half of the county, and later, the German Reformed, Evangelical, and other denominations came in.

Lumbering is probably the largest industry today, along with some coal mining, manufacturing, and farming. Sullivan County is better known for its scenic beauty, streams, and hunting, which make tourism a major industry.

One

Cherry Township

Cherry Township was organized at the May session of the court of quarter sessions of Lycoming County in 1824. It was formed from Shrewsbury Township and comprised all of what are now Cherry Township, Dushore Borough, Colley Township, and a portion of Laporte Township. The first settler in Cherry Township was Amos Ellis in 1816. In 1818, Andrew Shiner built a sawmill on Birch Creek and settled at Shinersville (now Sugar Hill). On July 4, 1819, local settlers gathered at the home of Ezra Payne where a tall liberty pole was raised and the stars and stripes unfurled. Since the pole they raised was said to be of cherry, they called the hill where Payne and Freeman Fairchild had built their homes Cherry Hill. Perhaps this suggested the name for the township. Cherry Township lies in the northern part of Sullivan County with Bradford County to the north, Colley Township to the east, Laporte Township to the southwest, and Forks Township to the west.

What is now Dushore was first permanently settled by John Mosier in 1825 after he bought this land and moved from Shinersville. First called Mosier Hollow or Jackson Hollow, Dushore was named for Aristide Dupetit Thouars, one of the French who arrived in 1794 and settled at the French settlement of Azilum along the Susquehanna River near what is known as Frenchtown (Bradford County). He was given land (accounts indicate 20, 300, or 400 acres) where Dushore is now located and cleared and farmed it until word came that Napoleon Bonaparte wanted the royalists to return to France. Being a French naval officer, he reentered the service. He was killed at the age of 38 in the battle of the Nile where Lord Nelson defeated the French fleet in 1798.

The name Duthouars was anglicized to Dushore for easier pronunciation.

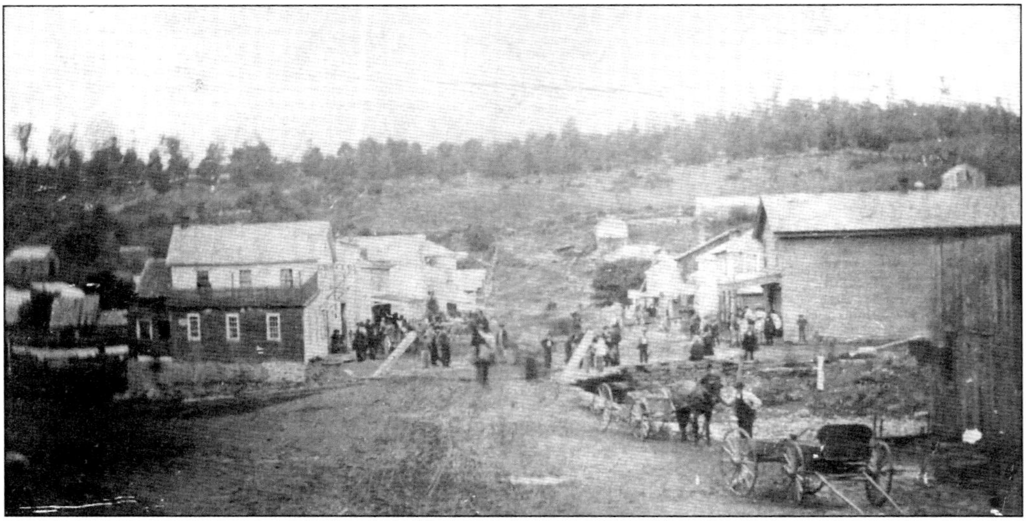

This section of the old Susquehanna and Tioga Turnpike, or Main Street in Dushore, led in front of Samuel Jackson's store (first on the right, after the creek) and a blacksmith shop (first on the left). Frenchman's Spring was at the end of the street (left) before starting up Mosier Hill. The creek (foreground) is the Little Loyalsock. The absence of St. Basil's Catholic Church (right, background) dates this photograph before 1860.

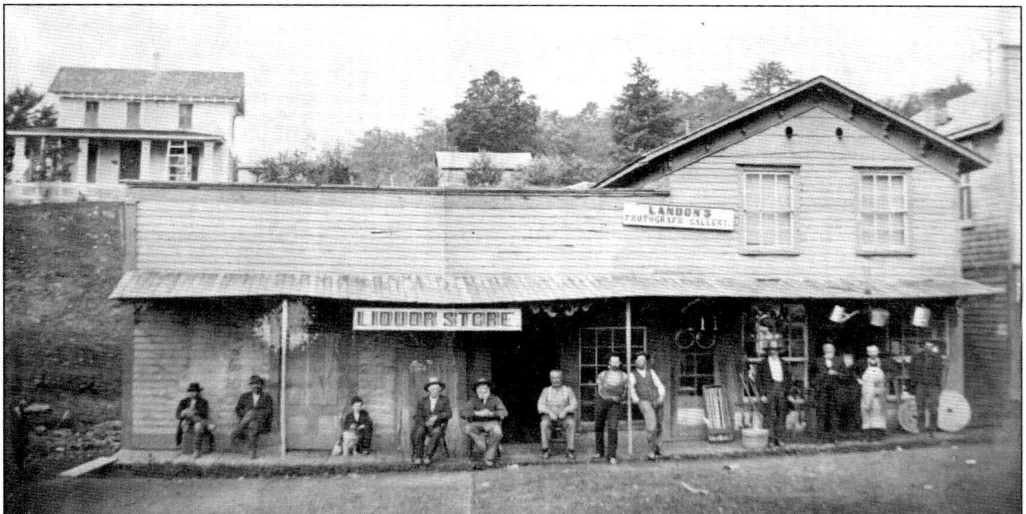

Landon's Photography Gallery and Liquor Store sat along the old turnpike in Dushore. Pictured from left to right are Sol Mosier, Bill Cook, George Deegan (boy with dog), Cornelius Donahue, Myron Wilcox, Henry Heisz, Daniel Pealer, Bill Fairchild, Freeman Thrasher, Amos Reeser, James Cunningham, and Cyrus Connors. The unwalled Little Loyalsock Creek ran behind the building (left). The old Cronin home (top) is still a private residence.

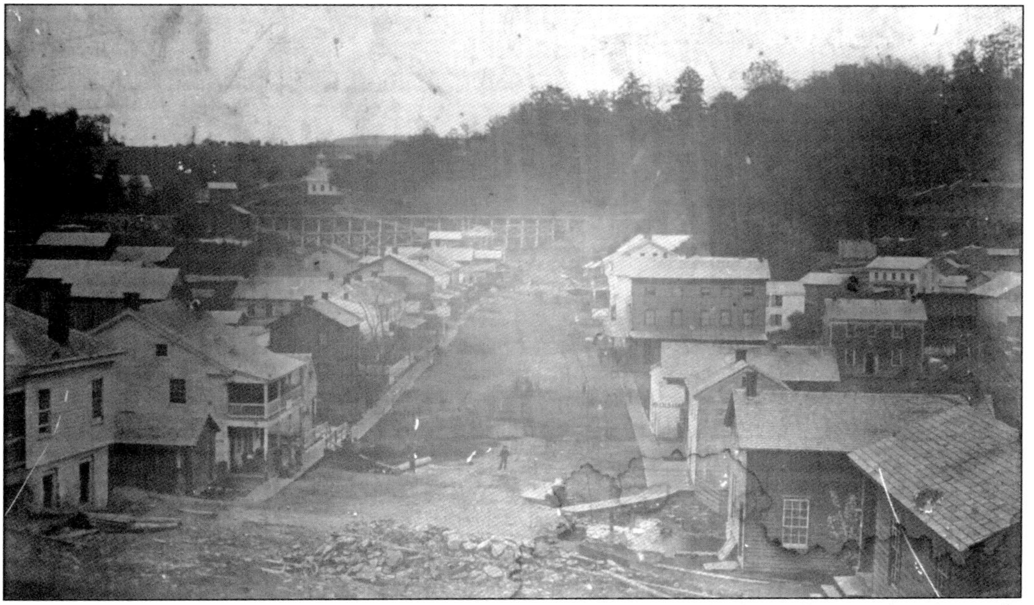

This view of Dushore, early 1870s, looks east toward the Lehigh Valley Railroad trestle (background). The New Methodist Church (background, above the trestle) was eventually used as storage for Cole Hardware before it was torn down. Joan Pond's grandparents and great-grandparents (Albert and Ethel Hoag and Robert and Sarah Hoag) lived on the hill (back, right) above the trestle that was rebuilt in 1872.

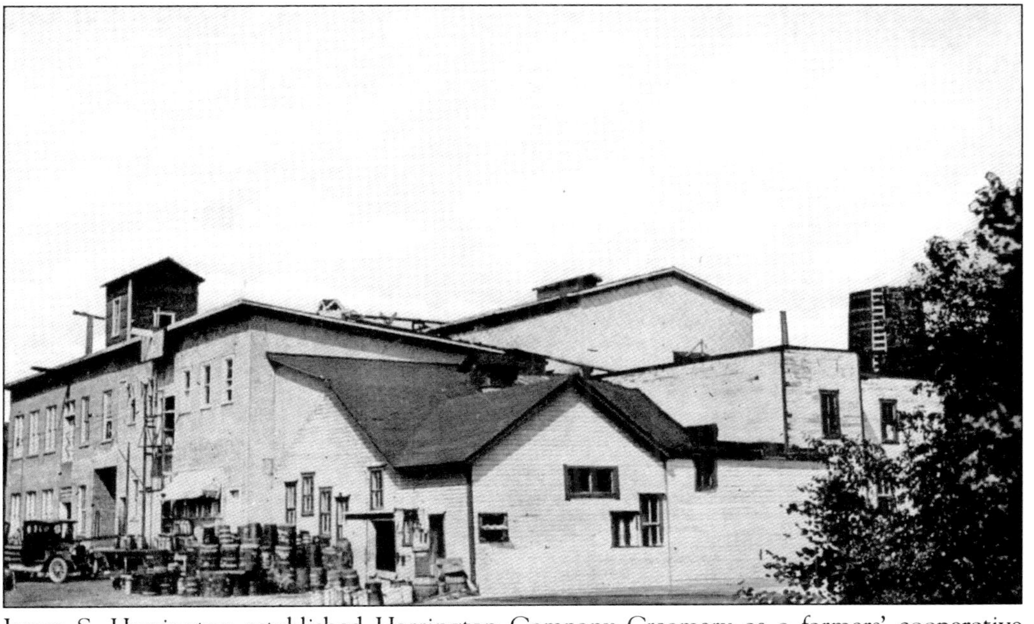

James S. Harrington established Harrington Company Creamery as a farmers' cooperative creamery in 1907; he retired in 1910. In 1919, it was incorporated with his son Maurice J. Harrington as president. Harrington's ice cream was famous at the nearby resorts of Eagles Mere, Lake Mokoma, and Harvey's Lake and in northeast Pennsylvania and southern New York State. In 1946, the business was sold to Philadelphia Dairy Products.

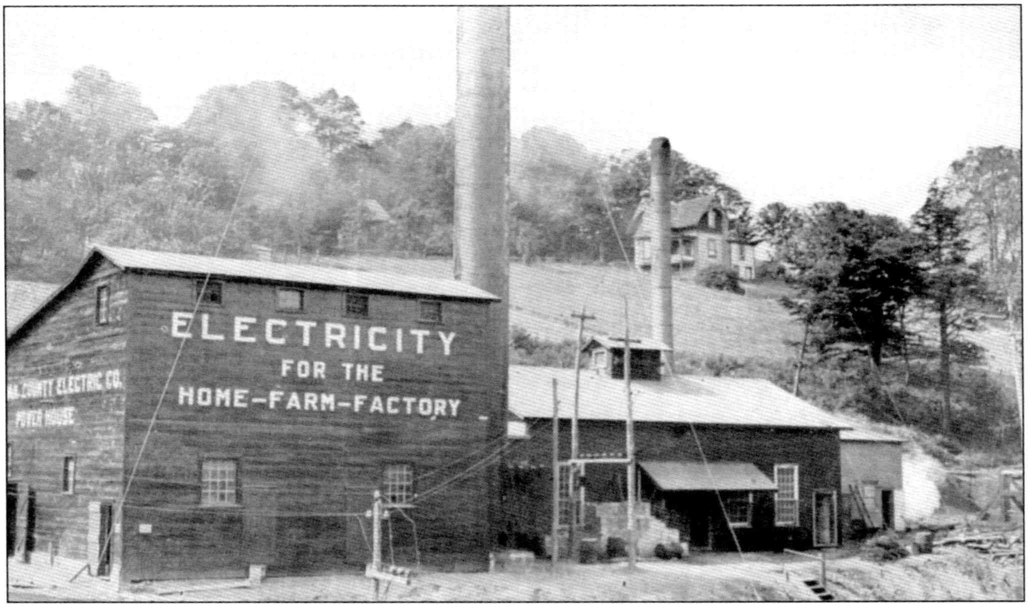

The Dushore Electric Company, later the Sullivan County Electric Company (1920), was established in 1906 with John Black as owner and manager. The plant stood on the hill near the railroad trestle just above the switch that took coal and grains out to Obert's Mill in Headleyville. This facility supplied power to most of northeast Sullivan County and parts of Bradford and Wyoming Counties.

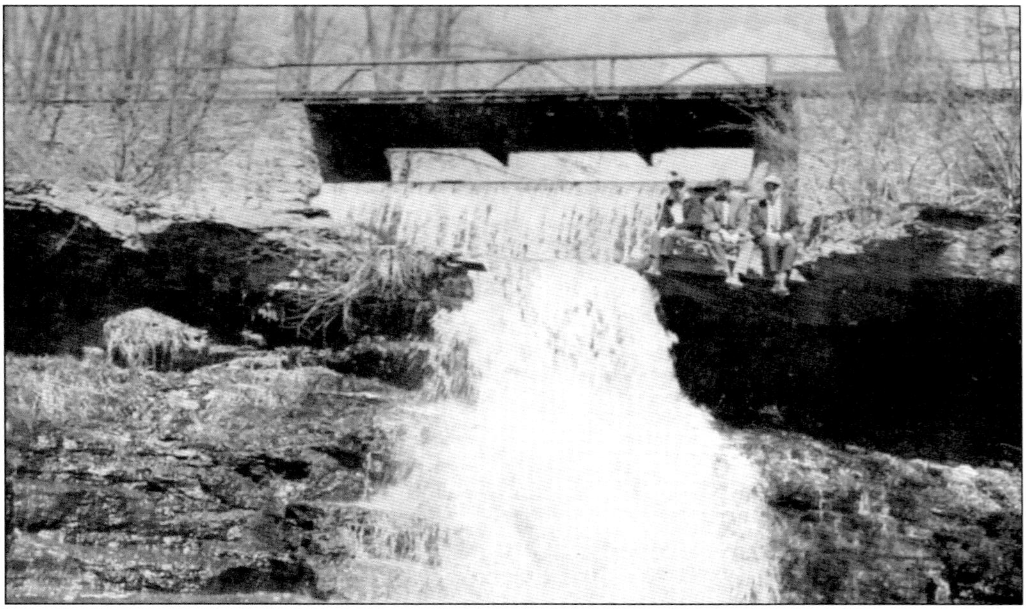

About 1820, Theodore Phinney built a sawmill at the "falls below the dam." Later John Dieffenbach sold out to Samuel F. Headley after a damaging 1850 flood. Headley rebuilt the dam and mills and then sold his store to James Deegan in 1852. Water from the Little Loyalsock was stored in the millpond overnight so the mill could operate in the daytime. The area was called Headleyville.

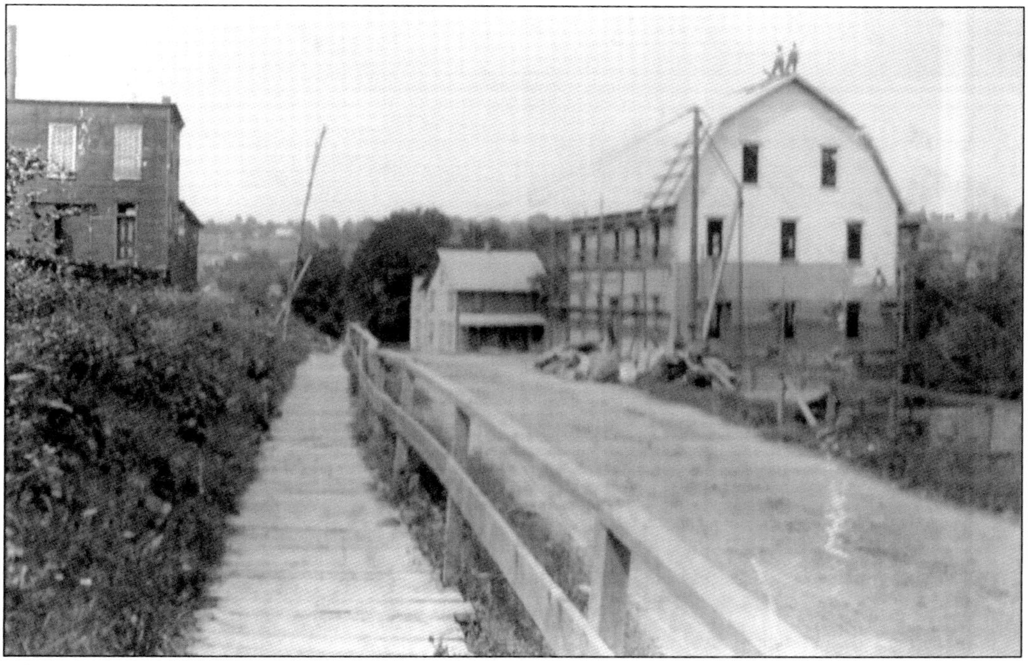

This view looking west along Mill Street in Dushore (Headleyville at the time) shows the iron foundry (left), later the lingerie factory, and the Obert Mill (right), which was just being built in September 1900. It was torn down in 1971. The Mosier home is in the distance.

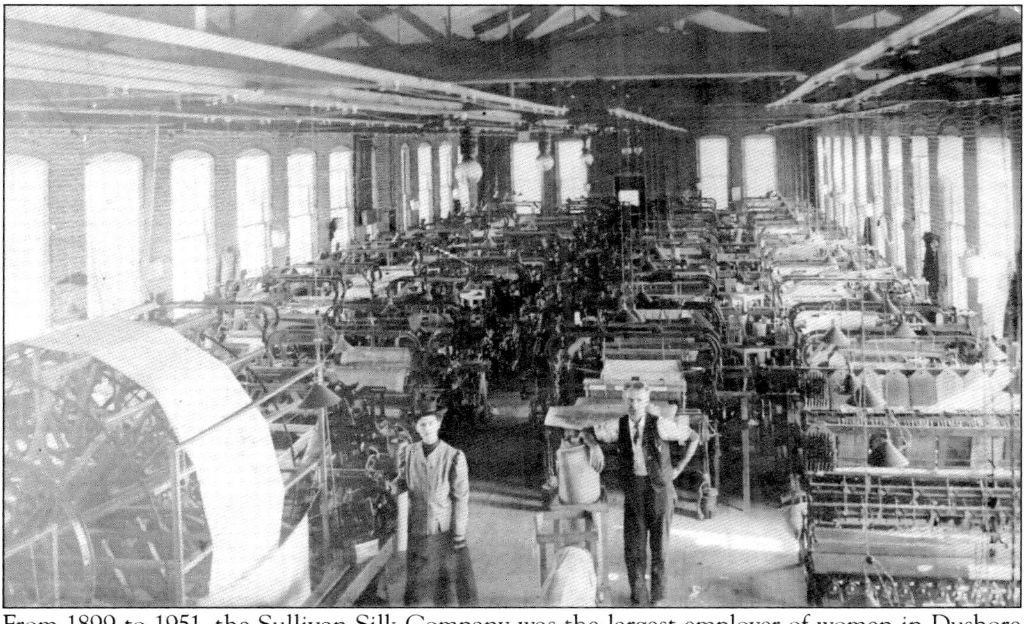

From 1899 to 1951, the Sullivan Silk Company was the largest employer of women in Dushore Borough. The company operated 70 looms; its output included dress silks, satins, and linings. Operations were suspended when nylon and rayon substitutes caused a decline in the market as well as high prices of raw material and transportation difficulties. Mason's Silk Mill was erected in Lopez in 1914.

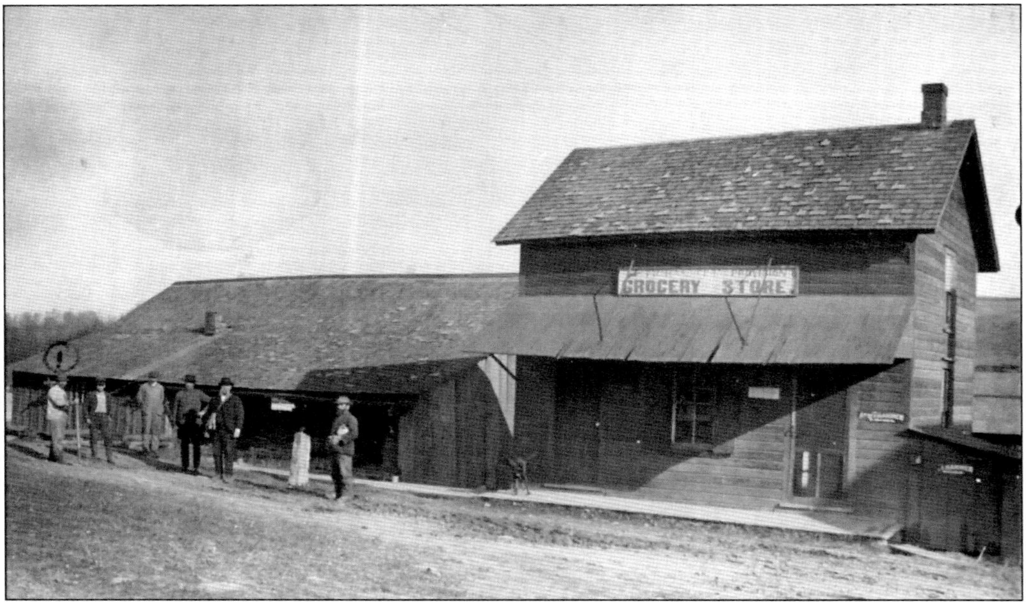

Hunsinger's Corners, located one mile from Dushore on present-day Route 87, contained a store, a sawmill, and a cider press. A blacksmith shop was owned by Raymond Kschinka, who was widely known for shoeing horses. The settlement was founded in the early days when the Thrashers and the Hunsingers settled in this vicinity. Porter Wilson Hunsinger (far left) was a son of Levi B. Hunsinger, who was a carpenter by trade; the rest are unidentified.

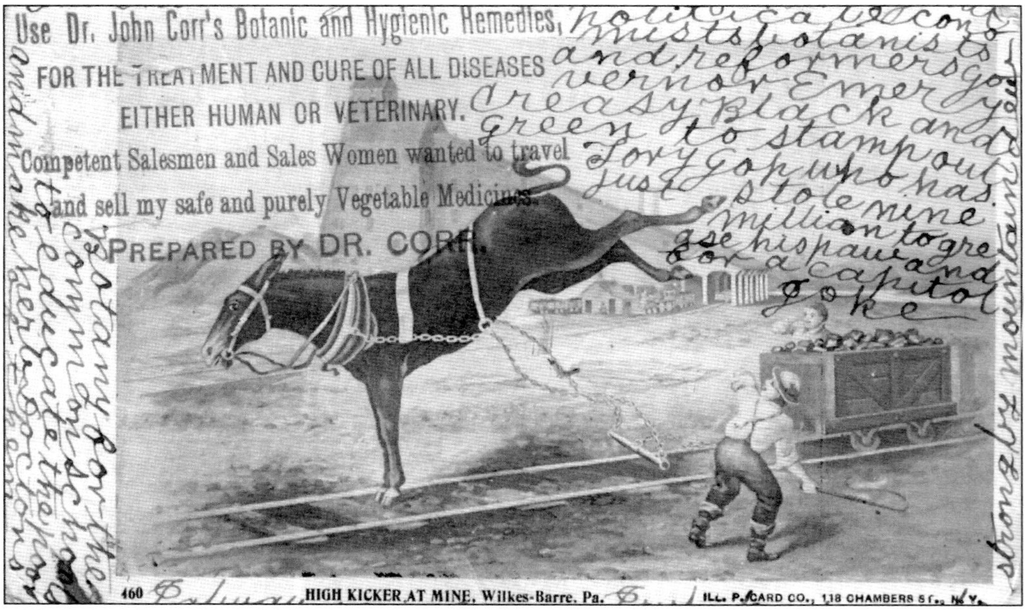

"Obscene matter" sent through the mail service often led to the sender's arrest. Dr. John Corr advertised to local businessmen in his campaign for a state legislature seat in the late 19th century. The postcards contained political advertisements and "Botanic and Hygienic Remedies" not considered obscene by today's standards. Corr (also spelled *Carr*) tramped Sullivan and Bradford Counties in the late 1800s and the very early 1900s.

Local legend held that Corr's mother was a wronged mistress of a Scottish or Irish nobleman who was sent away to this country. Another account held that his mother was a witch doctor in the Wyalusing (Bradford County) area. Corr was kind but considered queer and eccentric in his habits. The title doctor was self-assumed. He died in 1908.

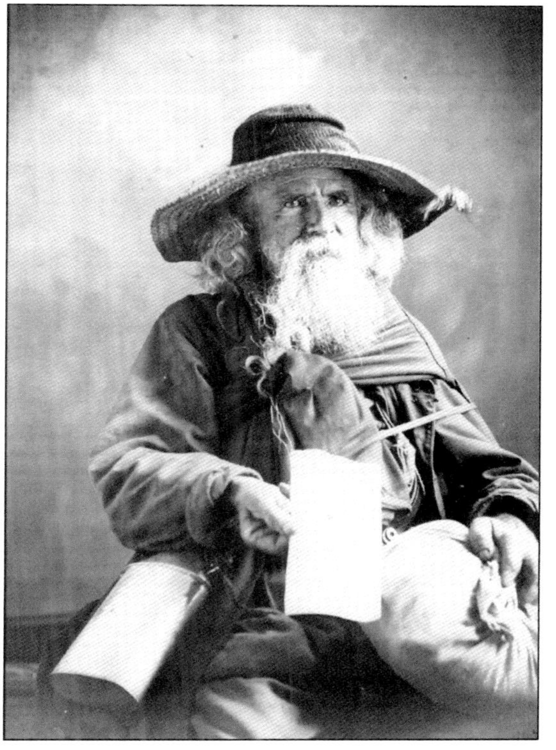

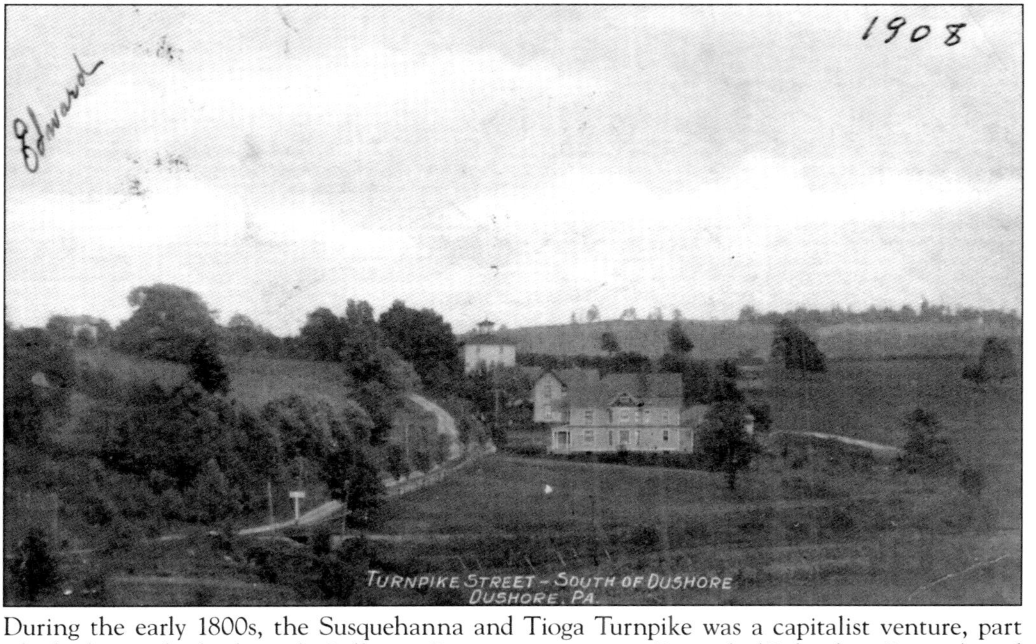

During the early 1800s, the Susquehanna and Tioga Turnpike was a capitalist venture, part of which was built through Sullivan County connecting Berwick (Columbia County) and Newtown (present-day Elmira, New York). By 1819, the Susquehanna and Tioga Turnpike road was completed across North Mountain as far as Birch Creek in Bernice and Mildred. This view of Turnpike Street, located in the southern part of Dushore Borough, was taken about 1908.

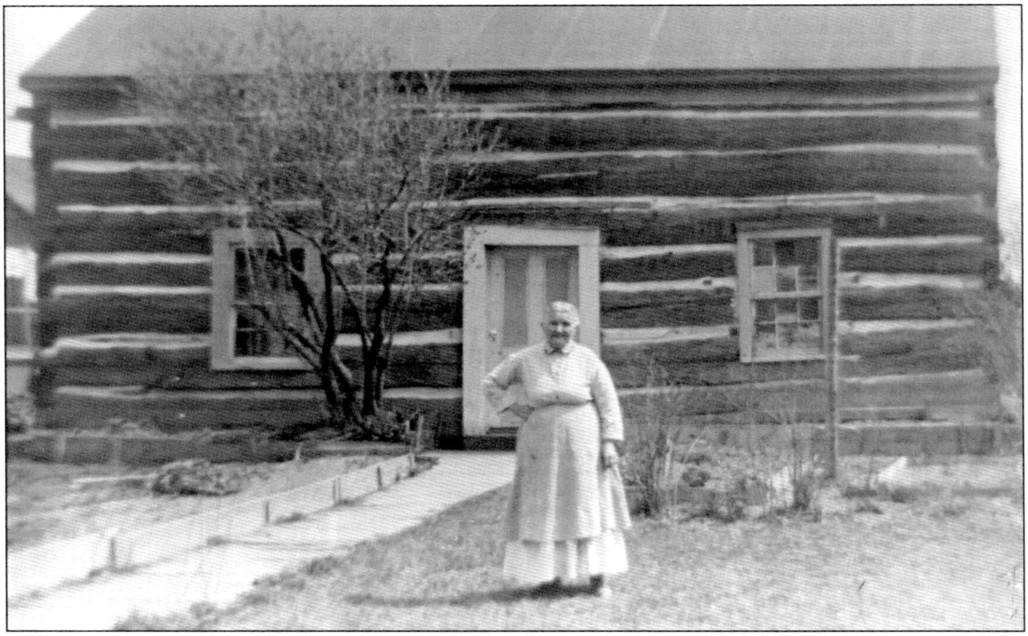

This might be Mary Simmees Cunningham at her log cabin on Mildred's Main Street in the 1890s. At the time, this was one of the few remaining houses built when the town was first called Shinersville in the 1820s. The house was later occupied by Dr. George C. Swope (1874–1940), a physician who served the Bernice-Mildred area for many years.

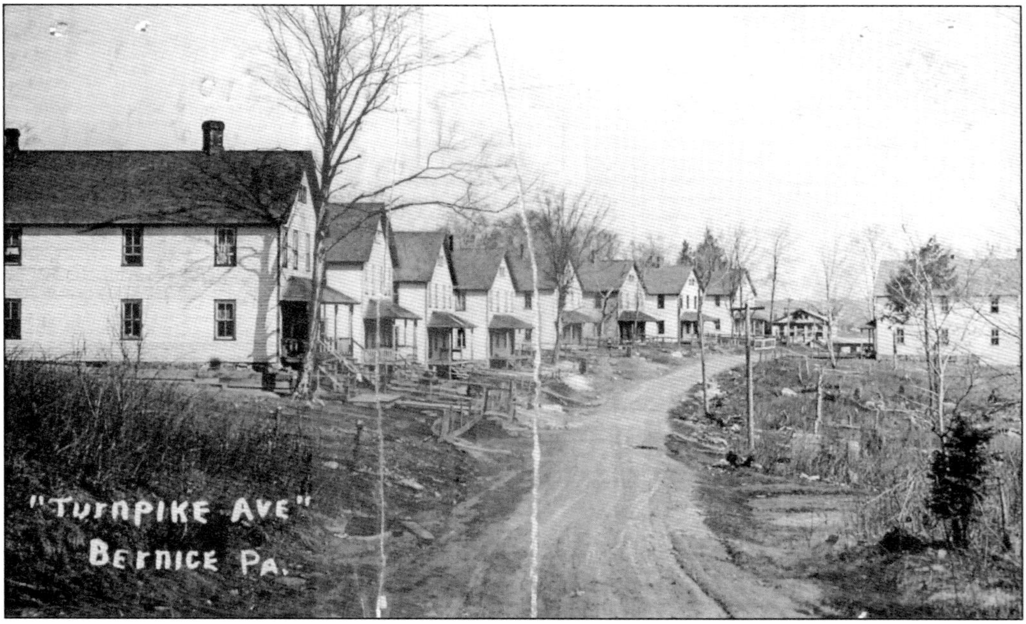

Connell Coal Mining Company homes lined Turnpike Avenue about 1905, housing foremen and supervisors who worked in the nearby mine. Its present name, Chinatown, came from Al Meehan. Only three of these homes remain today.

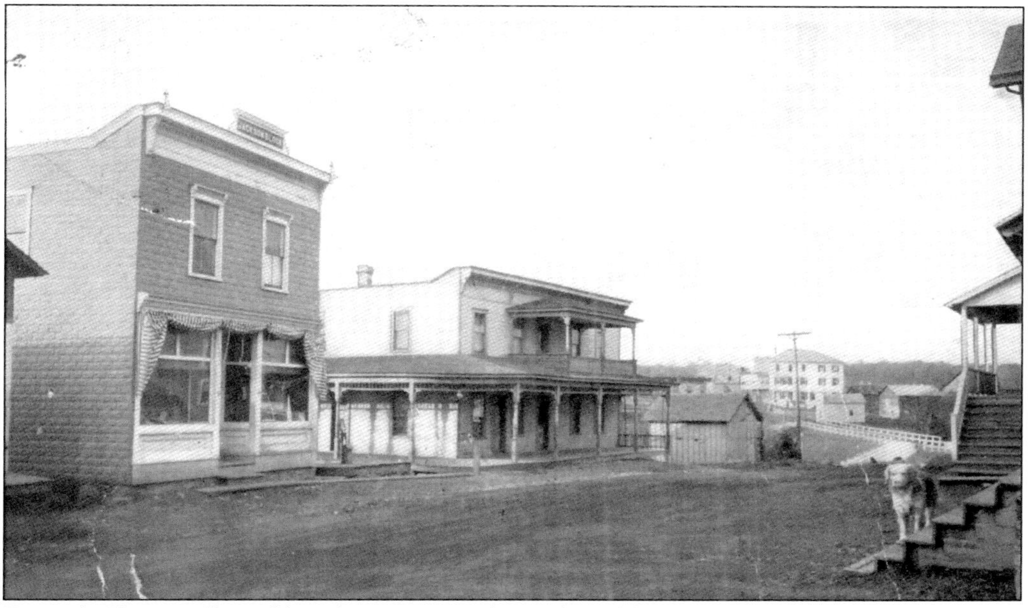

Formerly Shinersville and later known as Birch Creek, Mildred was founded in 1870 and thrived as a mining town for over 30 years. Shown are Stilley White's billiard parlor (left) and Tony Boll's bar/boardinghouse (second from left). The dog (right) is on the steps of Tony Zangara's barbershop, and the next porch is Morris Hoffman's Clothing Store. Mildred and Bernice are often called Ber-Mil. (Courtesy of Edward Cilvick.)

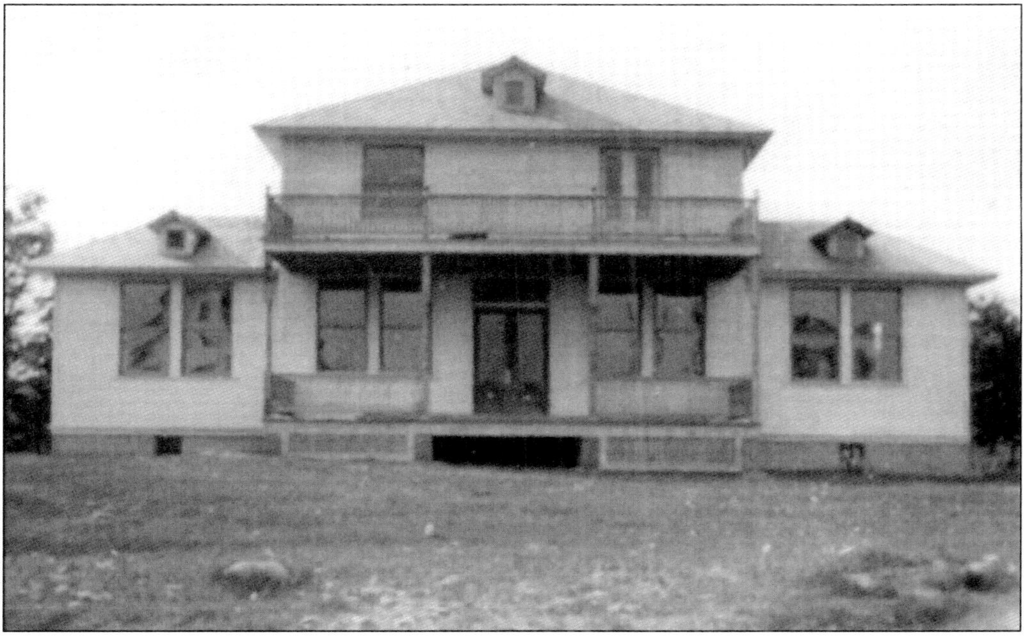

The Bernice Hospital was built by the Connell Coal Company around 1908 primarily for Connell Coal Company employees in the Mildred area. Miners from Dushore and surrounding communities worked in Mildred. The hospital burned down in the early 1930s. This is the only known photograph in existence.

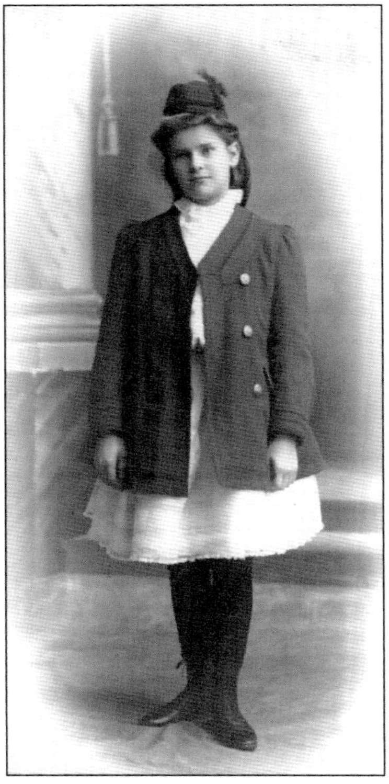

One story goes that the village of Bernice and all the company-owned buildings that grew around the first Bernice coal breaker were named after Bernice Woodruff Jackson, wife of George Duggan Jackson, a Dushore and Bernice businessman. She was born in 1832 and died in 1899. The young girl pictured here lived in the late 1800s and was most likely a granddaughter.

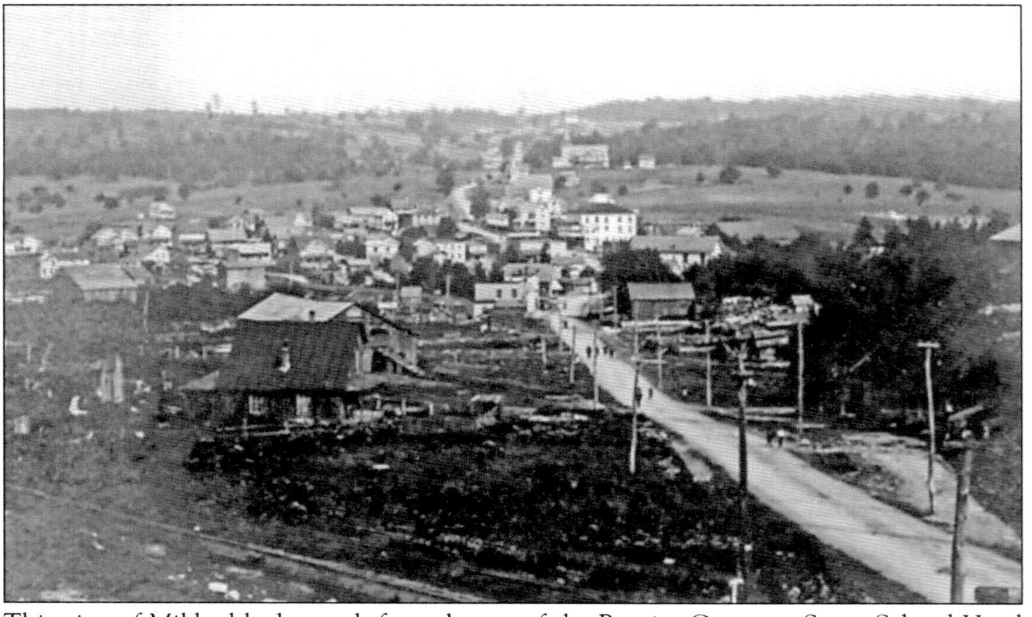

This view of Mildred looks north from the top of the Bernice Company Store. Schaad Hotel is the three-story building (above, right of center) with the two churches beyond that. The Mildred high school (right, out of picture) burned in the 1930s. The Trasco homestead is in the foreground. The road is the old Susquehanna and Tioga Turnpike, later Main Street, through Mildred and Bernice.

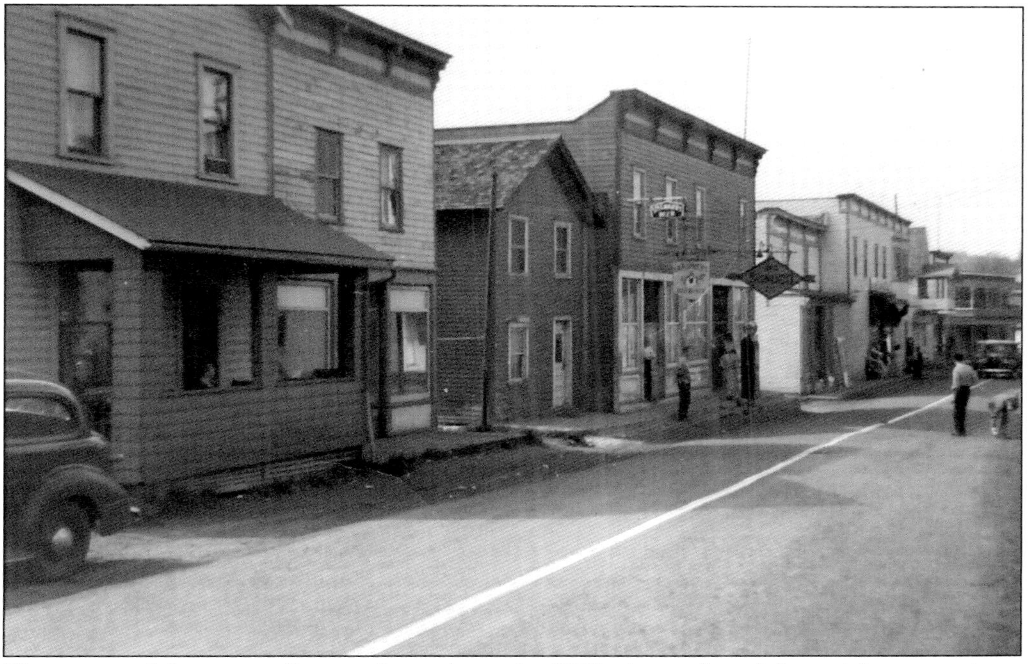

This image of downtown Bernice from about the 1930s shows, from left to right, two private residences, Perozzi's Bar and Grill (third and fourth structures), Charniski's Grocery, Joe Barnosky's Luncheon, Stilley White's billiard hall, and the Boll Hotel.

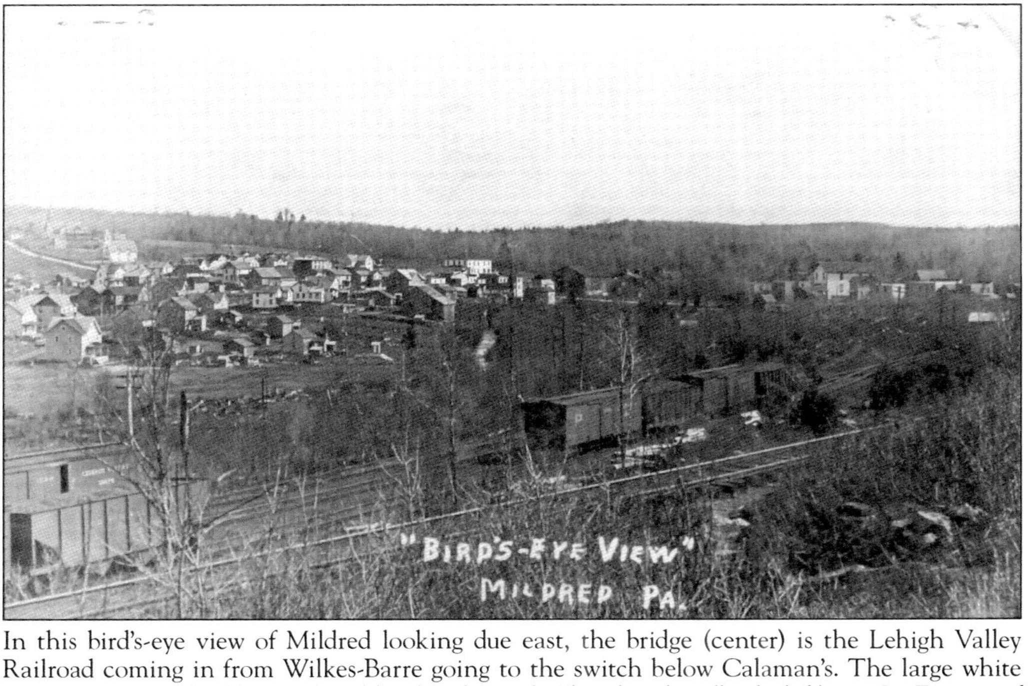

In this bird's-eye view of Mildred looking due east, the bridge (center) is the Lehigh Valley Railroad coming in from Wilkes-Barre going to the switch below Calaman's. The large white building (center, back) was the old Schaad Hotel. The churches (back, left) are St. Francis of Assisi Catholic Church (left) and Trinity Lutheran Church (right).

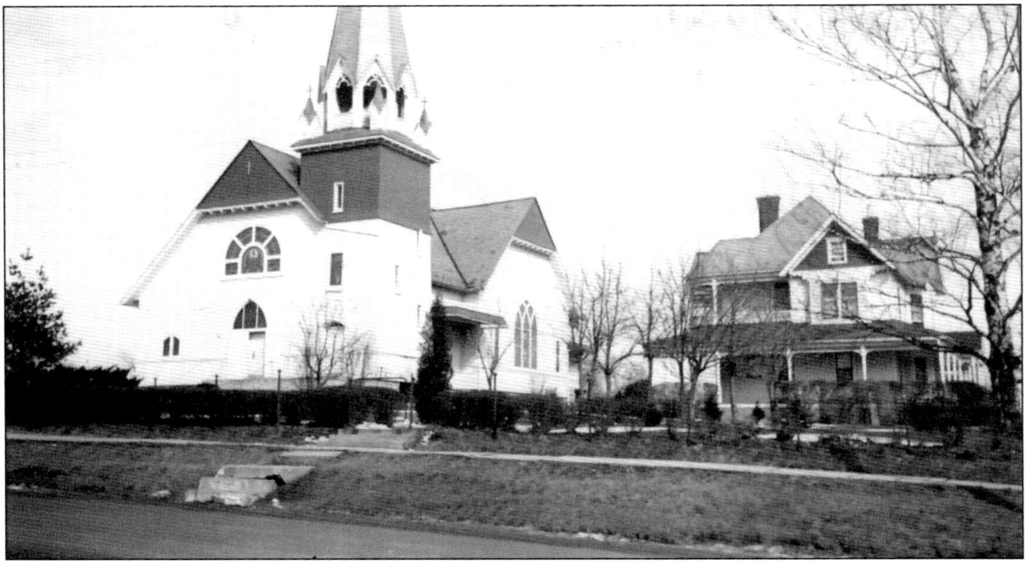

Catholic services were held in Mildred-area homes long before the cornerstone of St. Francis of Assisi Catholic Church was laid in 1895. The church was completed in 1897. The first priest was Rev. John A. Enright (1894–1922).

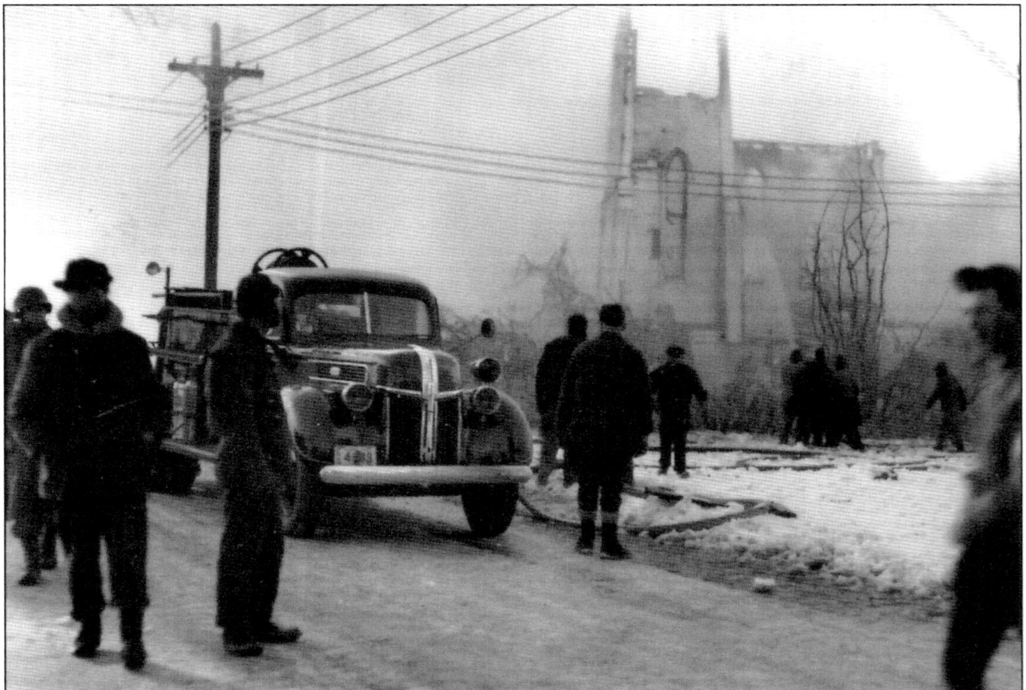

St. Francis of Assisi Catholic Church and rectory burned on Good Friday in the mid-1950s. Fr. Luke Haley was the priest at this time. Still talked about today is the 1953 fire that destroyed the Mildred Theatre, Steven's Restaurant, and the Calaman building, sweeping along Main Street in Mildred.

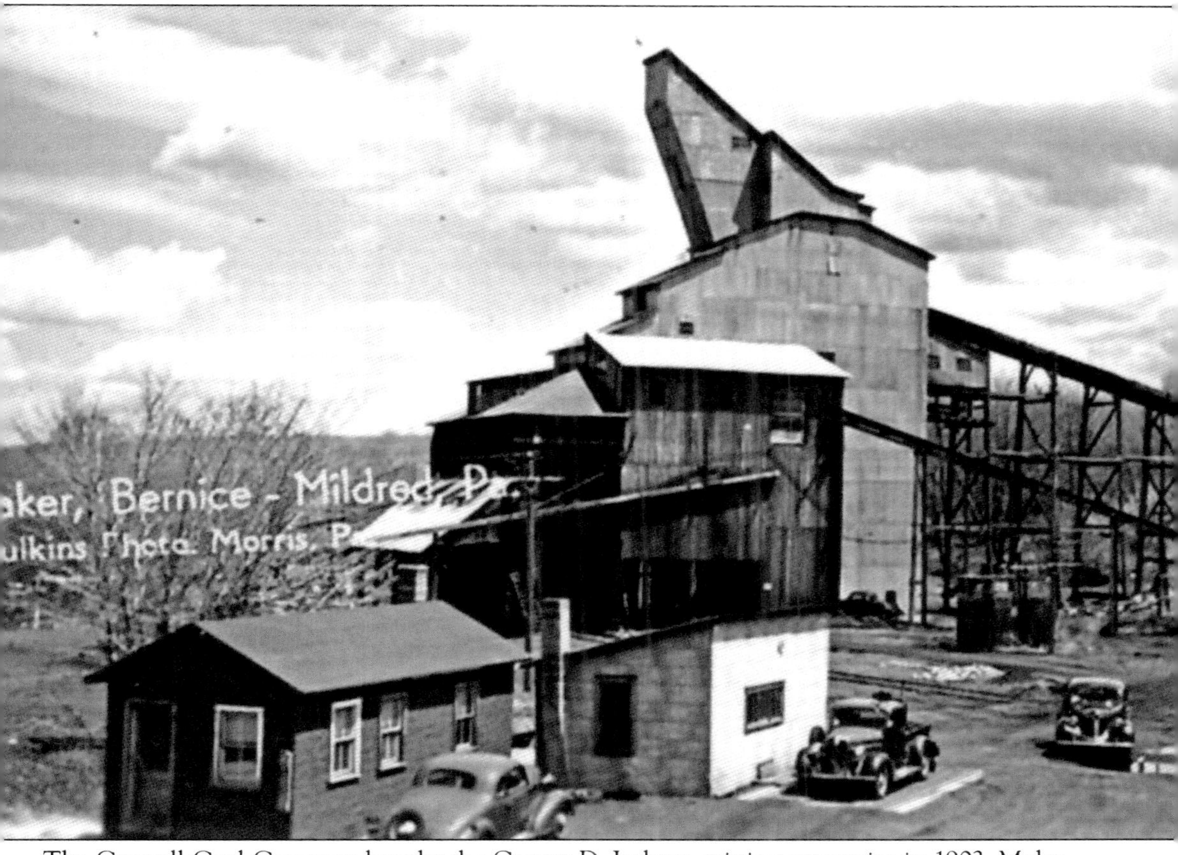

The Connell Coal Company bought the George D. Jackson mining enterprise in 1903. Mules brought coal to the bottom of the slope. Cars, hooked together, were pulled by a mine motor up the slope to the tipple with the aid of a gear and rack rail. This was the third and last breaker built in Mildred in the late 1930s. At the time, Erland Perozzi was the way master, and Bill Monahan of Laporte was the mine foreman and a part owner. The 1938 DeSoto (right) belonged to Joseph Taber.

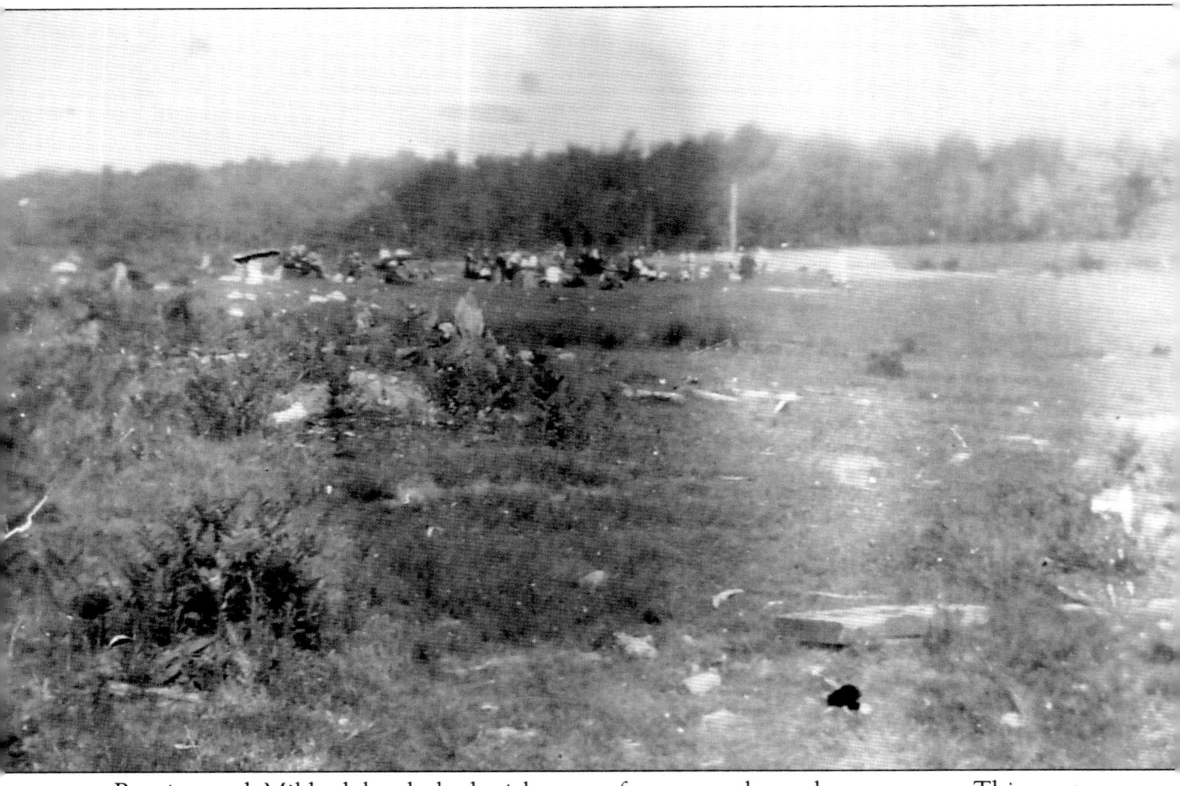

Bernice and Mildred locals had nicknames for areas where they grew up. This spot was affectionately called the Chinatown ballpark (the old baseball diamond) by Bernice locals. At that time, home plate was near the Lehigh Valley Railroad tracks, and the batter faced due west.

Two

Colley Township

Colley Township was established in 1849 by a decree of the court of quarter sessions of Sullivan County at the December term. The territory was taken from Cherry Township and named in honor of William Colley, one of the early settlers of the township. It is located in the eastern section of the township with Bradford County to the north; Wyoming and Luzerne Counties to the east and southeast; and Davidson, Laporte, and Cherry Townships to the southwest and west. The Susquehanna and Tioga Turnpike is a modern township boundary separating Colley from Davidson and Laporte Townships.

The first improvements in Colley Township were at Long Pond (Lake Ganoga) about the time the turnpike was built (1809). The first attempt at a permanent settlement was made by Hugh Bellas of Sunbury in 1813 at Shady Nook, three and a half miles up the Loyalsock Creek from Lopez. The settlement's name was changed to Lee Settlement for three brothers, Jesse, Nathan, and Absalom Lee, who settled there. What is known as the Colley Settlement was made along the North Branch of Mehoopany Creek in the northern section of the township.

Worth and Cortez Jennings came to Sullivan County in 1881 and purchased large timber tracts from James McFarlane. In 1887, the Jennings brothers operated a sawmill on Taylor Creek near Seeman's Hotel just west of Lopez. After they moved to Lopez (1897) and established their business, they built 40 homes along the Pigeon Creek Road and on the hillside north of the Loyalsock. Lopez's population was well over 1,000 by 1890. Businesses were established to meet the needs of the people. Most of these historic buildings were destroyed in the fire of 1982. Lopez was the only lumbering town in the county that sold liquor. On payday, "woodhicks" from Ricketts and other nearby communities spent their hard-earned cash at the four hotels there. Lopez Manufactory (1896) made clothespins, broom handles, curtain poles, mine rollers, cant hook handles, dowels, and wooden novelties. Originally known as "Tar Bridge" then "Saw Dust City," today Lopez is touted as the "Ice Box" of Sullivan County.

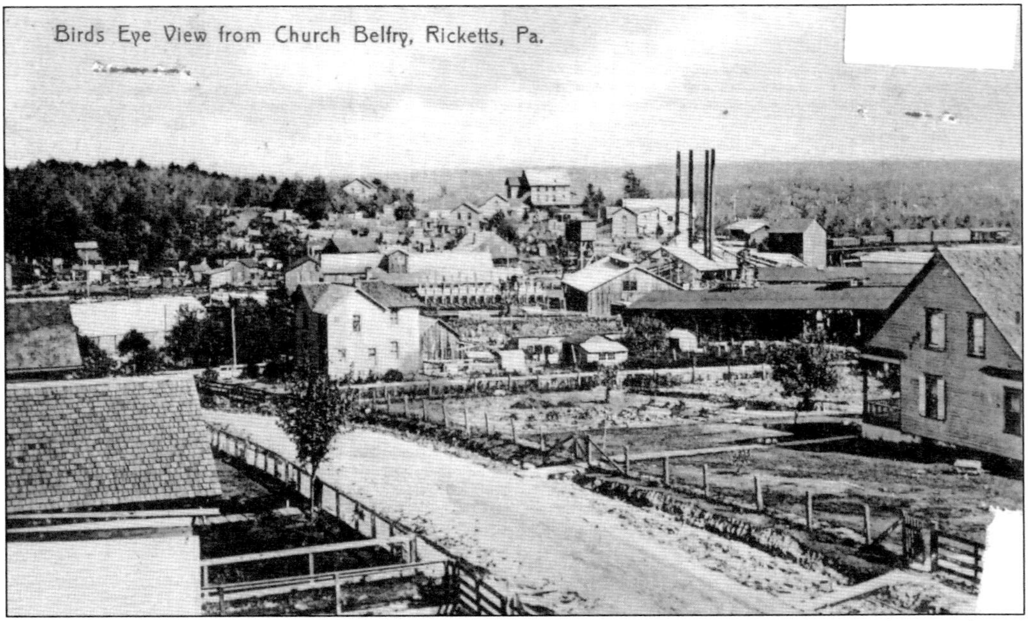

In 1891, the town of Ricketts grew around the Albert Lewis Lumber Company mill that employed 150 men. The same year, Harry Trexler and Harry Turrell built a large mill that had a daily capacity of 100,000 feet of board, a stave factory, and an excelsior mill employing 150 men and a few girls. Located just north of Lake Jean, Ricketts was a ghost town by 1914 after the trees were all cut.

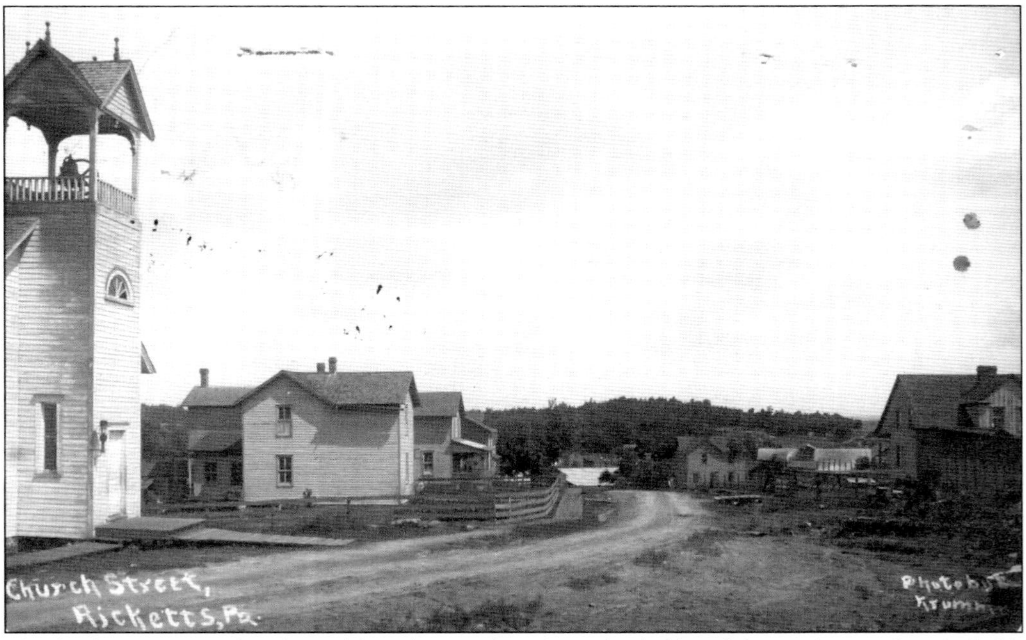

The bird's-eye view of Ricketts (above) was taken from the belfry of the Lutheran church (left). The town was located in Wyoming and Sullivan Counties with two schools (one in each county), one church, and a company store to serve locals.

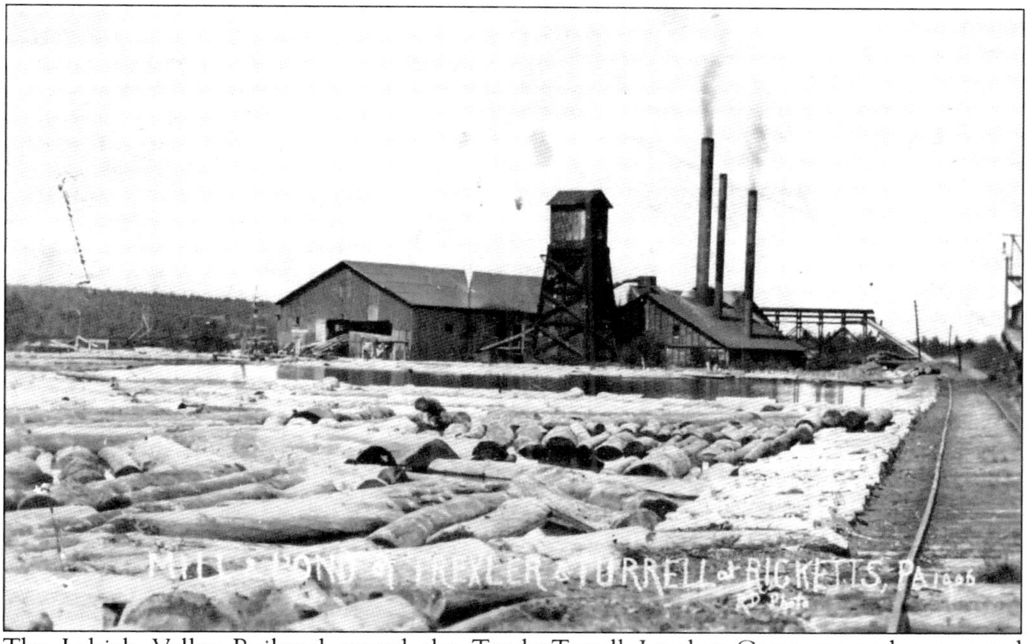

The Lehigh Valley Railroad served the Trexler-Turrell Lumber Company and connected Lopez and Ricketts by 1890. The pond and stave mill of the Trexler-Turrell operation in 1906 made staves for coopers to make barrels. The Ricketts mill was the second largest in northern Pennsylvania. Lopez was the largest.

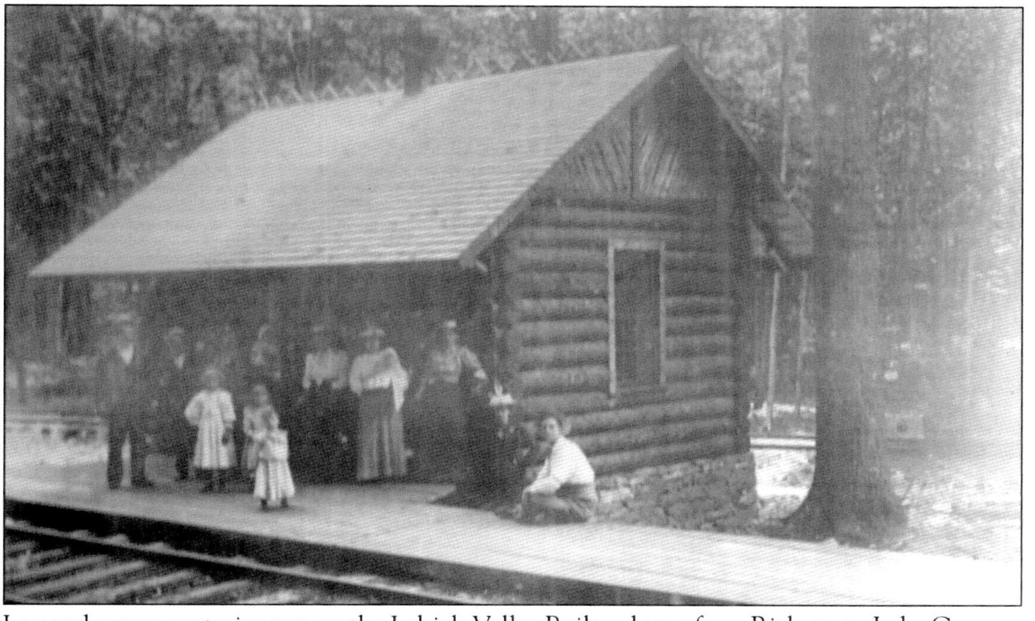

Log and passenger trains ran on the Lehigh Valley Railroad spur from Ricketts to Lake Ganoga. In this photograph taken in 1895 at the Ganoga Lake train station, the smallest child (front) is "Cappy" Jay Campbell, who died 1971. He was a World War I veteran, a state highway department engineer, a member of the New Albany Band, and a mayor of New Albany in Bradford County for nine years.

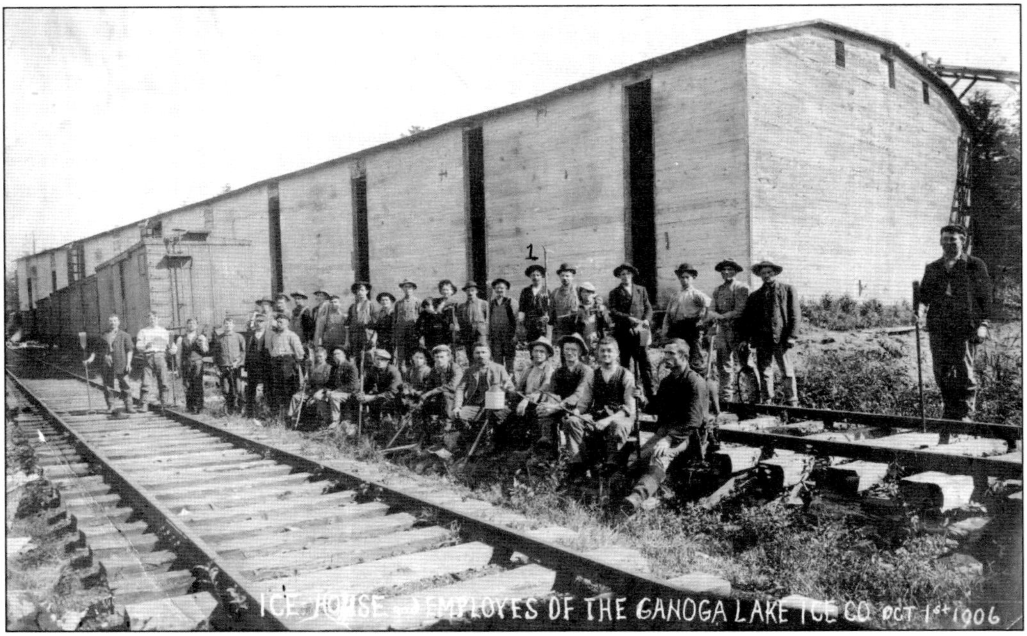

Built in 1904, the Ganoga Lake Ice Company icehouse was 1,000 feet long and 50 feet wide with 35 2-by-12-foot joists. Sawdust sheeted up the interior between the studs. Cut marsh grass was placed across the ice in depths of three to four feet. A ramp and loading platform brought up ice where it was loaded into freight cars. Only George E. Covey (1) is identified.

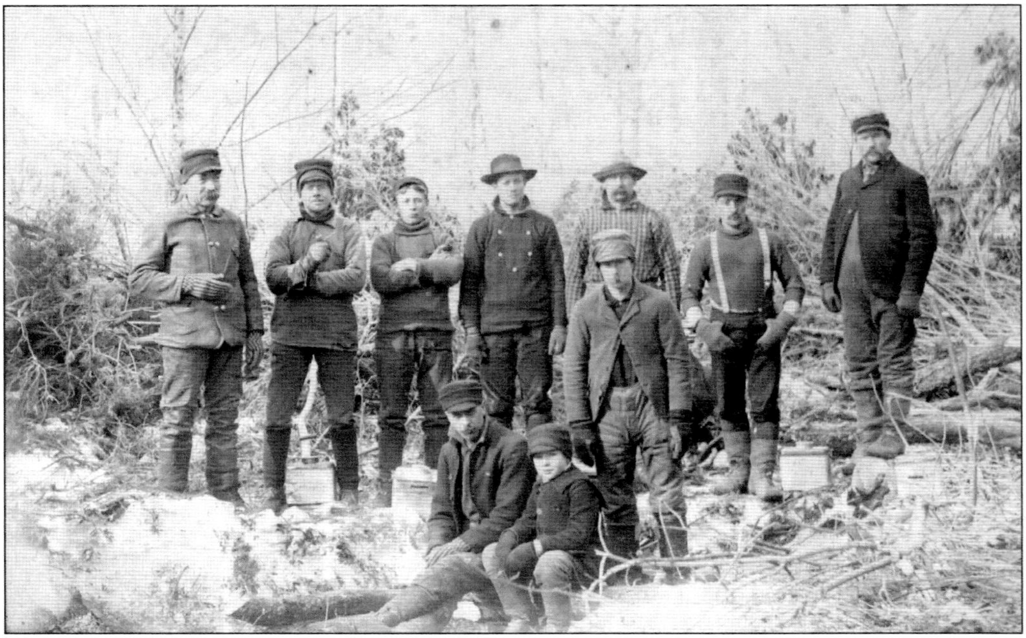
John Dennis Lane (left, in front) and his son James (boy in front) are identified in this Ganoga Lake Camp crew. James was born in the Dorsey Hotel at Ricketts. The hotel was owned by Daniel Dorsey whose wife, Margaret, was Lane's sister. The majority of logging was done during the winter when it was easier to skid out logs on ice and snow. (Courtesy of Jo and Jerome Lane.)

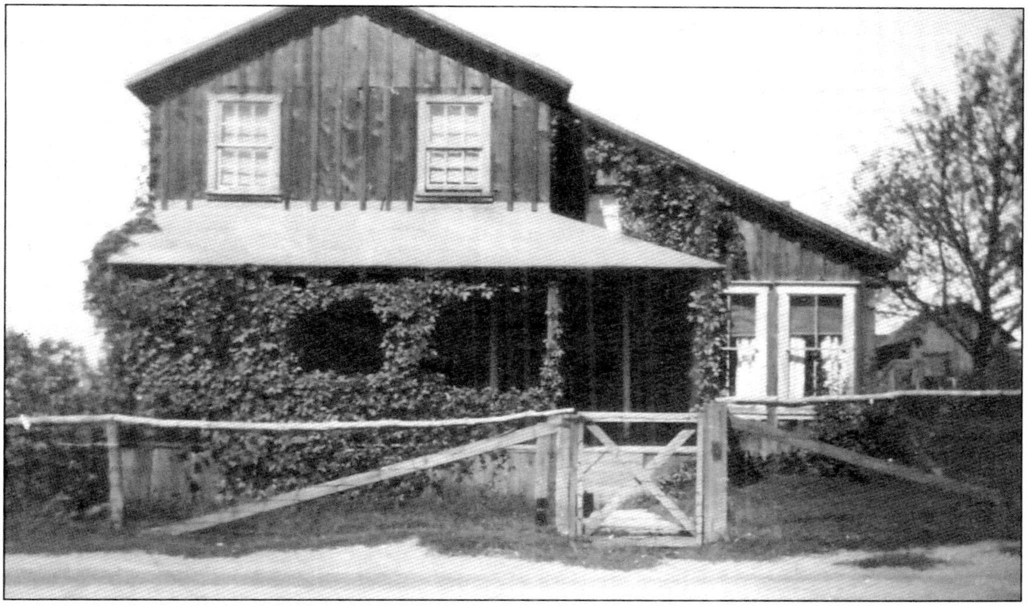

Built in 1901, Murraytown built up around a coal breaker that stood 169 feet high, the largest in the United States at the time. The town boasted 25 large, comfortable houses (the one shown was photographed about 1920), a company building, a store, and a post office. The Williamsport and North Branch Railroad laid a switch near Lopez to the Murray Mines in 1902. From 1903 to 1932, 600 men were employed.

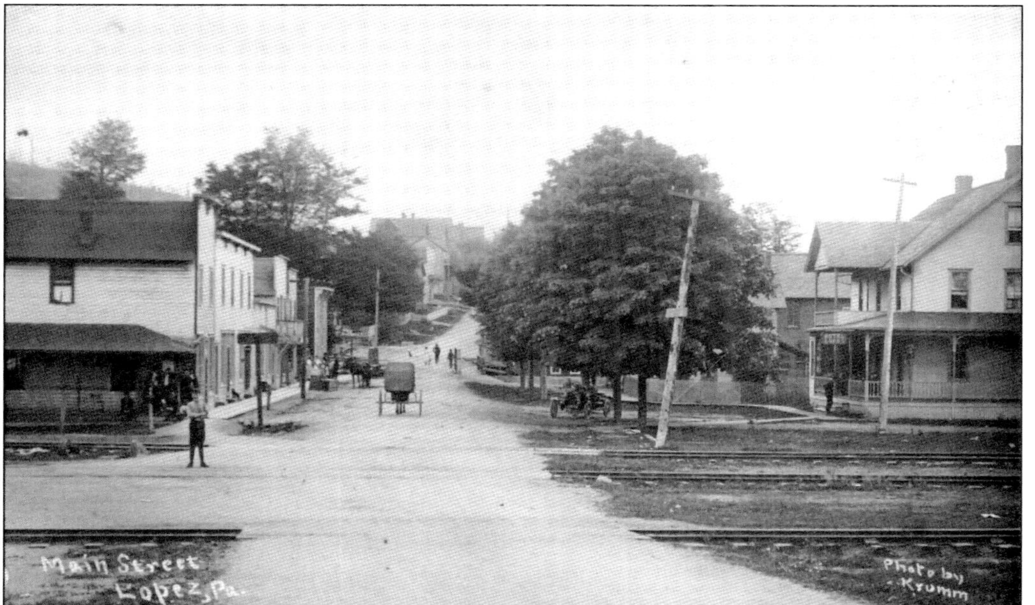

Lopez's Main Street, photographed about 1907, shows McGee Hotel, the post office, Ohrt's, McGuire's, and Stavisky's on the left and Hotel Lopez/Rouse's on the right. Three tracks of the Bowman's Creek branch of the Lehigh Valley Railroad are seen in the foreground. The railroad depot is to the left behind the photographer. The identification is relevant to the 1950s.

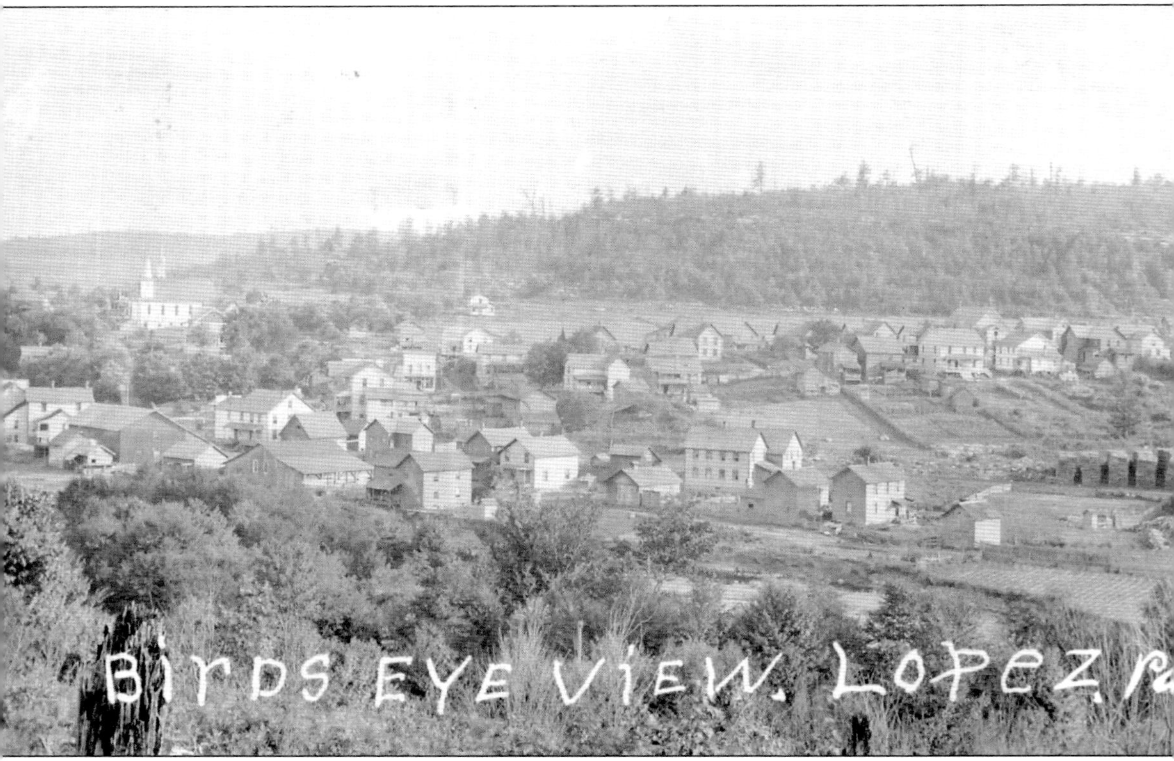

Church Row, named because it was the first street to have a church, is by the Evangelical church (left, background). The Methodist church, later becoming St. Vladimir's (behind houses, right), is discerned by a white cross on its roof. The last kindling wood factory is by the stacked lumber (right, center).

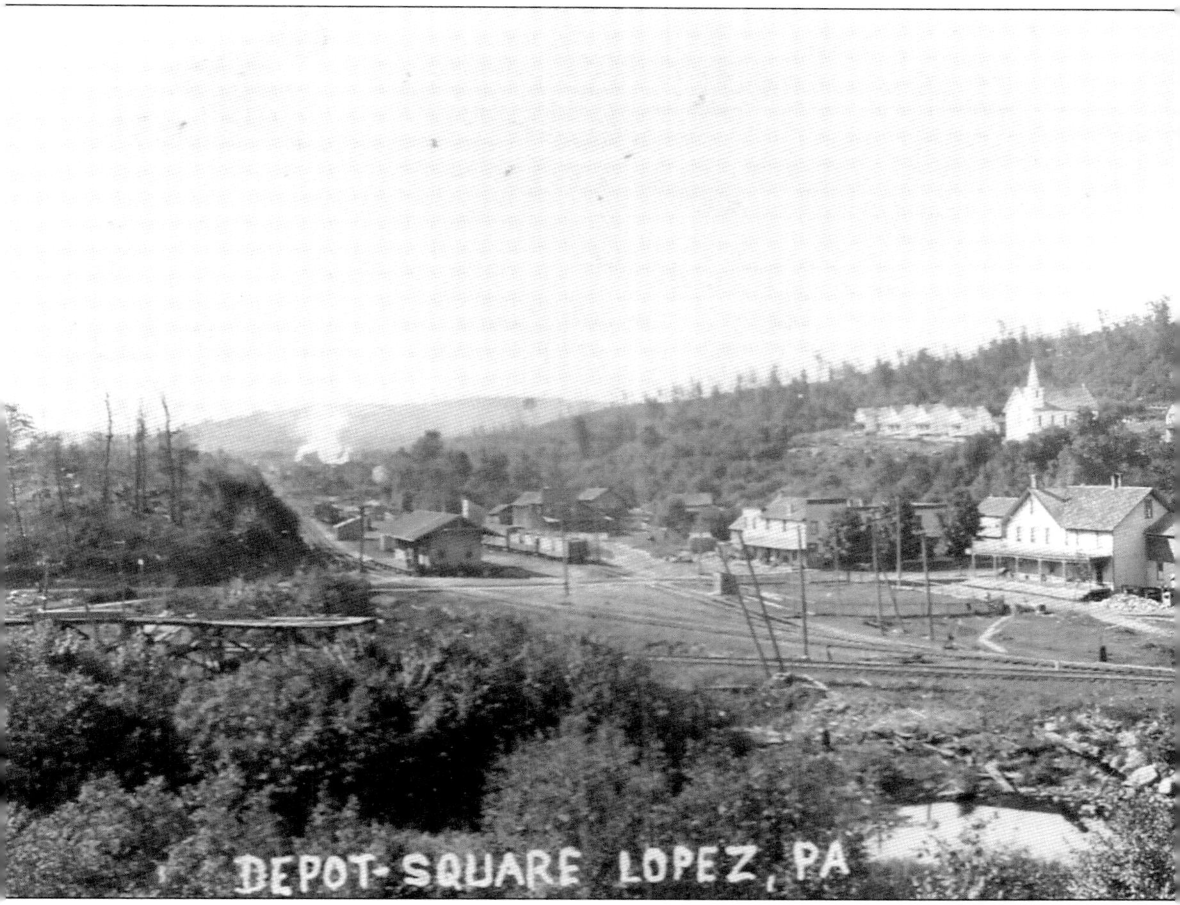

The Depot Square in Lopez is pictured with Church Row (upper right). Turrelltown is in the area of the smoke behind the depot. This picture was taken about 1900 from the porch of Jennings Brothers Company Store looking due south. A part of the Jennings Brothers lumber mill was along here. Pigeon Creek, one of the headwaters of the Big Loyalsock Creek, is in the foreground.

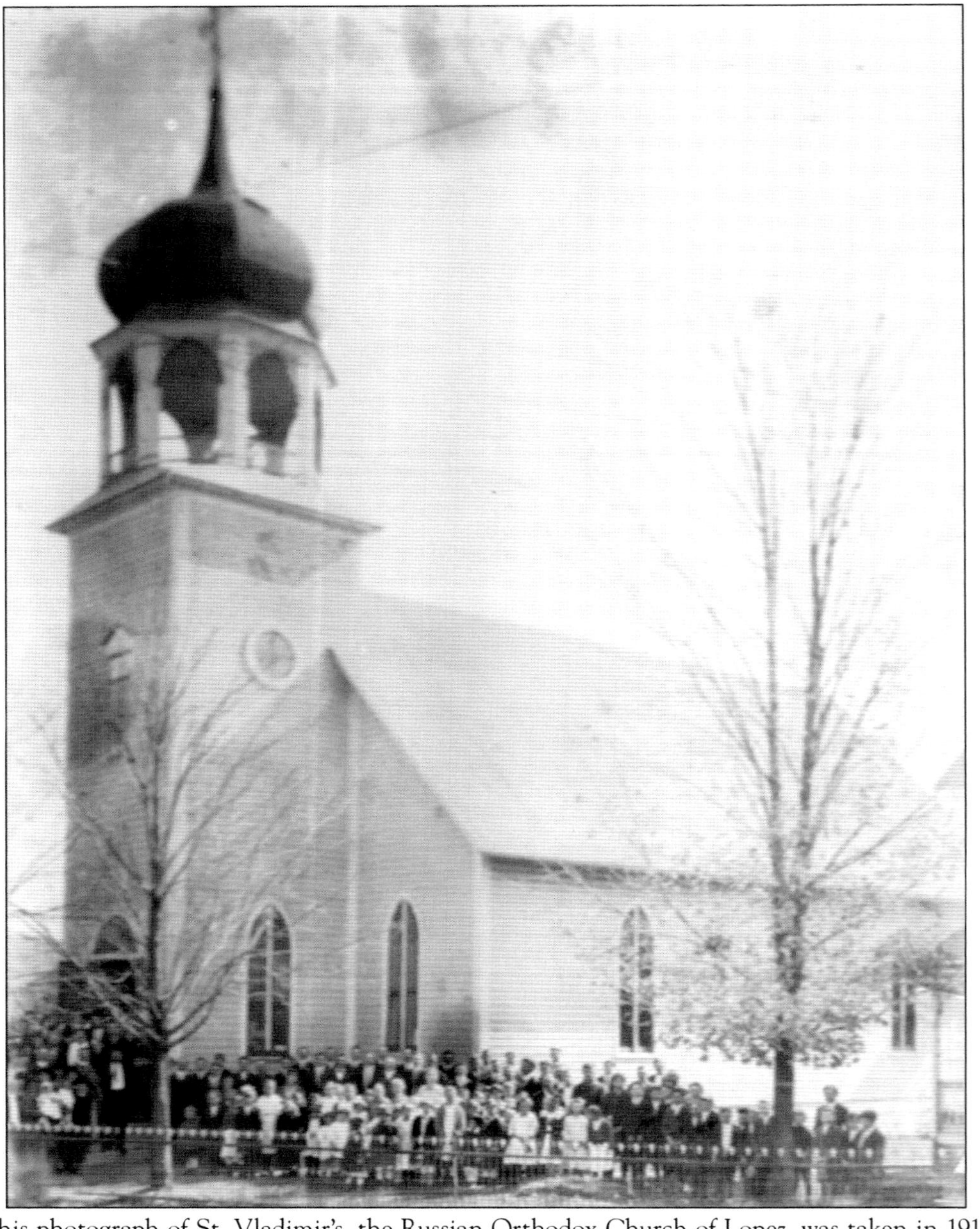

This photograph of St. Vladimir's, the Russian Orthodox Church of Lopez, was taken in 1911 when the belfry was completed. Local Methodists built the church in 1899, and Lutherans were allowed to hold their services there. Membership dropped as jobs and families moved. Albert Dyer purchased the building and sold it to the Russian Orthodox denomination for $700 in 1907. St. Vladimir was chosen as patron saint of the new parish. The Society of St. Nicholas was formed under the direction of Dimitri Evanoyko and consisted of Evanoyko, Thomas Maykovich (McCobin), Stephen Betsy, Elias Betsy, Andrew Huray, Theodore Shymansky, and later Peyko, Dimitri Borick, John Kozemko, Alexander Stavisky, Adam Stavisky, William K. Gulick, Samuel Yarosh, and Thomas Stavisky. In August 1955, fire destroyed the interior of the church. (Courtesy of the Andrew Huray family.)

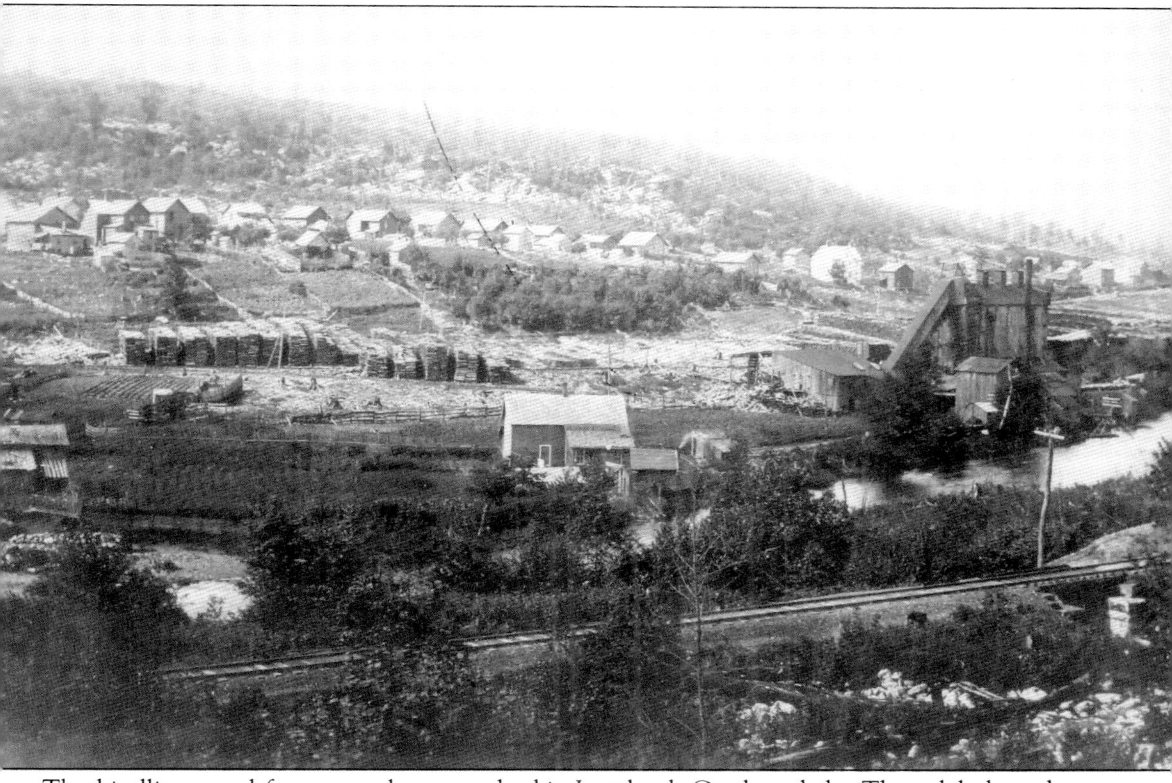

The kindling wood factory sat between the big Loyalsock Creek and the Thorndale branch of the Lehigh Valley Railroad west of Lopez. The town of Lopez sits to the left just out of the picture. The first kindling wood factory was built in 1888 by McCartney and Hall and burned two years later before it was rebuilt. It was later sold to the Standard Kindling Wood Company of New York City. The railroad tracks went to Thorndale.

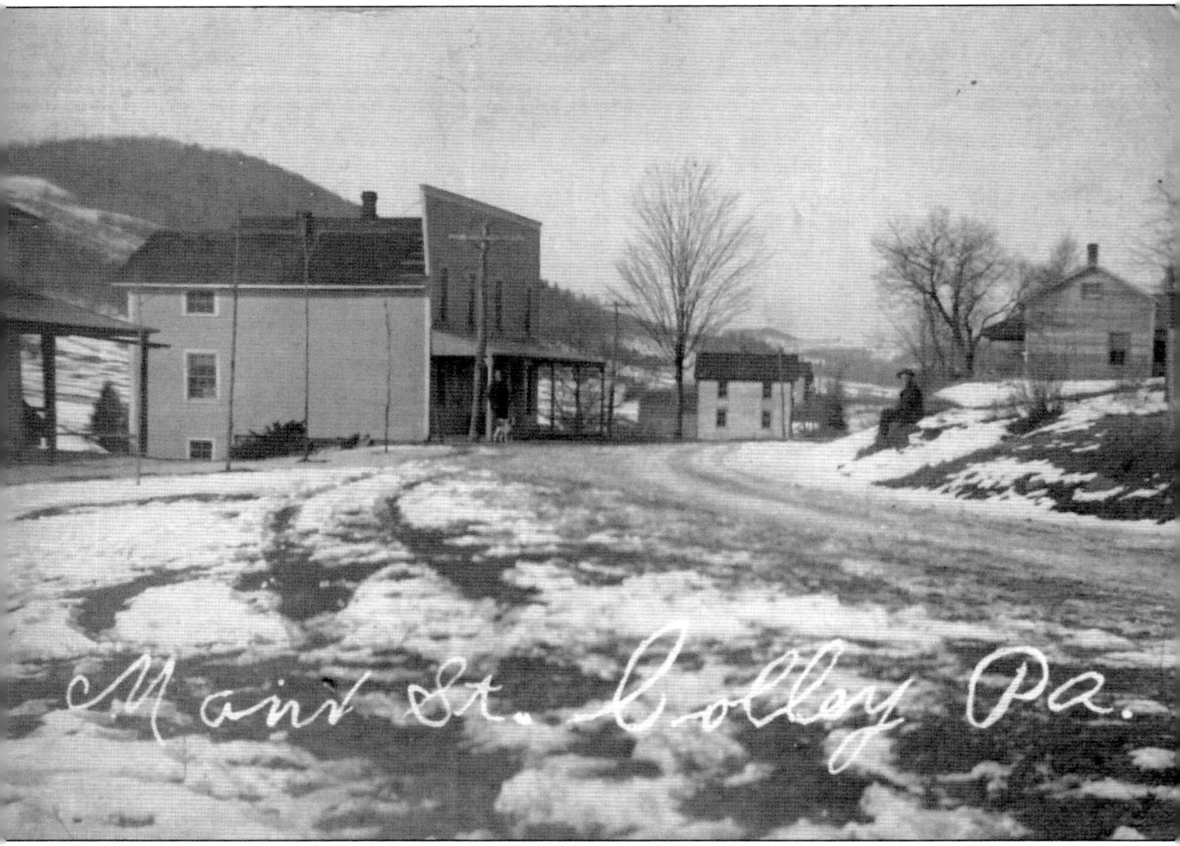

This view of downtown Colley looks west where present-day Pond/Panther Lick Road intersects with Route 87 and shows the Lewis Ross residence (left, porch roof visible). The Winters family and George Smith were subsequent owners. The old general store and post office (second from left) was owned by George Dieffenbach, who was also the postmaster, then David J. Gephart I and later James Haman. A tavern was eventually added. Some 300 feet beyond the Preston Crawford residence (center, back) was the Colley Hotel, which later became the Colley blacksmith shop run by Edward Butts. The Claire Reeser house seen on the right no longer stands. Behind this home's foundations are the remnants of an old buggy lane. Pond Road (right) was once the main road through the village. (Courtesy of Jim Fox.)

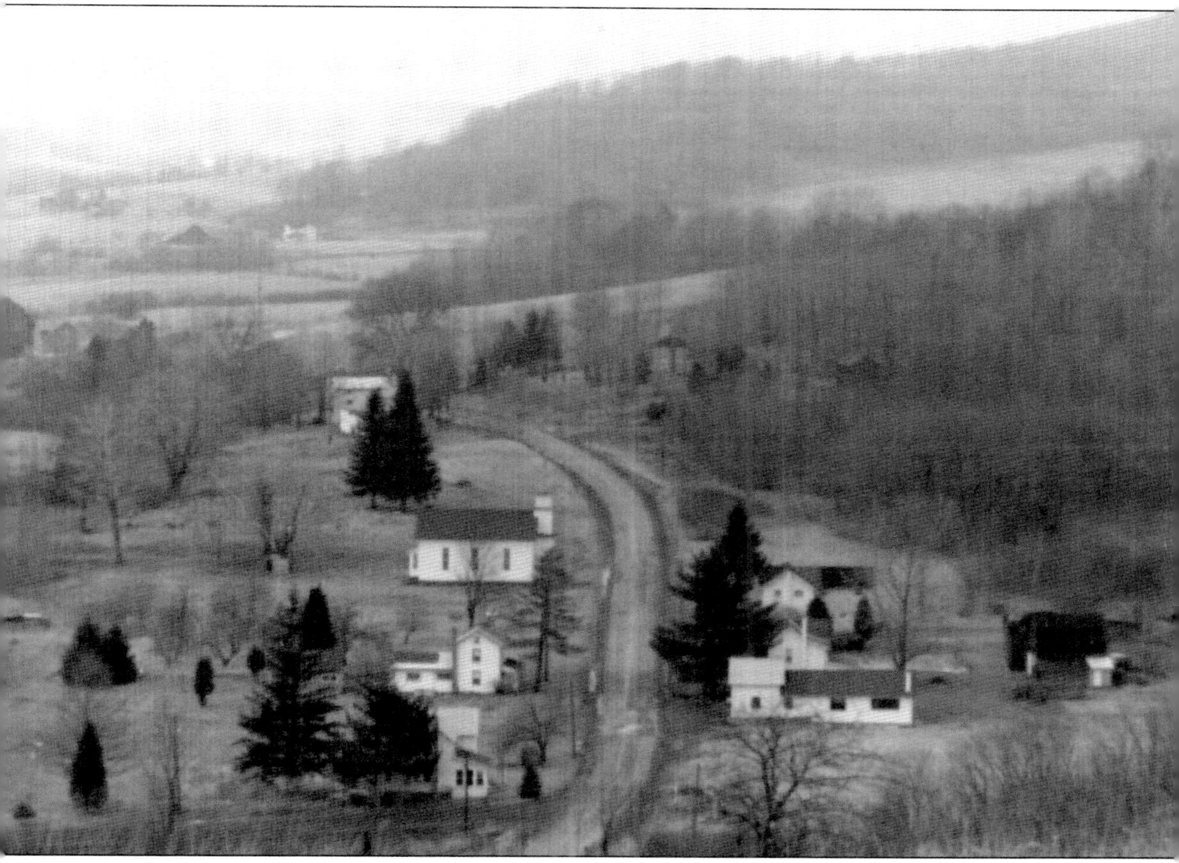

This 1974 photograph of Colley resembles a painting and shows how little the village changed since the 1930s. Pictured clockwise from left are George and Minta Dieffenbach's home, Thomas Hunsinger's home, Colley Church, Colley General Store and Post Office, Nelson McCarrol's home, Mr. Foote's home (first name unknown), Mary and Walter Dunn's home, and an old garage. The Colley Church was built in 1890 as the union church, which meant that the building was available to any denomination. The church subsequently became Evangelical, Evangelical United Brethren, and then United Methodist. The building was badly damaged in a snowstorm in January 1996 and was torn down. (Courtesy of David J. Gephart II.)

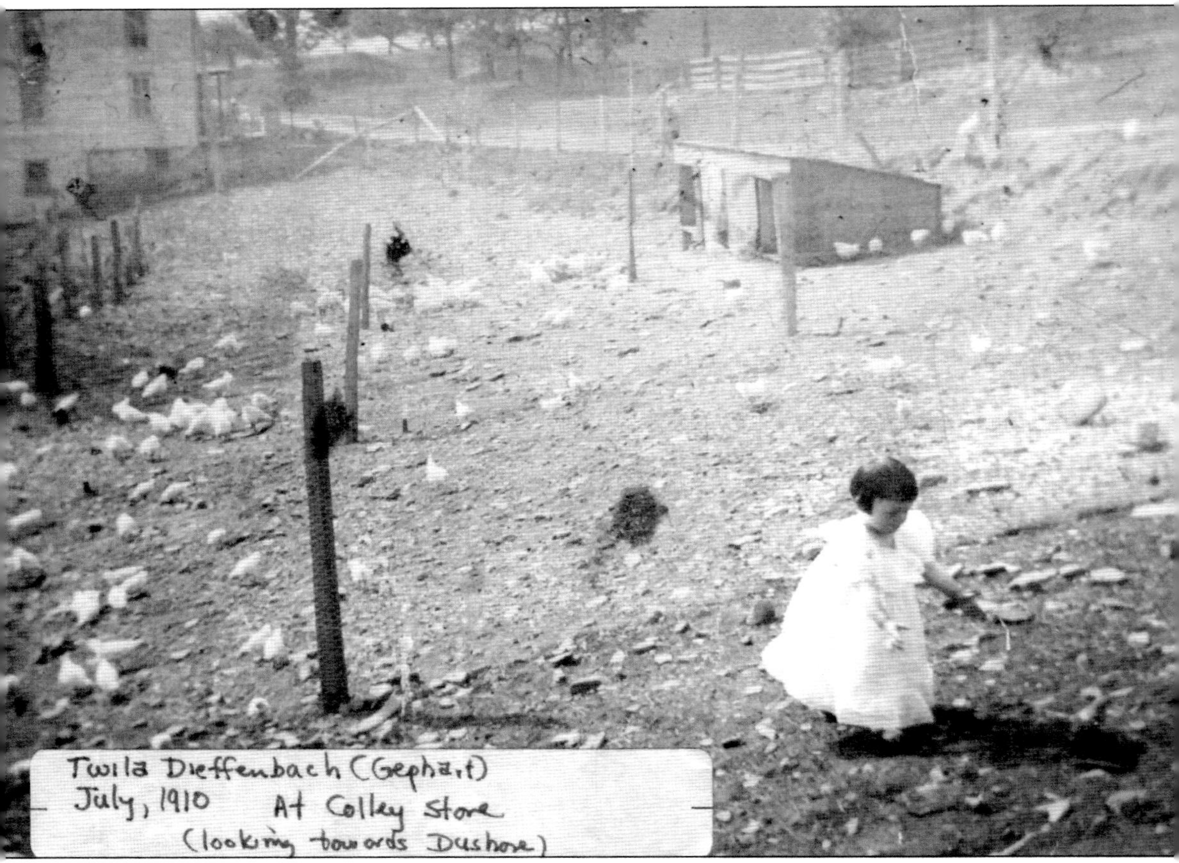

Twila Dieffenbach Gephart, the mother of David J. Gephart II, was two when her picture was taken in July 1910 at the Colley store. The view looks west toward Dushore. The Colley store is behind the photographer. The house in the back is the old Nelson McCarrol house. The dirt road was replaced with Route 87, which now runs where the old chicken coop once stood. (Courtesy of David J. Gephart II.)

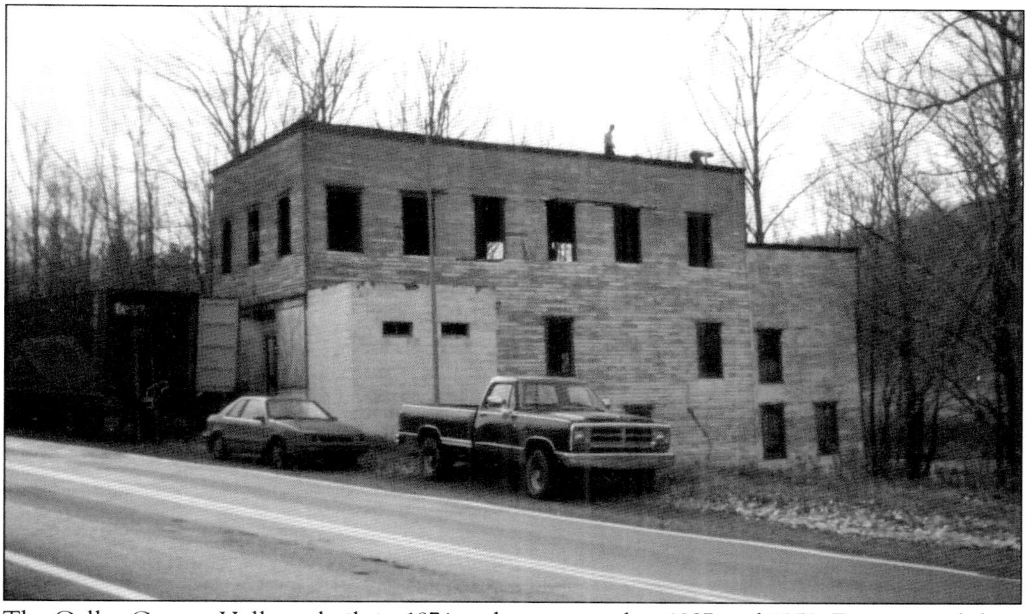

The Colley Grange Hall was built in 1874 and reorganized in 1937 and 1950. Farmers and their families purchased items from a store in the back, and there was a free library. One way of making money included borrowing a lantern. If it was not returned promptly, a 10¢ fine was paid. In the mid-1990s, the building was condemned and torn down. (Courtesy of David J. Gephart II.)

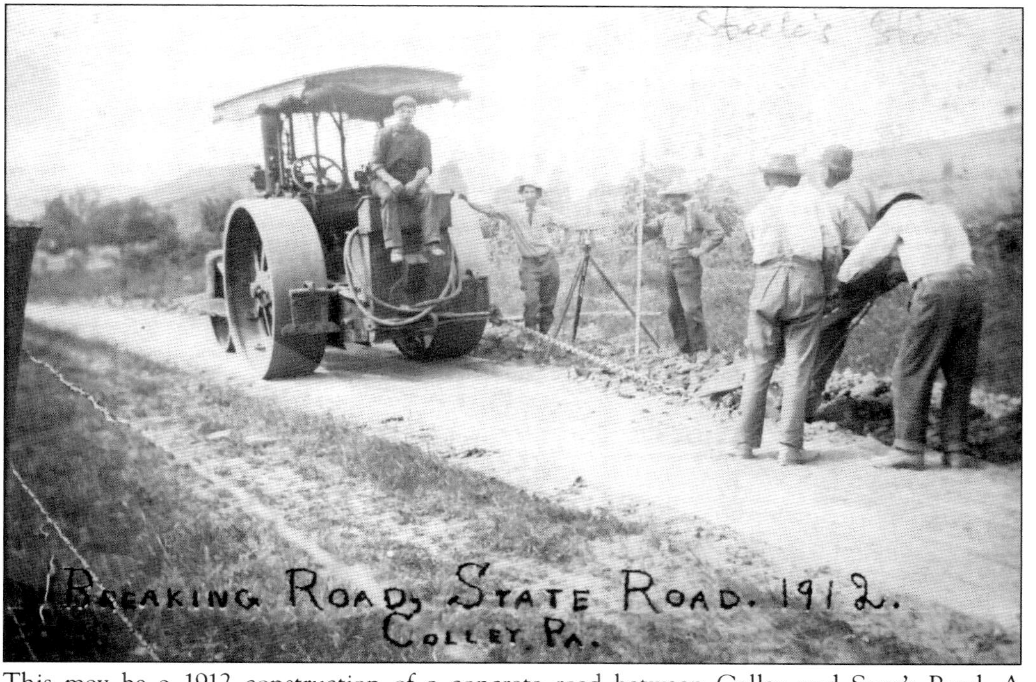

This may be a 1912 construction of a concrete road between Colley and Saxe's Pond. A steam-powered, smooth-wheeled roller pulled a plow to break up the old road. The distance was one mile. No one is identified. (Courtesy of David J. Gephart II.)

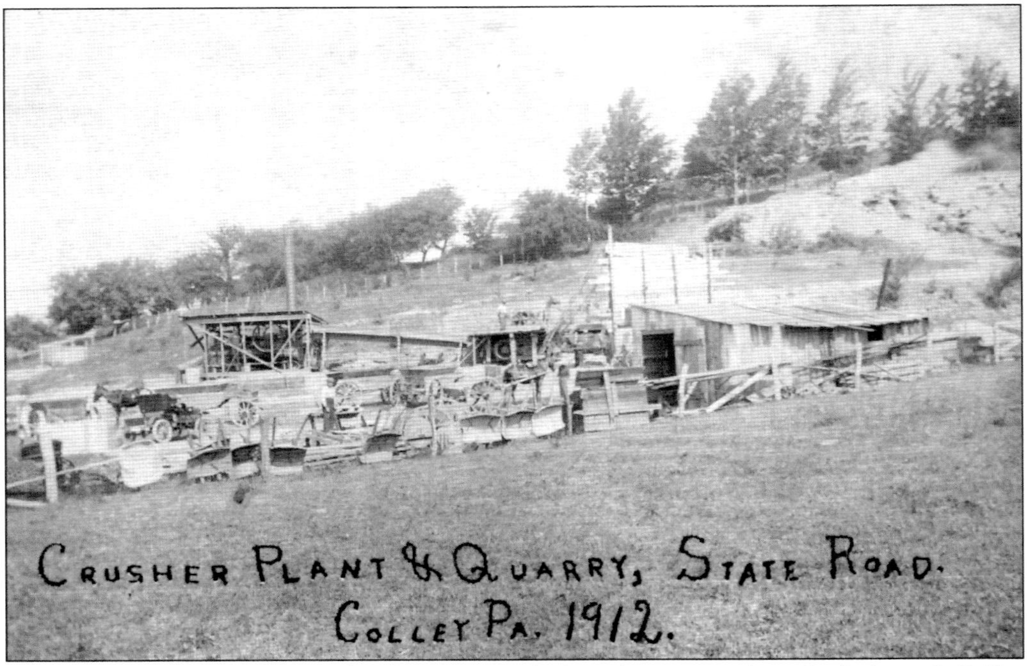

The crusher plant and quarry (above) are pictured when the state road was built through Colley in 1912, and (below) the work crew is grading the road by hand. A rock-crushing machine was used to make ballast for the road. No one is identified. (Courtesy of David J. Gephart II.)

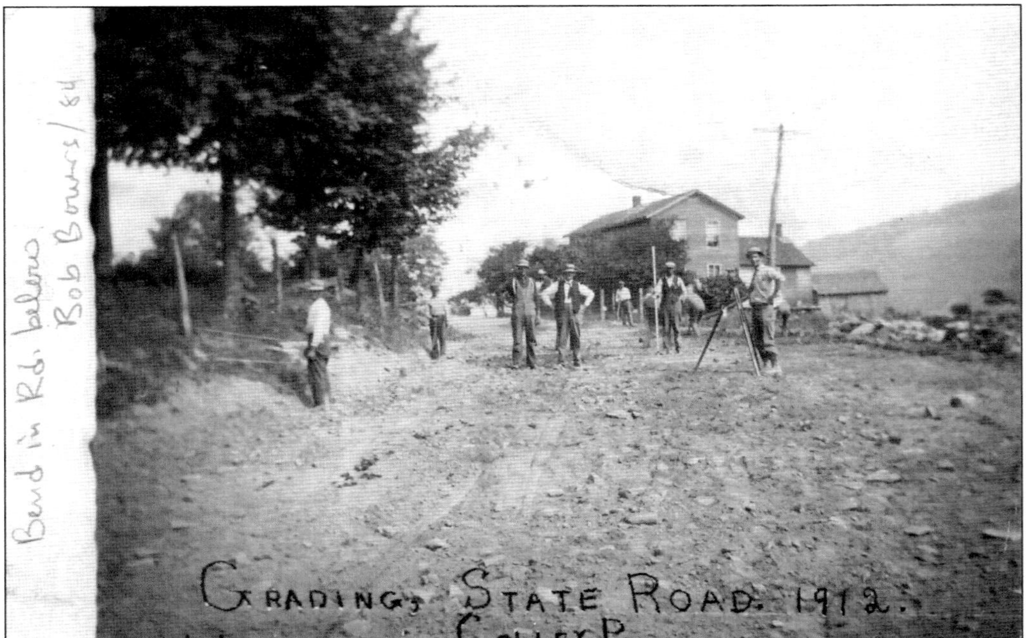

Three

Davidson Township

Davidson Township was established in 1833 by a decree of the court of quarter sessions of Lycoming County. The territory was taken from Shrewsbury Township and originally comprised a portion of what is now Laporte Township. David Richart, a Colonel Derr, and Nathan Howell found this fertile valley at the base of North Mountain in 1808. They returned with their families and were the first settlers here. The township was named for Asher Davidson, an associate judge of that court. Located in the southeastern section of Sullivan County, it borders Luzerne County with Colley Township to the east, Columbia and Lycoming Counties to the south, Shrewsbury Township to the west, and Laporte Township to the north. North Mountain towers above the surrounding hills at an elevation of 2,200 to 2,400 feet and lies in the center of the township in an almost east–west direction.

The Susquehanna and Tioga Turnpike, built in 1808, forms the eastern township boundary. The road brought in most of the early settlers of this township. At the time the Northumberland Road was built from the North Mountain settlement to Columbia County, the area comprising Sullivan County was still a part of Northumberland County. The Northumberland Road could have been the one extended to the Shrewsbury and Lewis Lake settlements. People who settled the Elk Lick area cut their way through, crossing from the turnpike at Long Pond, or came across the mountain from the Fishing Creek settlement in Columbia County.

Sonestown was named for George Sones, who built a sawmill in 1843.

Muncy Valley takes its name from Muncy Creek. Landowner Robert Taylor offered substantial inducements to have a tannery located there, and in 1867, L. R. Bump built a small tannery with a capacity of 150 cowhides a day. The tannery burned down five years later and was rebuilt. It went through several owners until D. T. Stevens and Son sold out to the United States Leather Company in 1893.

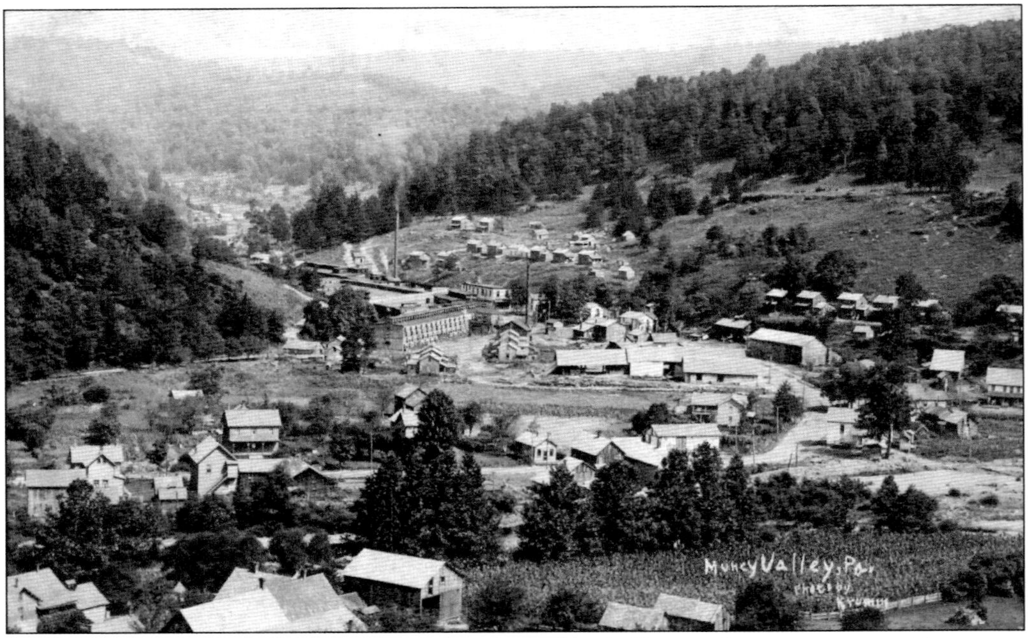

In the 1890s, the Muncy Valley tannery (smokestack at left) was a large operation with its own smithy, barn, bark shed, and schoolhouse (right, center). A priest from Blossburg gave mass in Mike Scarbeck's home located on the hill (center, background). Bark mounds were located behind what is now the Muncy Valley Inne. Highway 220 will later be located in the foreground.

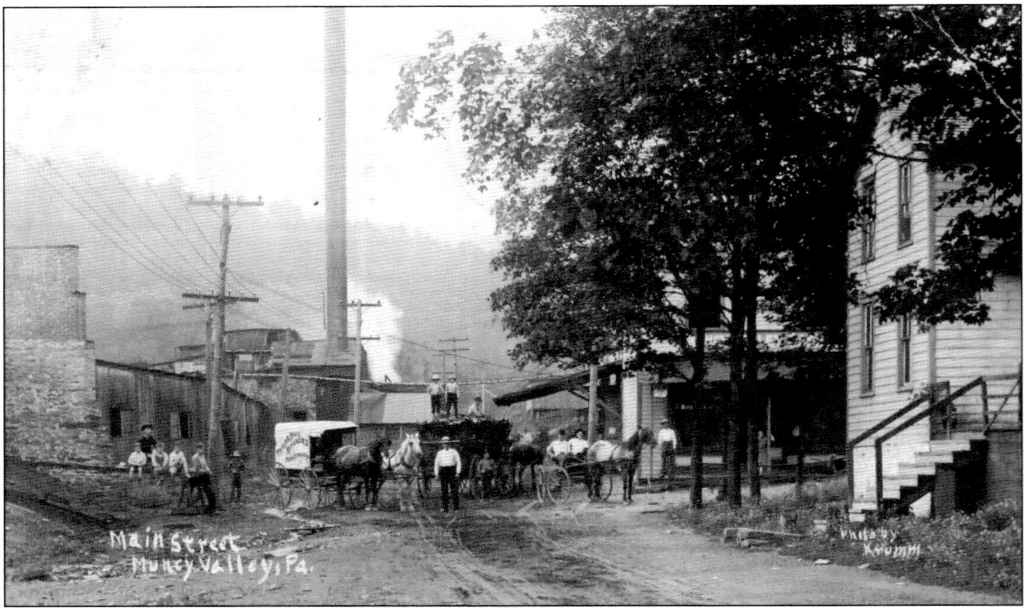

This view of Main Street in Muncy Valley shows a part of the tannery (back, left). Note the bark wagon (center). The mound of bark (far left) was located behind what was later Moran's Ford Garage and Dealership, now the Muncy Valley Inne. The white-top wagon (left) belonged to Taylor Brothers Butchers of Muncy Valley. Their store was located about where the present-day post office now stands. (Courtesy of Carol St. Clair.)

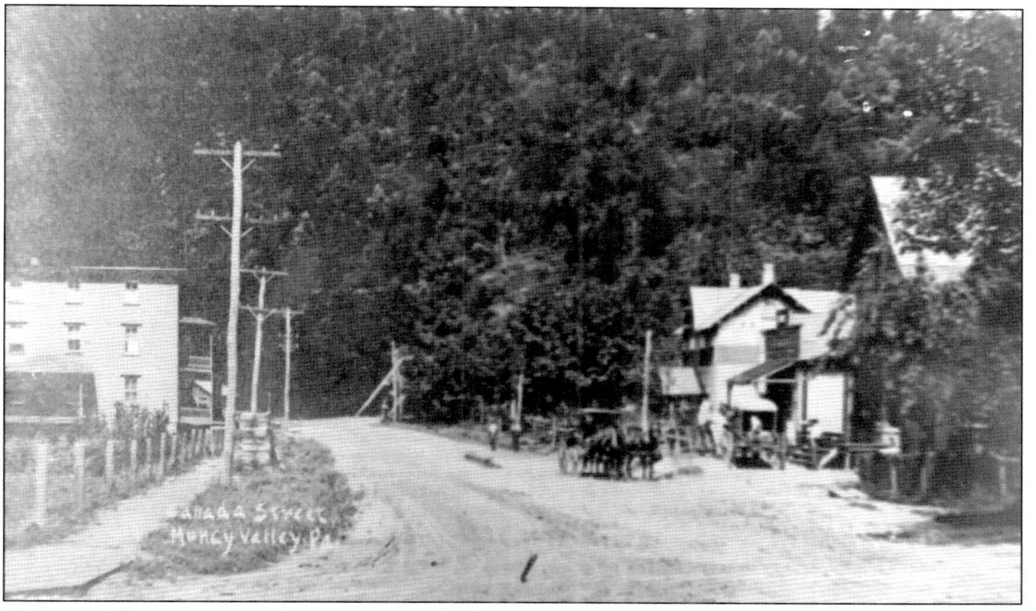

Muncy Valley's Canada Street, pictured about 1900, is where Alvah T. Armstrong, son of Celestia's founder Peter Edward Armstrong, built a store "over in Canada," meaning across the creek where Harvey Buck and Frank Magargel managed general stores. For years, when locals in this area spoke of "going to the tannery," they meant going to Muncy Valley. But when the tannery went about 1920, so did the population.

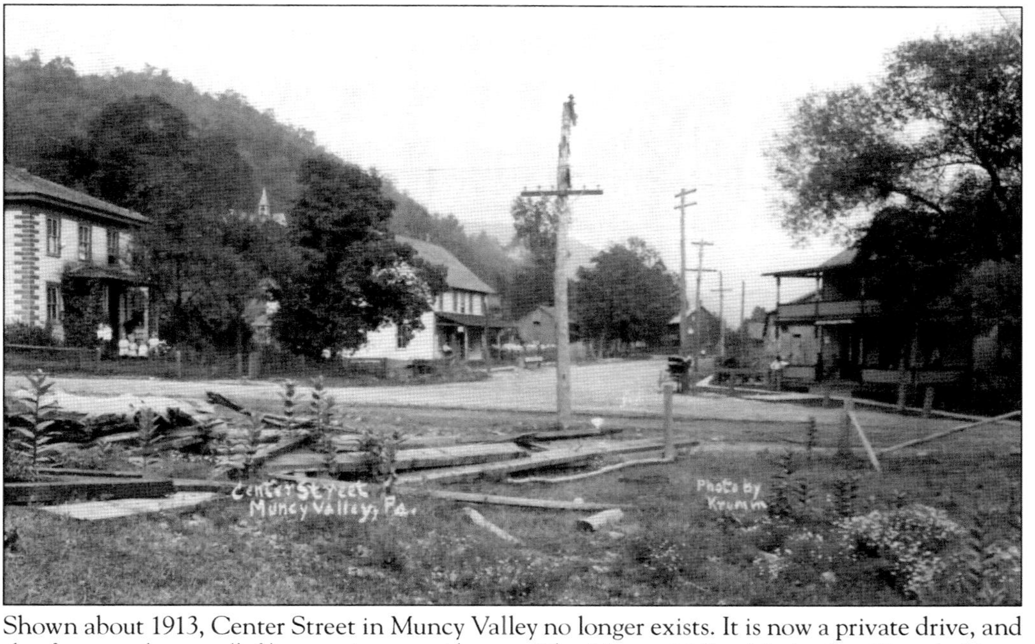

Shown about 1913, Center Street in Muncy Valley no longer exists. It is now a private drive, and the first two houses (left) are private residences. The Muncy Valley Methodist Church (since demolished) is seen on the hill. The houses (back and right) were torn down to make way for Route 220. Highway 42 will later be located in the foreground. The house on the right was a tourist home run by the Bradley family.

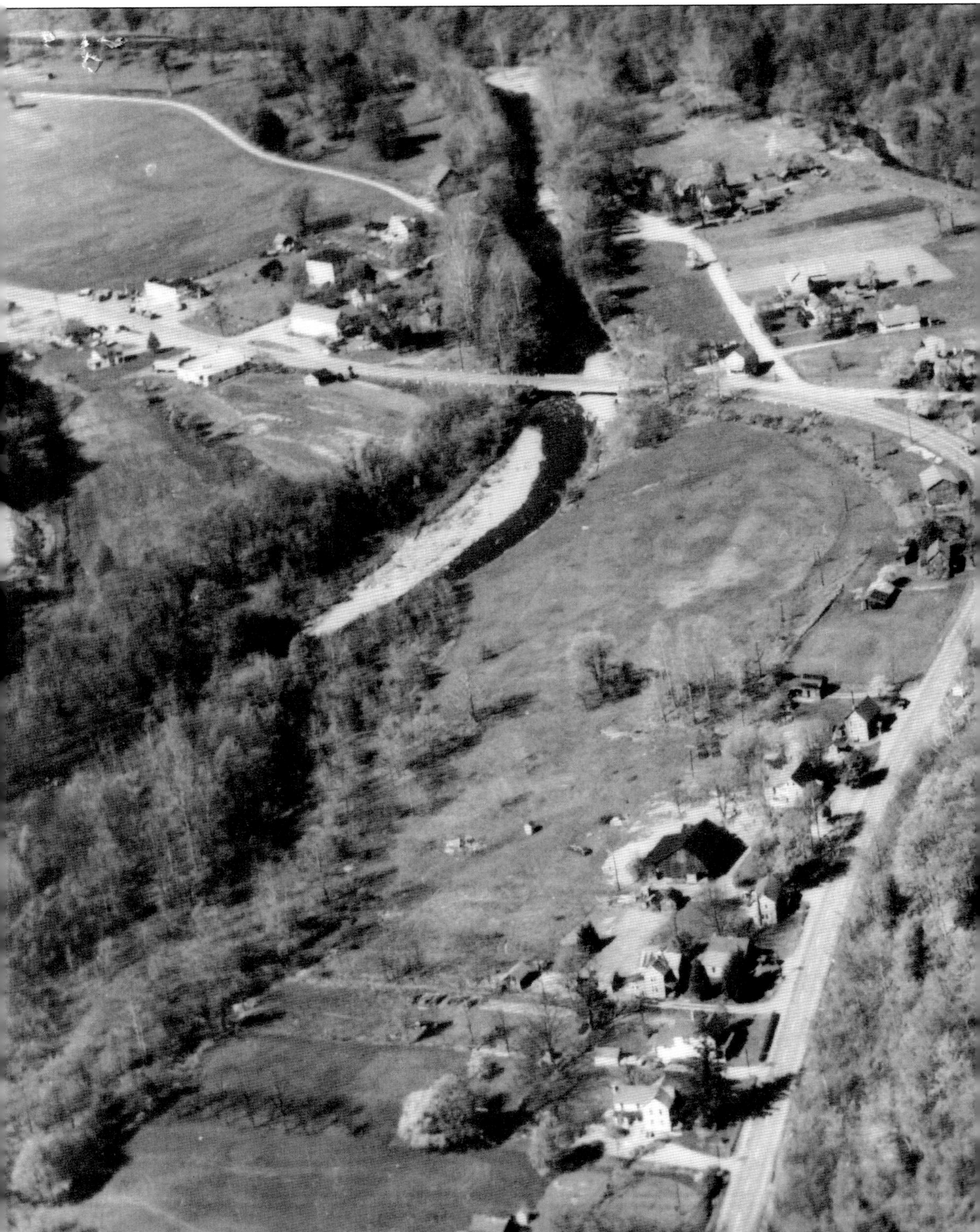

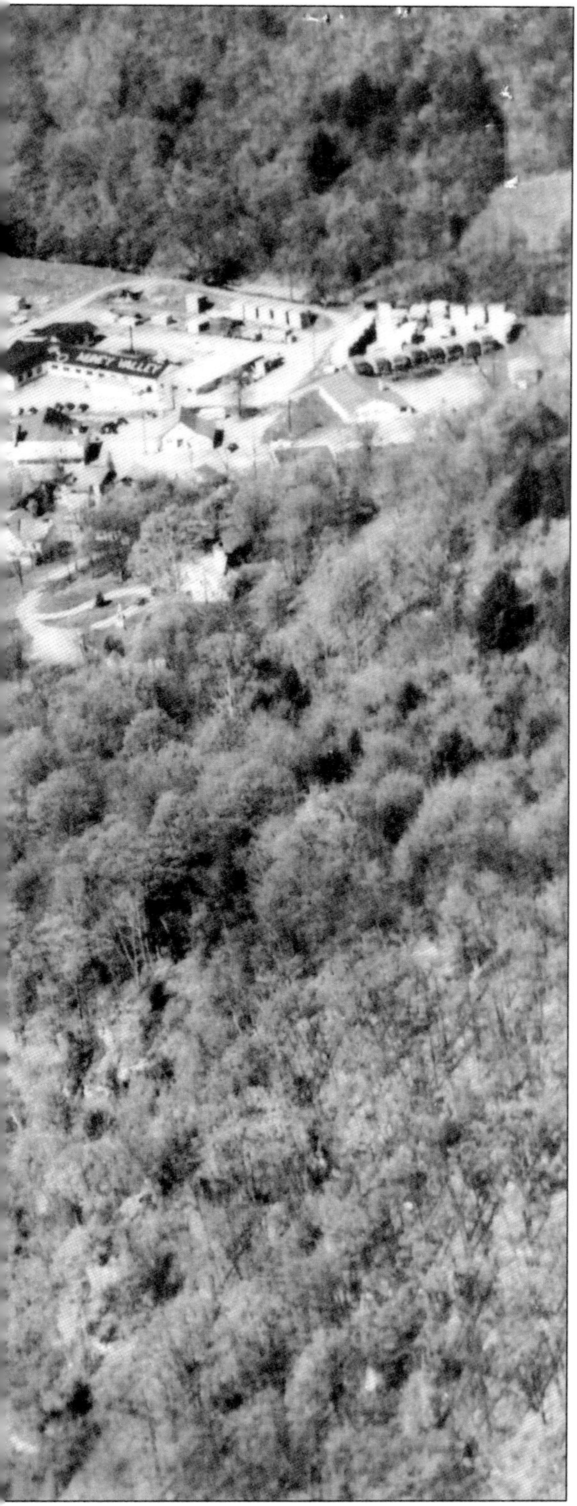

This aerial view of Muncy Valley, taken about 1950, shows the Muncy Valley Industries (upper right), which made spools for wire rope. It was owned by Harold V. and James Lundy, father and son, and employed about 40 local men. It was built in 1948. Route 220 is the L-shaped road, and Highway 42 is at the top of the bend and headed to the right toward Eagles Mere. Muncy Creek is to the left. Center Street would have been located in the curve.

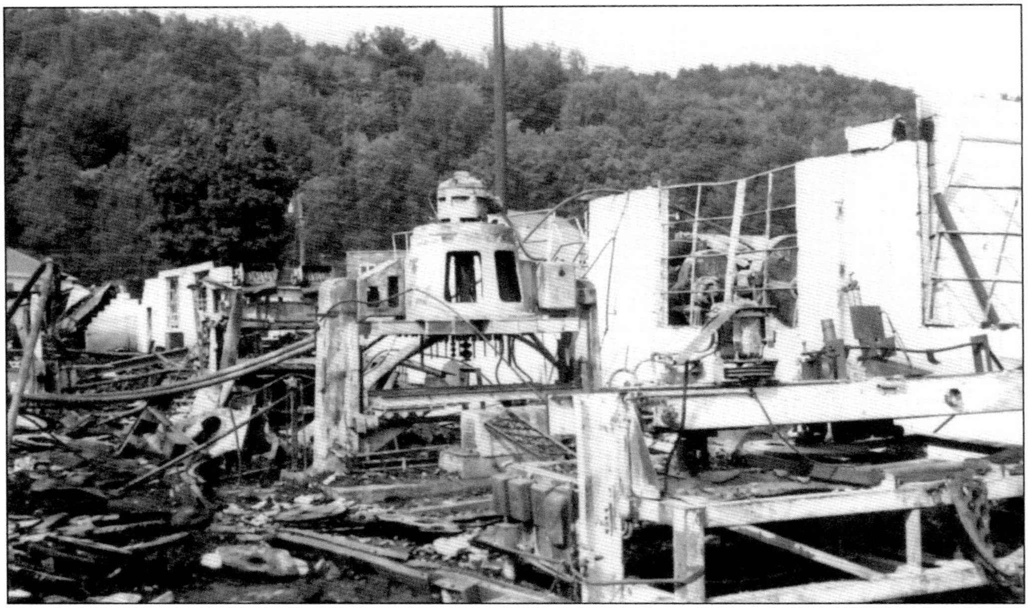

Muncy Valley Industries manufactured products involving the use of wood, plastics, rubber, glass, steel, and related raw material and manufactured reels ranging in diameter from 12 to 80 inches. The business was built on land once owned by the Muncy Valley Tannery. A Dutch oven heating plant was used for sanitation and reducing fire hazards, but the business burned down in 1965.

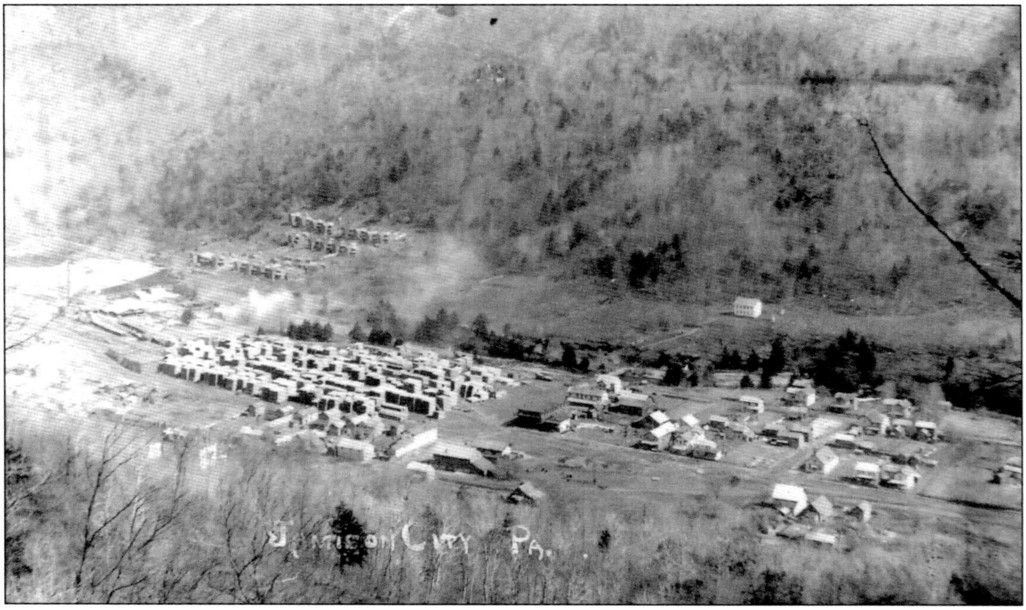

Jamison City was located along Fishing Creek. Named for Col. John Jameson, it was later changed, honoring Philadelphia financier Benton K. Jamison. The Bloomsburg and Sullivan Railroad was completed at this point in 1887. Jamison City became a noted lumber and tanning town from 1889 to 1912, with its population hitting 350 in 1893. After new tanning methods were developed, businesses began closing. The tannery closed in 1925.

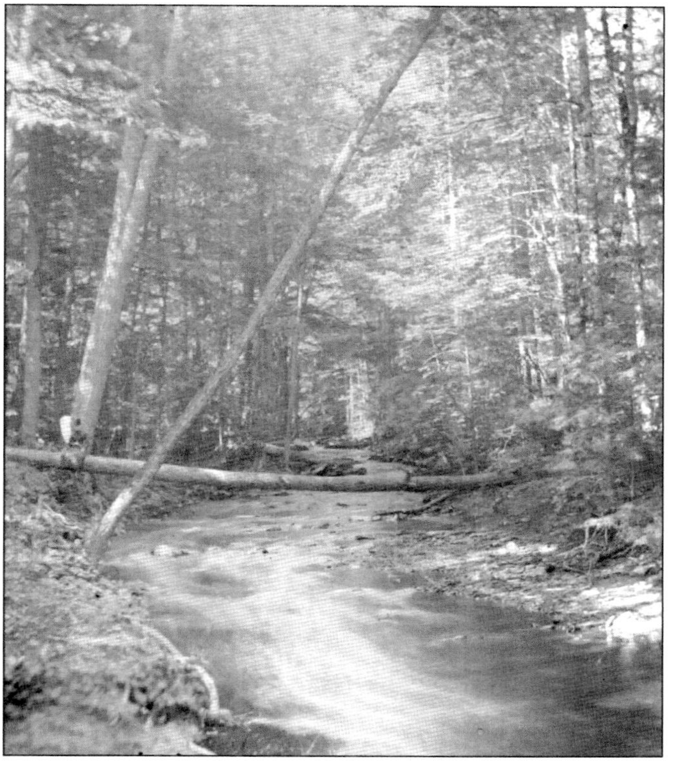

The Bloomsburg and Sullivan Railroad ran up Fishing Creek from Catawissa, the junction of the Pennsylvania and Reading Railroads. Financed by Jamison, it was constructed between 1886 and 1889. During the same years, construction began on the first sawmill and tannery in Jamison City.

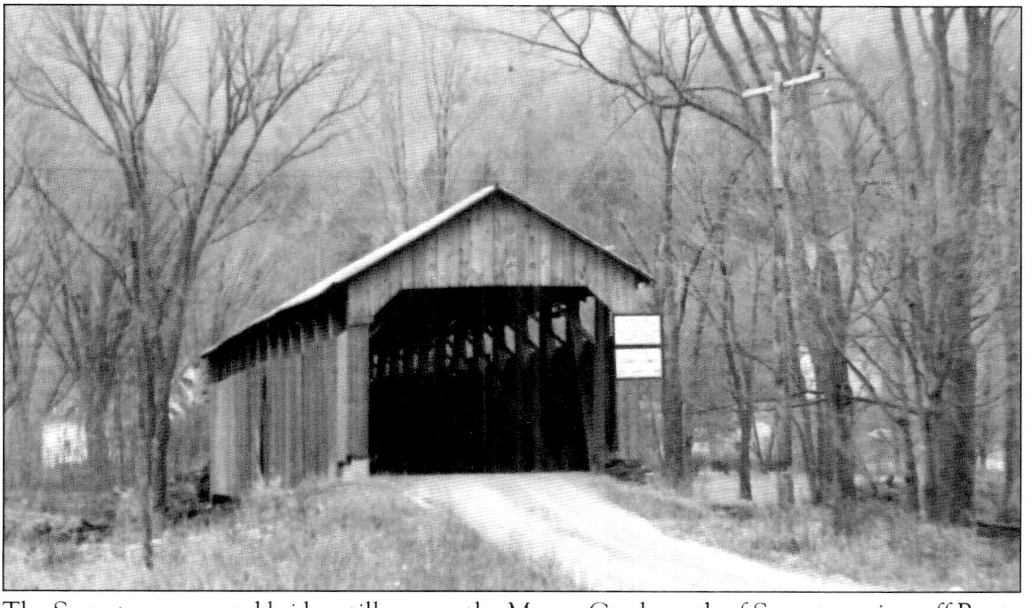

The Sonestown covered bridge still crosses the Muncy Creek south of Sonestown just off Route 220. Constructed in the 1880s, it was originally built to reach John F. Hazen's gristmill. The covered bridge replaced an old plank crossing that was used from the 1850s until the 1880s.

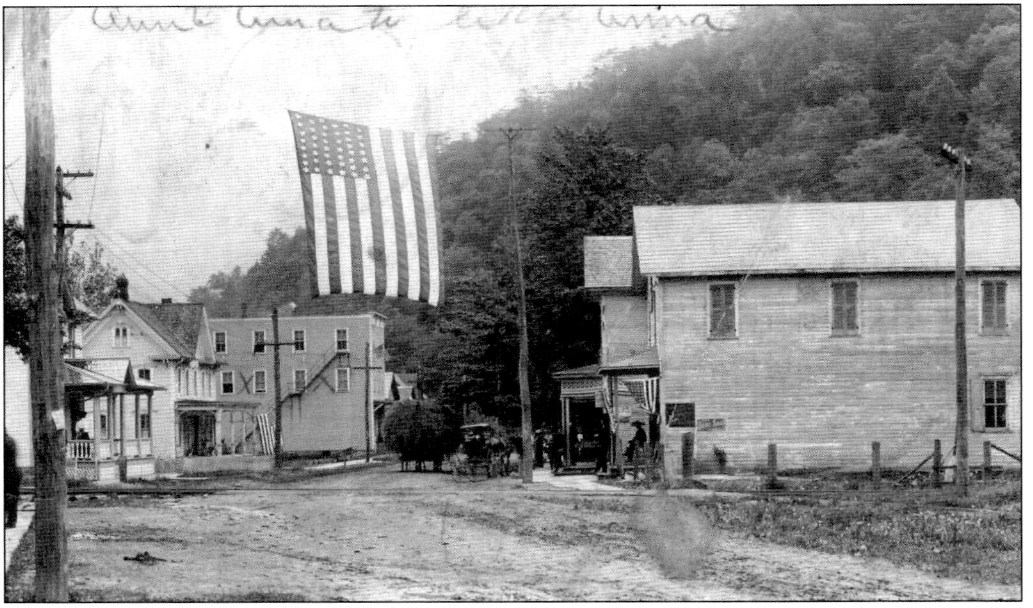

On Main Street in Sonestown, the buildings pictured from left to right are the doctor's house, Frank Magargel's residence, and the Lorah store. Across the street are Magargel's store (far back, right) and then sisters Anna (teacher) and Mabel (postmistress) Speary's store. The narrow-gauge railroad can be seen running across Main Street. The small railroad station, out of the picture, was to the right.

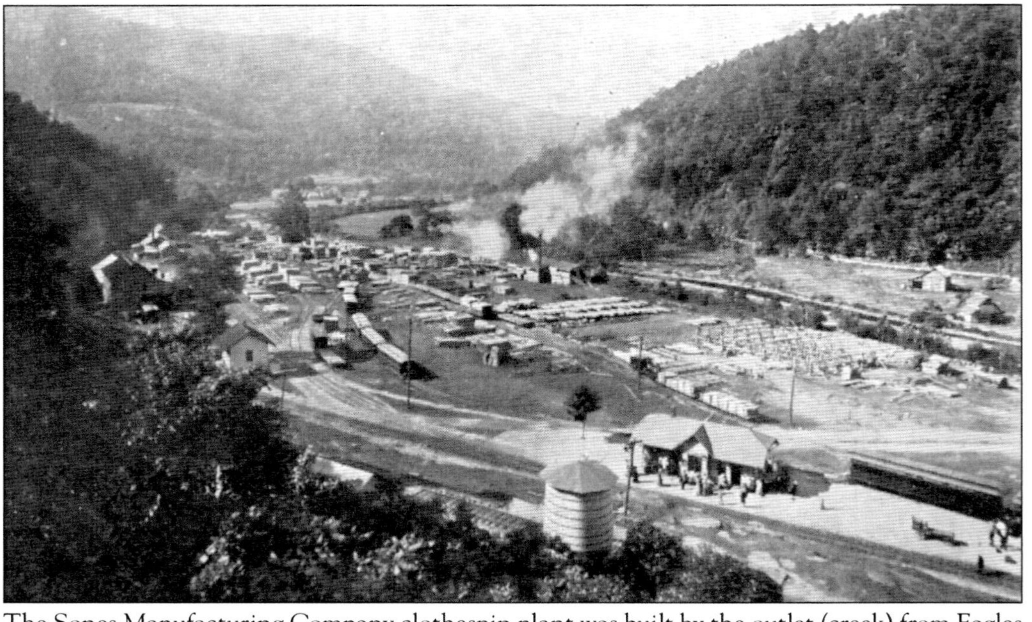

The Sones Manufacturing Company clothespin plant was built by the outlet (creek) from Eagles Mere Lake and burned in 1907. This view shows the second clothespin factory, which closed in 1922, the novelty mill, and the sawmill all located just to the south of Sonestown (out of picture, right). The Williamsport and North Branch Railroad water tower and station are seen in the foreground.

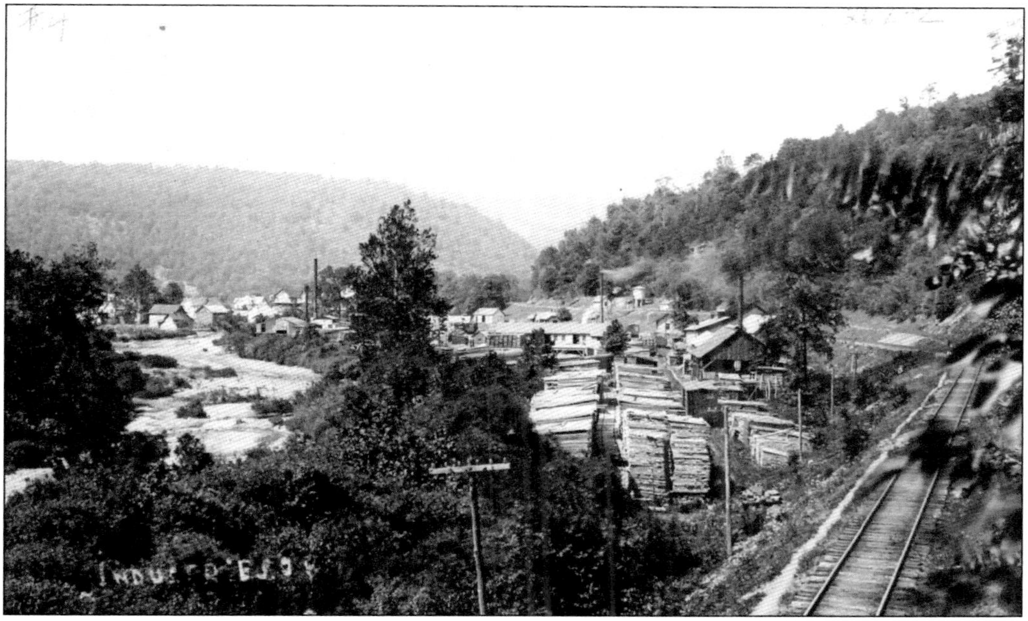

Sonestown's boom came in the 1890s with the arrival of the Eagles Mere narrow-gauge railroad. The station was located by the outlet, which drains Eagles Mere Lake. The Sonestown Mills and Williamsport and North Branch Railroad (right) hugged Muncy Creek. George Sones, whom the town was named for, built a sawmill here in 1843. Sonestown is in the background.

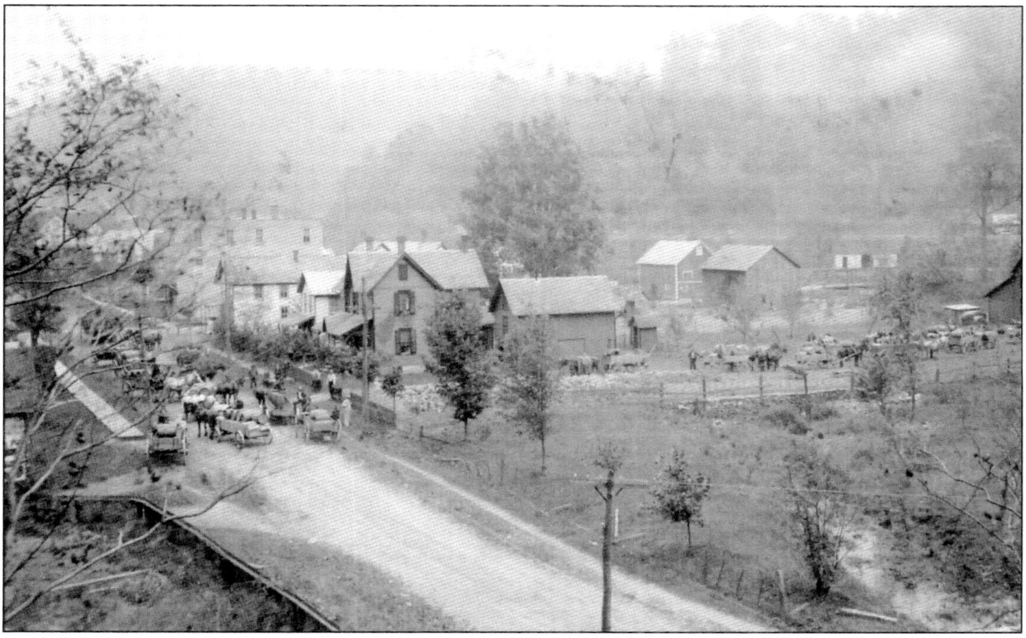

Local farmers with their wagons full of apples (note the barrels) line a part of Main Street to the cider mill (far right) at the southern end of Sonestown. The cider mill was erected in 1895 by John Converse. The press was fired by wood, and its hydraulic power pressed 100 tons of cider. (Courtesy of Carol St. Clair.)

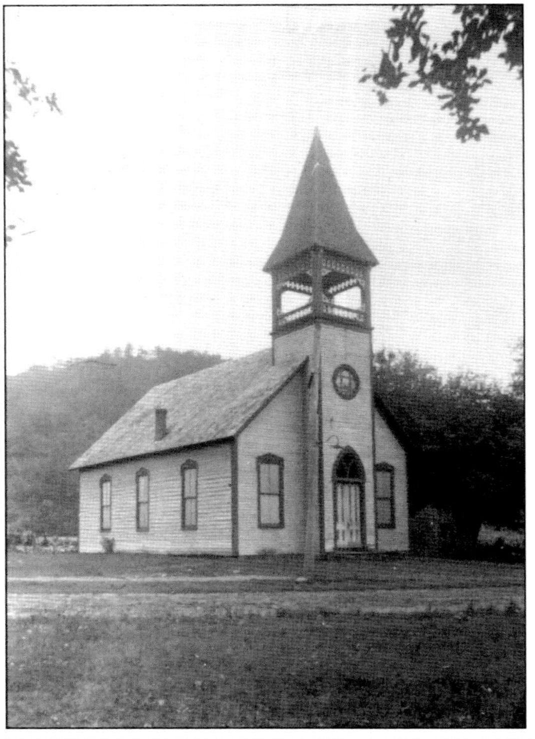

Sonestown Methodist Episcopal Church was incorporated in 1862, and the deed for the land where the building is presently located has a date of 1869. The Methodist church was probably served from the Forksville circuit but has been a part of the Muncy Valley circuit since 1871 or before. The building is now a private residence. (Courtesy of Carol St. Clair.)

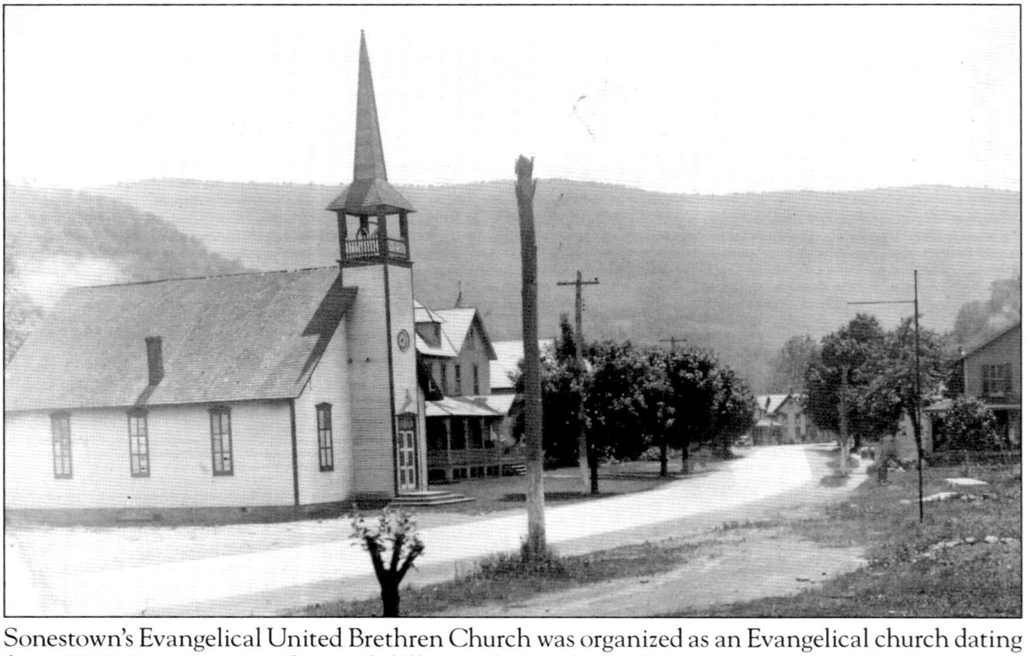

Sonestown's Evangelical United Brethren Church was organized as an Evangelical church dating from 1846. It was a part of several different charges before becoming a part of the Sonestown charge. The deed was made in 1889, so it is quite possible that members met in homes or in the schoolhouse before this date. The building was torn down in the late 1960s. (Courtesy of Carol St. Clair.)

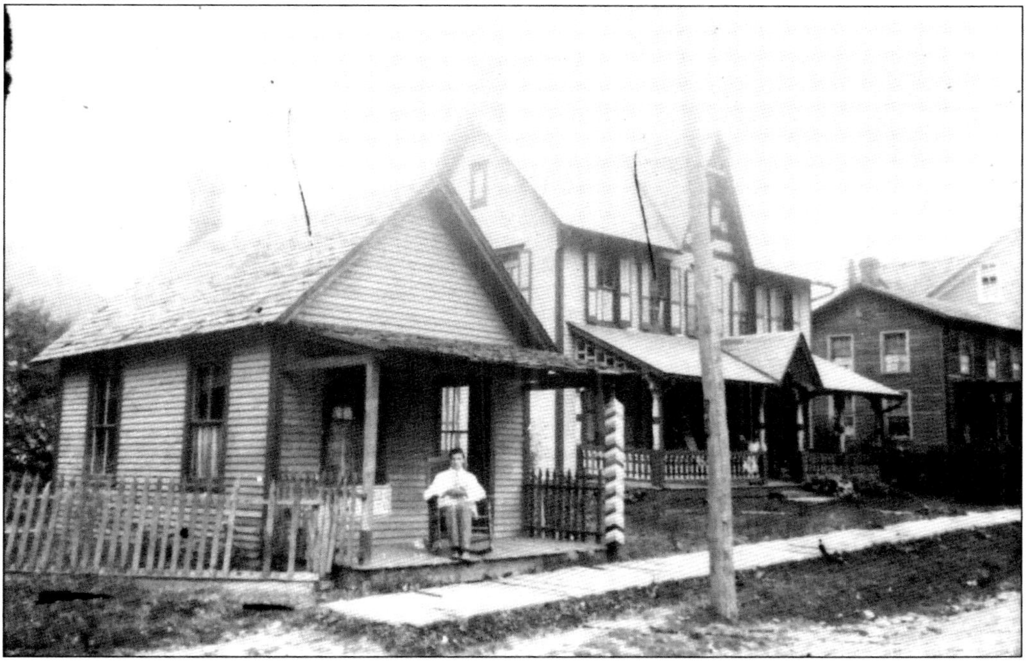

Sonestown's first post office (left) was on South Main Street before it moved to Speary's store. The identity of the man is unknown. The building no longer stands. The two houses (right) still stand and are private residences. (Courtesy of Carol St. Clair.)

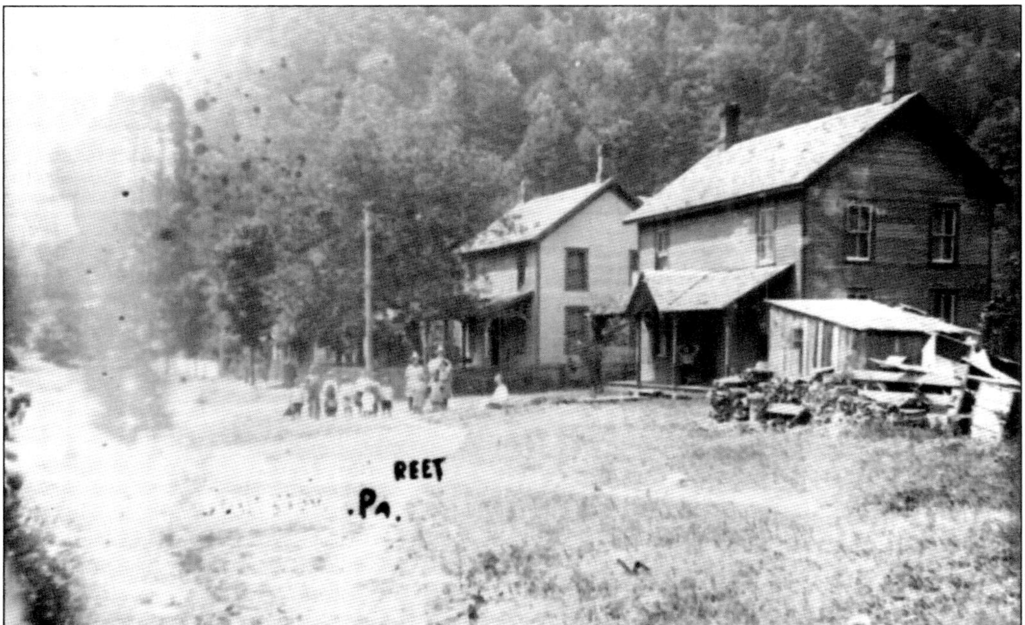

Swamp Poodle was swampy then and still is today. A heading mill and stave factory were located behind the houses near the railroad switch.

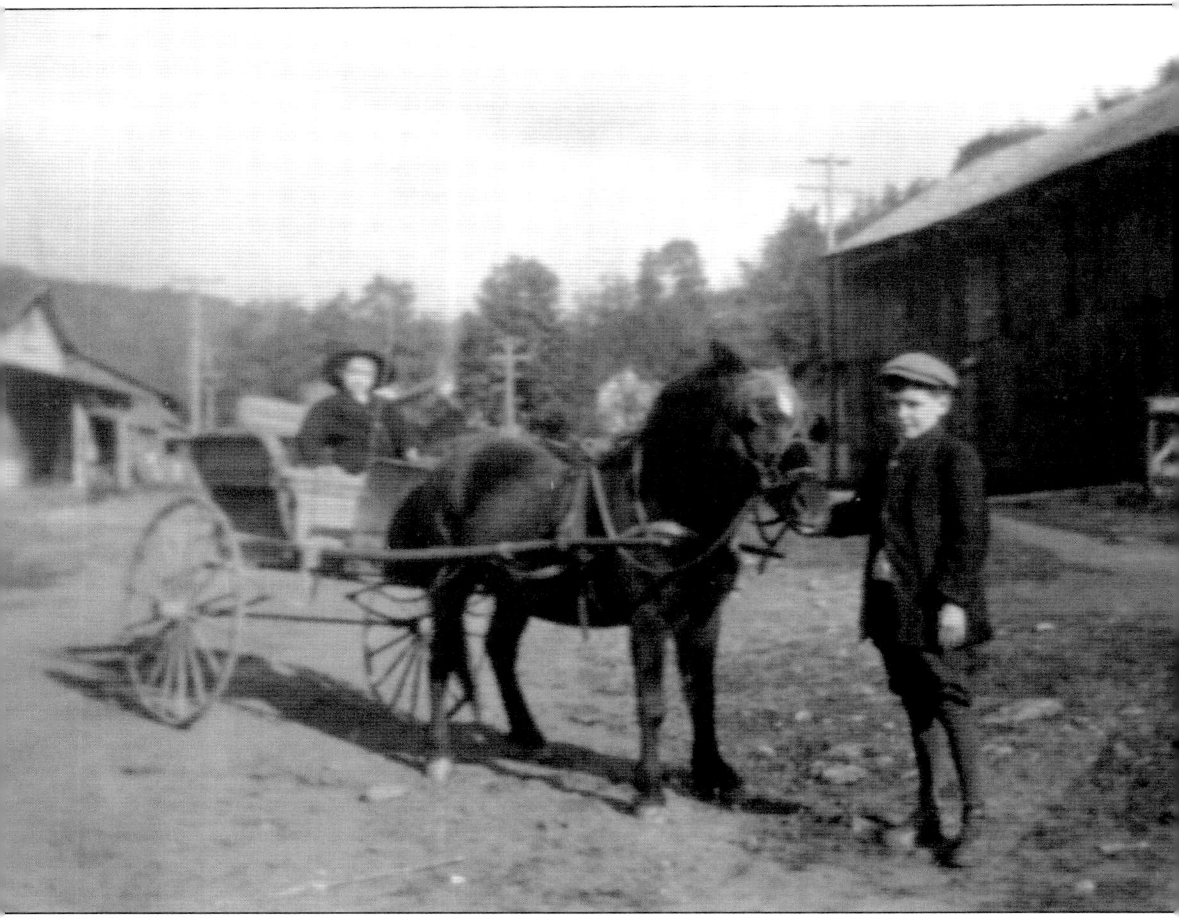

George and Josephine Taylor's wagon was pulled by their pony Trixie from Beech Glen to Muncy Valley where they attended school. Josephine's first husband was Wilford Buck. Her second husband was Howard Peterman, a county historian who died in 2008. This photograph was taken around 1910, probably at the Muncy Valley School. (Courtesy of Carol St. Clair.)

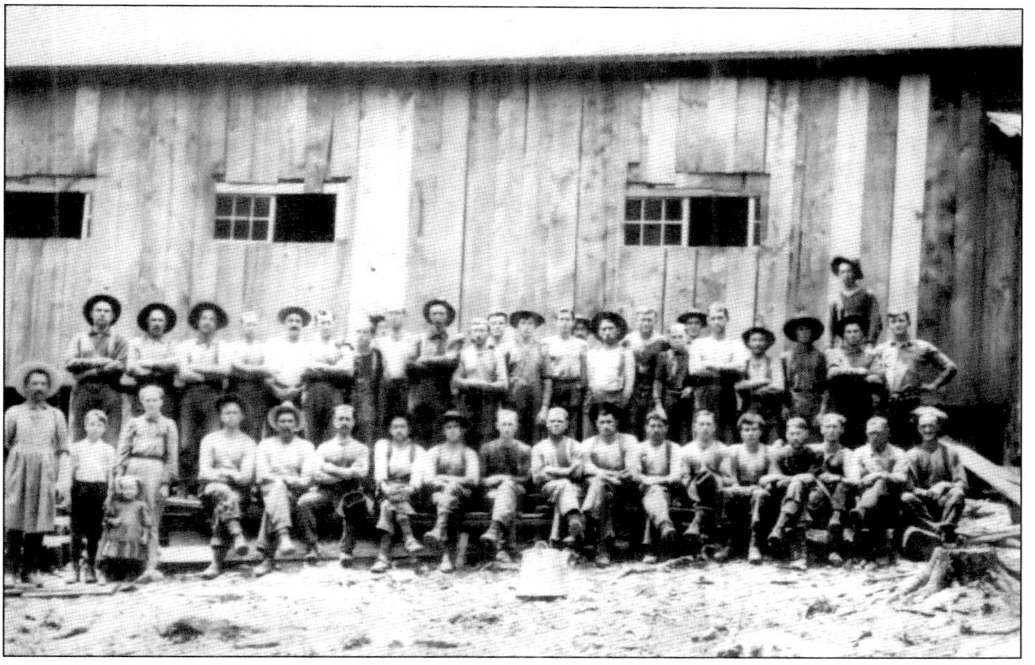

The exact location is not known, but this lumber camp was located along Big Run north of Sonestown. Big Run empties into the outlet from Eagles Mere Lake. Only Sam and Jessie (Rider) Kilgus (front, left) are identified. (Courtesy of Carol St. Clair.)

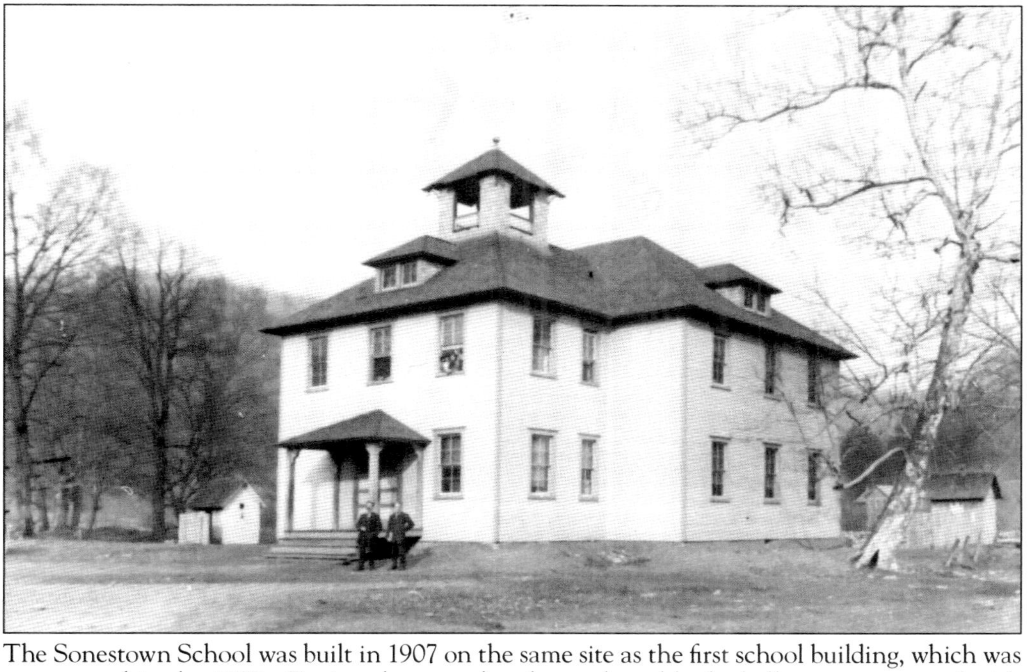

The Sonestown School was built in 1907 on the same site as the first school building, which was constructed in the 1880s. During the next decade, track and basketball teams competed with other schools at the Forksville Fair and at other county school sites. The first basketball games were played on outdoor courts since there were no gymnasiums.

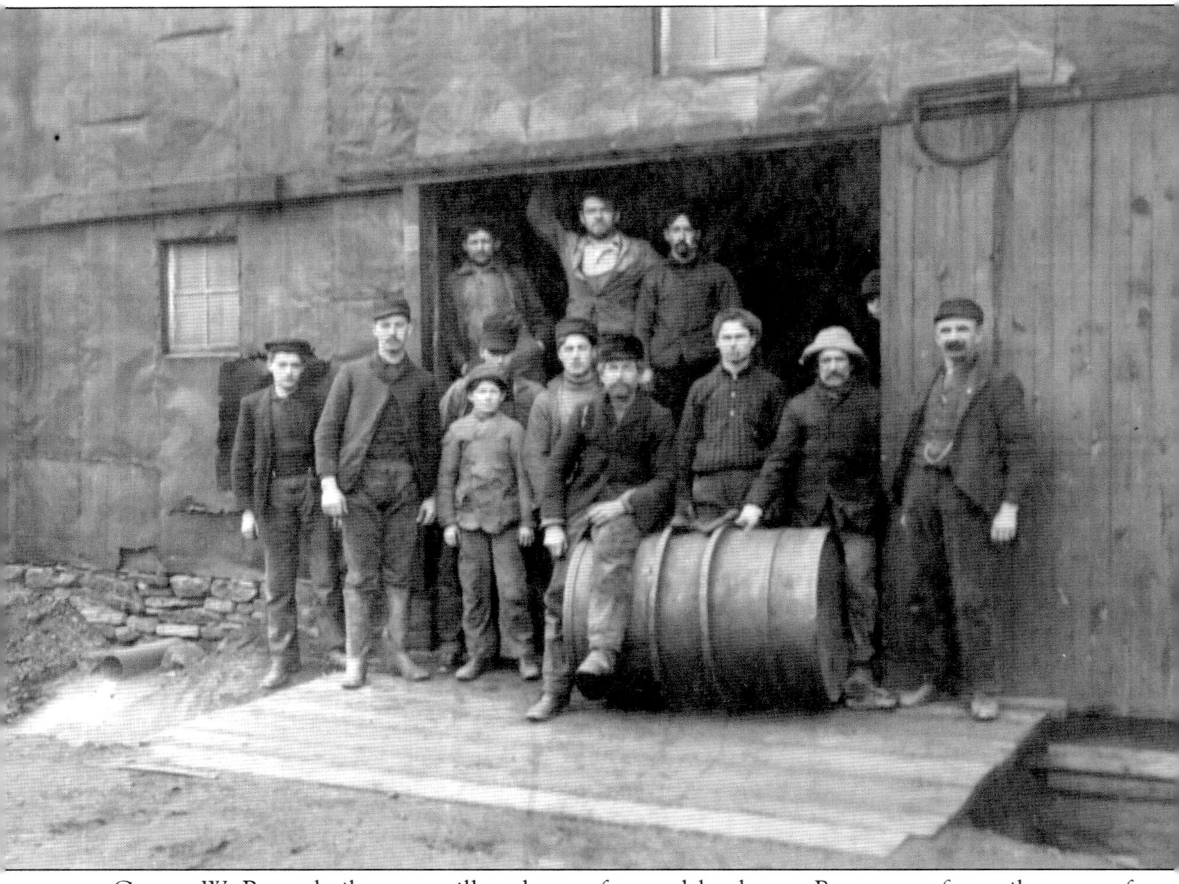

George W. Baum built a sawmill and manufactured lumber at Baumtown five miles west of Jamison City on the West Branch of Fishing Creek until the mill was destroyed in an 1850 flood. In the late 1800s, Sutton-Peck Chemical Company opened a chemical plant (acid factory) at Emmons. It later closed, and operations were moved north to Nordmont before 1900. The only people identified are Myron Dunn (first from the left), Johnny Wells (second from the left), Ezra Levan (third from the left, behind boy), Reuben Dunn (at the boy's left), and superintendent Stanley E. Dunn (far right). Reuben Dunn was Mary Tennant's grandfather, and Stanley E. Dunn was her great-grandfather. The first deed to the company was dated 1890. The company's office was listed as Carbondale. E. M. Peck was a secretary of Pentecost Lumber Company. Supposedly the name of Peck's son was Emmons, which is how the town got its name. Peck bought all the lands of this company in June 1910 for $1. Most of the people who worked at Emmons had died by the mid-1960s, and very few were interviewed. (Courtesy of Mary Tennant.)

Four

ELKLAND TOWNSHIP

Elkland Township was established in 1804 by a decree of the court of quarter sessions of Lycoming County. The territory was taken from Shrewsbury Township and originally comprised of what are now Elkland, Hillsgrove, and Fox Townships and a portion of Forks Township. Early settlers named it Elkland because of elk found in that region. The township is located in the western section of Sullivan County with Bradford County to the north, Forks Township to the east, Forks and Hillsgrove Townships to the south, and Fox Township to the west. The Big Loyalsock Creek forms a portion of the southern boundary.

The first road built in Elkland Township was known as the Genesee Road (Towanda Path), which was opened about the year 1800. Emigrants traveled the road from southern Pennsylvania to the valley of the Genesee River in New York State. Another road was built leading from the settlement at Forksville to the Genesee Road, with a third road leading from the Genesee Road to the settlement in Fox Township.

Joseph Priestley owned large quantities of land in Elkland and made a special effort to induce English people to locate in Elkland. As an inducement to the first 12 settlers, 150 acres of land was given to each, free of cost, on several conditions, one being that each settler had to build a log house within the first year and clear and improve 10 acres within five years. Edward J. Eldred, a British barrister in London, was a land agent of Samuel Wallis and Priestly for the lands known as the Upper Loyalsock and Elk Creek Holdings. His two-story log cabin was known as Liberty Hall and located on the Genesee Road near what is now Hugo's Corners in the north part of the township. Emigrants to the Genesee Valley in New York State stopped here overnight. Eldred represented the law in a scarcely populated area, settling disputes that ranged from threats and thefts to near murders. Another early settler was James Ecroyd, who moved from Hillsgrove and built a gristmill.

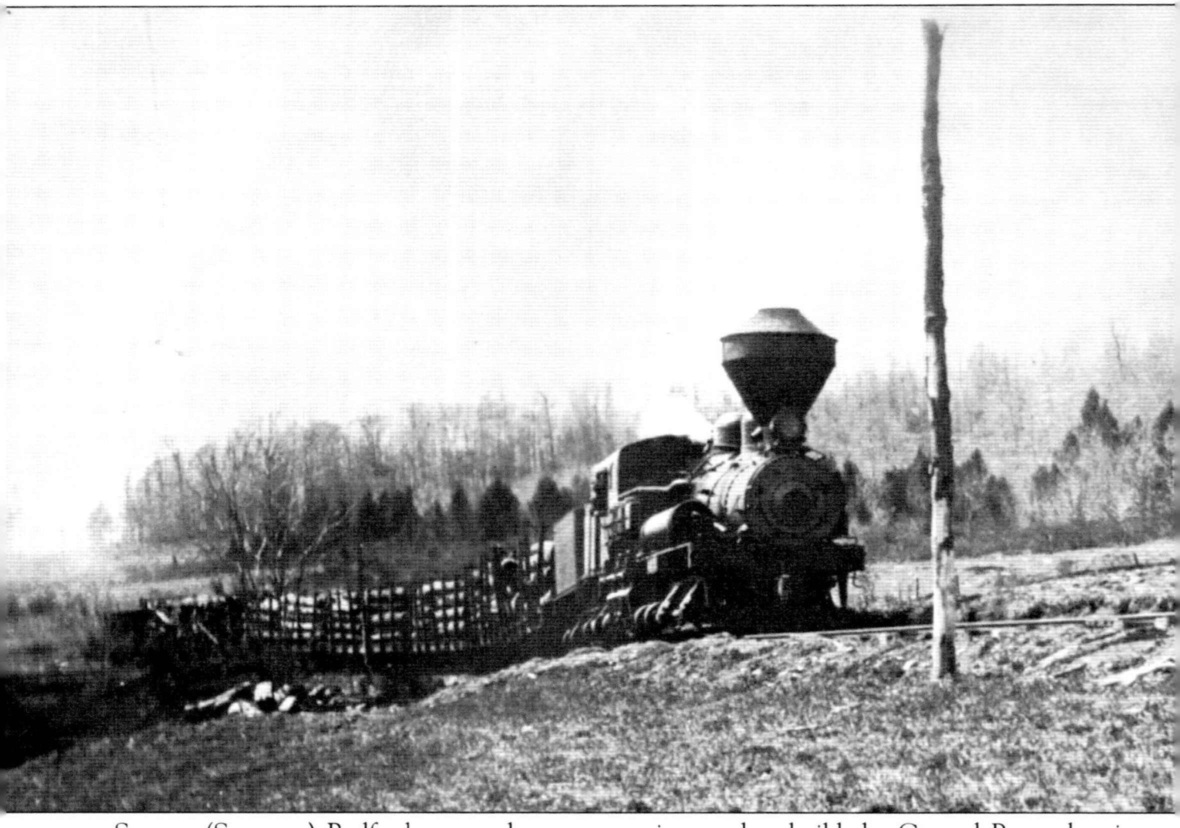

Semore (Seymour) Bedford operated a steam engine used to build the Central Pennsylvania Lumber Railroad from Millview to Laquin in Bradford County and worked as a fireman for the railroad until an accident broke his leg. This photograph of a train engine may have been taken on property belonging to Miles Barnes along Mill Creek. This railroad followed Mill Creek down to Millview and then across the flats to Mitstifer's lumber camp at Walkersville, which was timbered off in three years in the early 1920s. The camp was probably named for Clayton Mitstifer, who was a woods foreman for the Krimm Company that had operations in Lycoming County and Sullivan County. (Courtesy of Dale Bedford.)

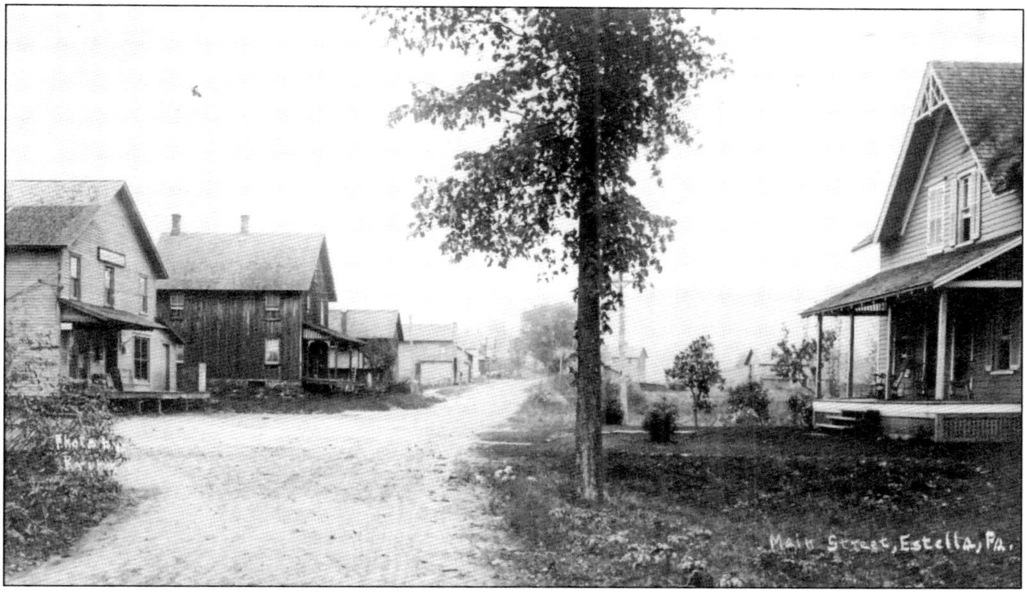

Above, along Estella's main street in 1900, from left to right are the Jennings store, the Baptist church parsonage, Raleigh Beinlich's, future State Route 4009, and Carl Collins' Ford dealership. The Jennings home is at far right. Ellsworth Jennings built his store in 1897 that included the post office and telephone exchange. The store (below, far right) at the opposite end of the village was subsequently owned by Gleason Lewis, Harland Baumunk, and Charles Leljedal. The Rosbach house is second from the right, then a barn, and the Ford dealership is fourth from the right. Charlie Kilmer bought the barn (far left), tore it down, and built a house. Beyond this (out of picture) was the creamery. With its main office in Forksville, the Sullivan Telephone Company line (1904) ran from Estella to Eldredsville, then from Keeney's Corners to Woodhead Corners, and to Bethel. Estella was first called New Salem.

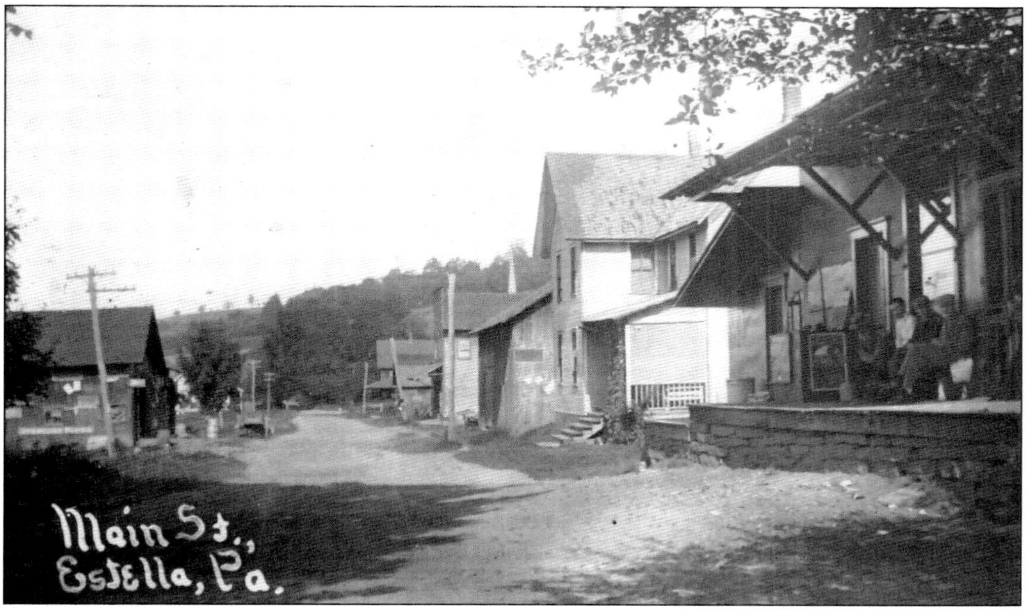

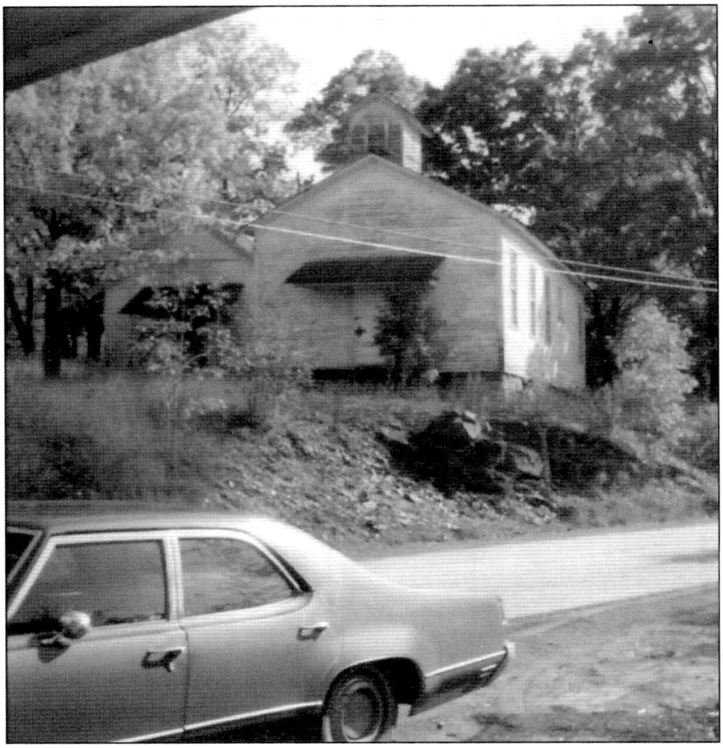

The old Estella high school (right) and lower school took in students from several miles around by 1900. The schools were built in 1898. Chaffee Hill Road to the left of the buildings once connected Bedford Corners with Estella before State Road 4009 was built. (Courtesy of Stanley M. Woodhead.)

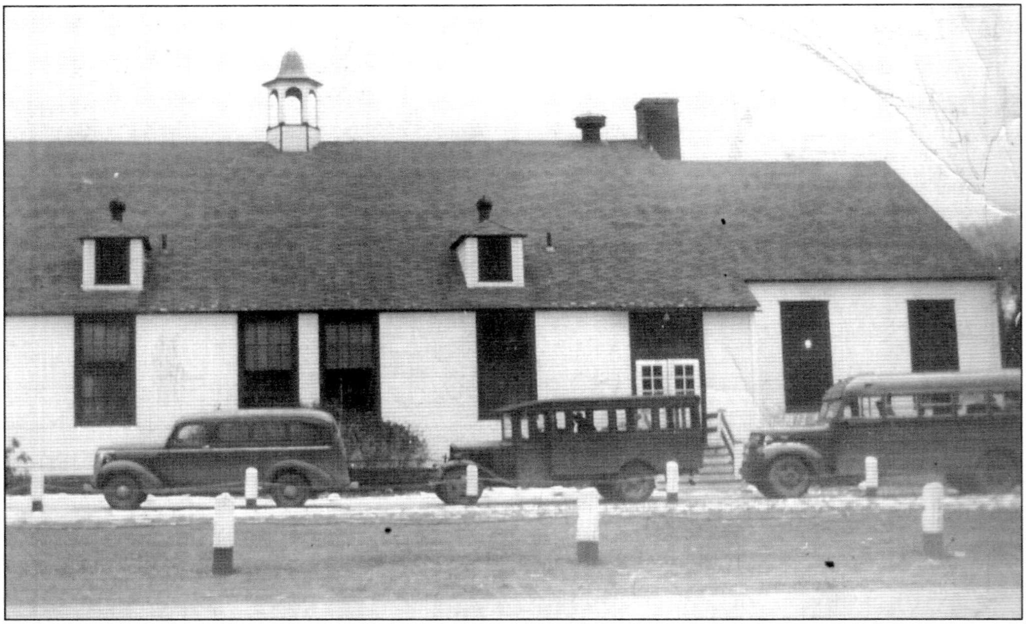

Estella School (now Dar-Way Elder Care) was built in 1930. The girls' restrooms and coat closet were on the left (where they also entered), and the boys' were on the right. The bus on the left was driven by Ralph Hugo, and the "egg crate bus" (center) was owned by Hugo but driven by Emery Norton. The bus on the right, from Shunk in Fox Township, was owned by Raleigh Beinlich.

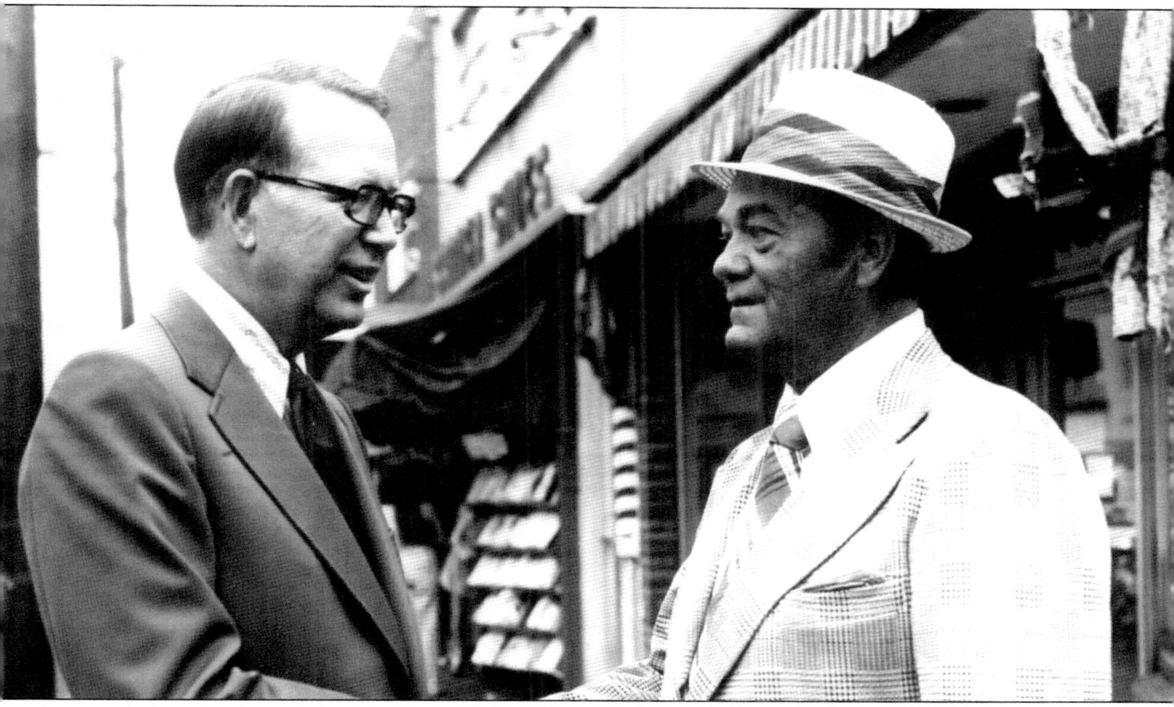

Kenneth Lee (left) said that in about 1937, the school board fired almost all the teachers in the school system. The student body went on strike and marched up to school superintendent Lyman Snyder's store in Eldredsville. Snyder was not impressed, but a new principal and teachers were hired. Shaking hands with Lee is Luther Davis, a former coach and teacher at the Estella high school. (Courtesy of Kenneth Lee.)

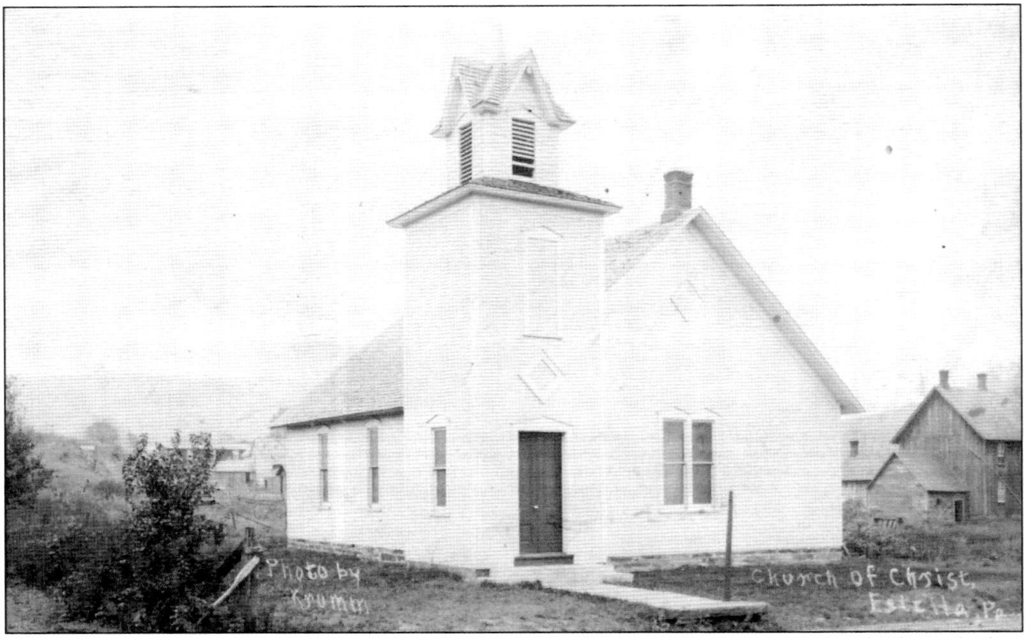

Now the Living Hope Church, the old Baptist church became the Church of Christ before it was rented by the Mennonites in 1956. The building was constructed in 1904. Ellsworth Jennings purchased the property in 1947. The old Baptist parsonage, no longer standing, is seen to the right.

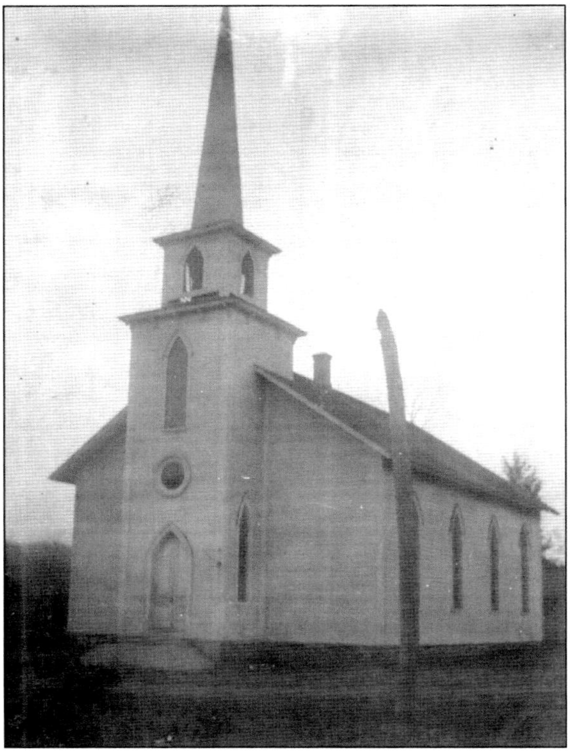

Built as a union church in 1888 by Sadler Rogers, the Estella Methodist Church served as a place of worship for the Methodist, Wesleyan, and Episcopal groups. John and Augustus Plotts assisted in the construction. Once a part of the Forksville-Hillsgrove-Estella circuit, it merged with the Forksville Church in 2003. The old church is now private property and stands on the corner across from Estella's general store.

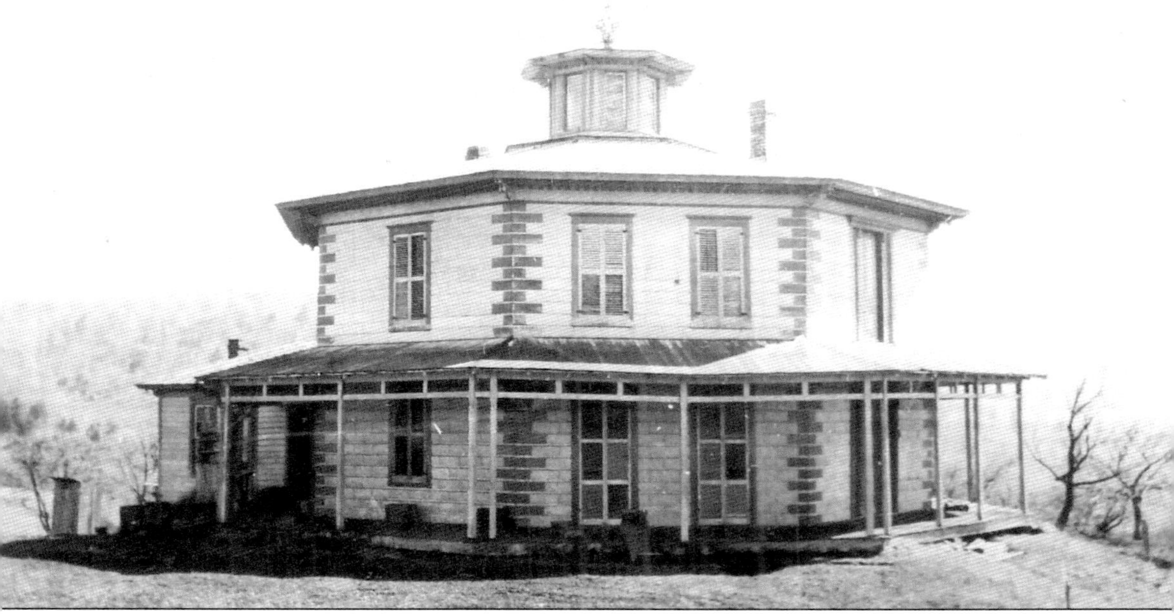

William Marsden of Philadelphia paid local carpenter Anthony Gleockler $3,300 to build the round house in the 1860s as a country home. Stories associated with the house include a hanging, unexplained deaths, funerals, and tenants hacking at thick heavy beams beneath the house for firewood. Cattle even walked through the open building. The octagonal-shaped home was restored by a local family and still overlooks Estella.

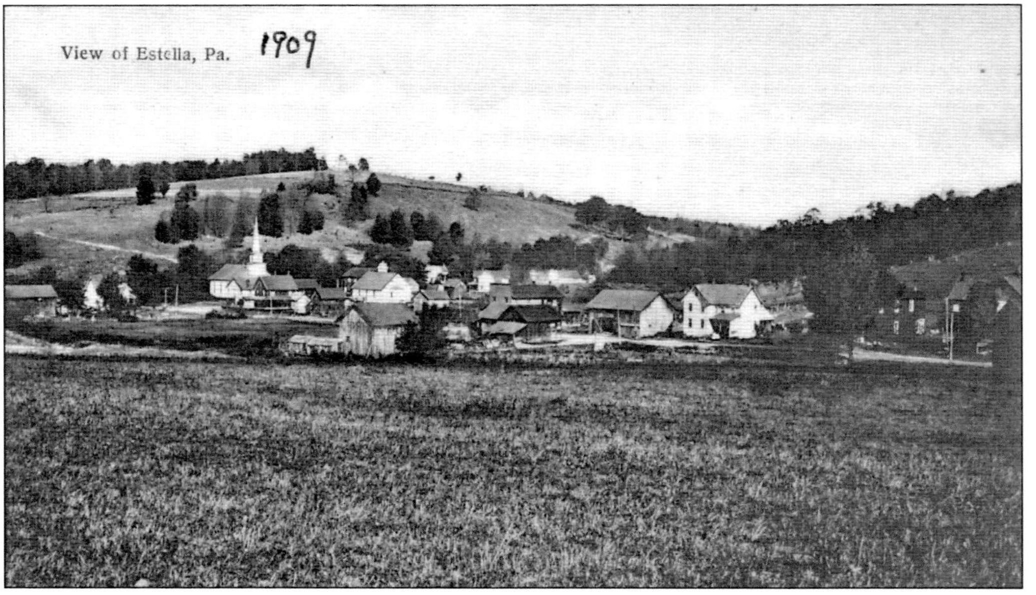

This bird's-eye view, looking northward, of Estella was taken sometime after 1907. The Estella Methodist Church (left of center), Jennings store, and the old Baptist church parsonage in front of the church are recognizable landmarks.

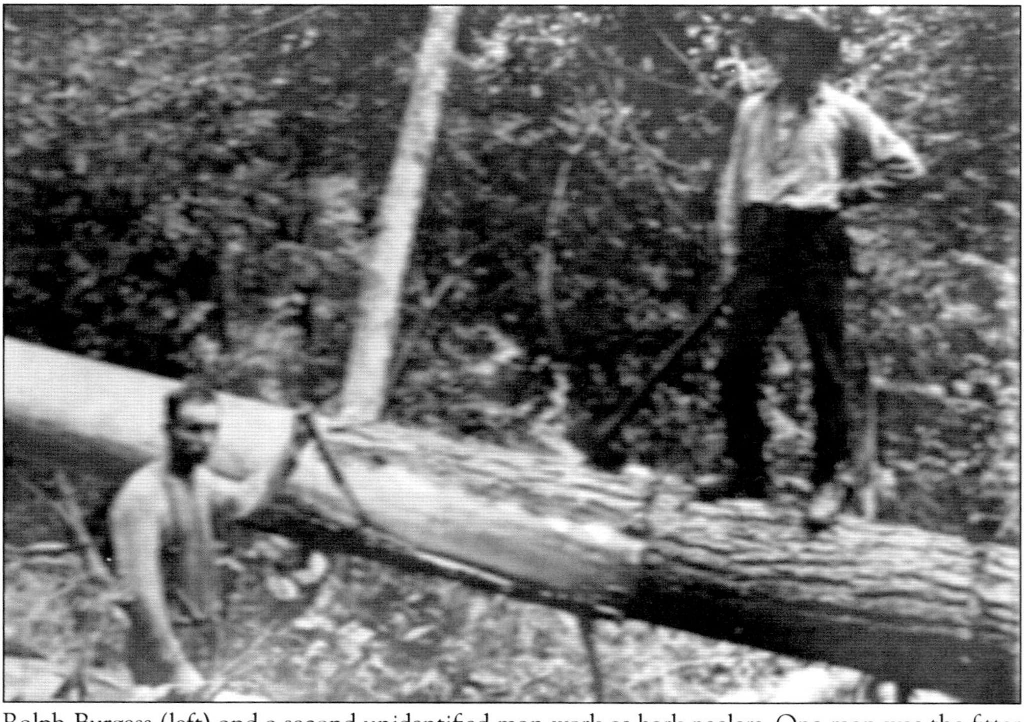

Ralph Burgess (left) and a second unidentified man work as bark peelers. One man was the fitter who climbed up the tree and slit the bark in rings. The other man was the spudder who went in with his spud tool and peeled bark down from around the tree. Burgess was the father of Bonnie Boyles of Elkland Township. The date of the photograph is unknown. (Courtesy of Bonnie Boyles.)

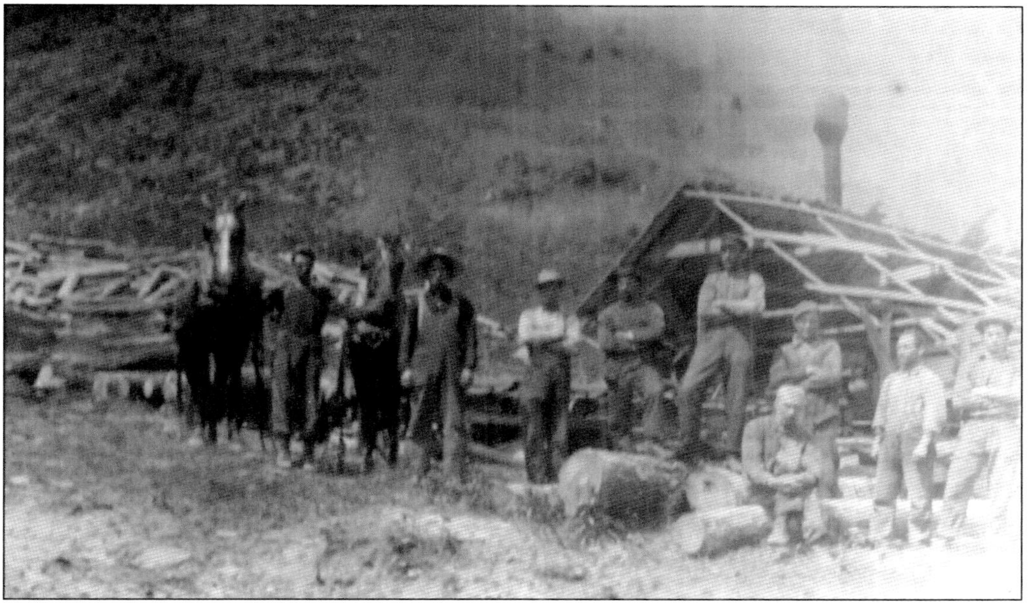

This horse-portable steam engine could be driven to any location near a water source. After assembly, the engine was connected to the sawmill by a belt. Water was fed into the boiler either by a water pump or steam injector, and fire or heat pushed through fire tubes. Many sawmill operations started like this—on a shoestring budget. (Courtesy of Dale Bedford.)

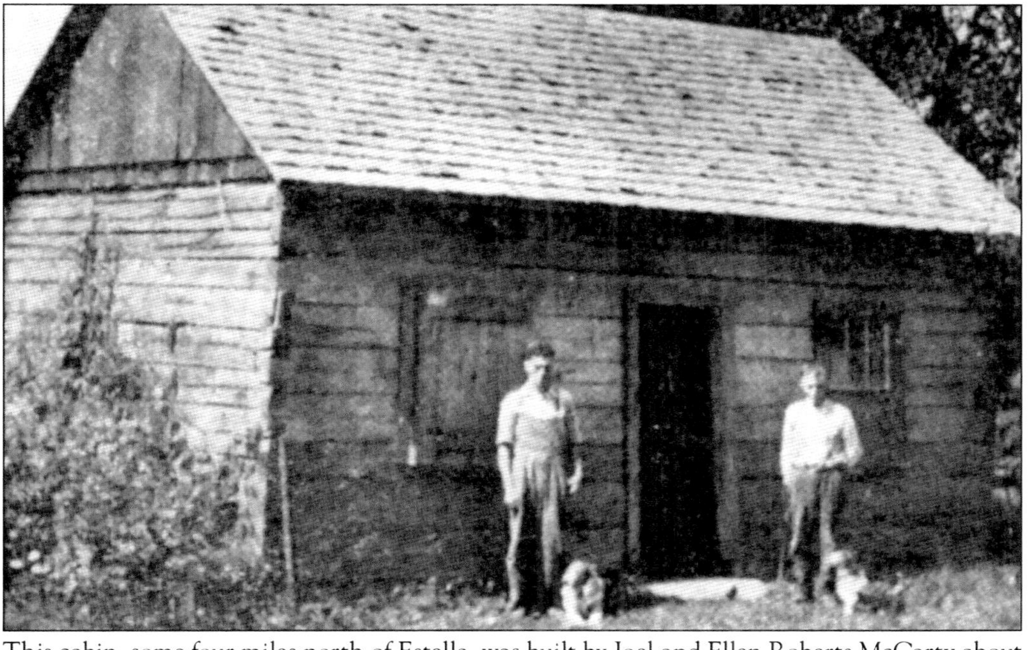

This cabin, some four miles north of Estella, was built by Joel and Ellen Roberts McCarty about 1800. The logs were cut square with dovetailed corners. It was sheathed inside with hewn planks, smoothed by a chisel called a "slick," and applied perpendicularly. The cabin was used as a woodshed after the newer farmhouse was built. Pictured are Nelson (left) and Hampton Pardoe. (Courtesy of Jake and Dottie Pardoe.)

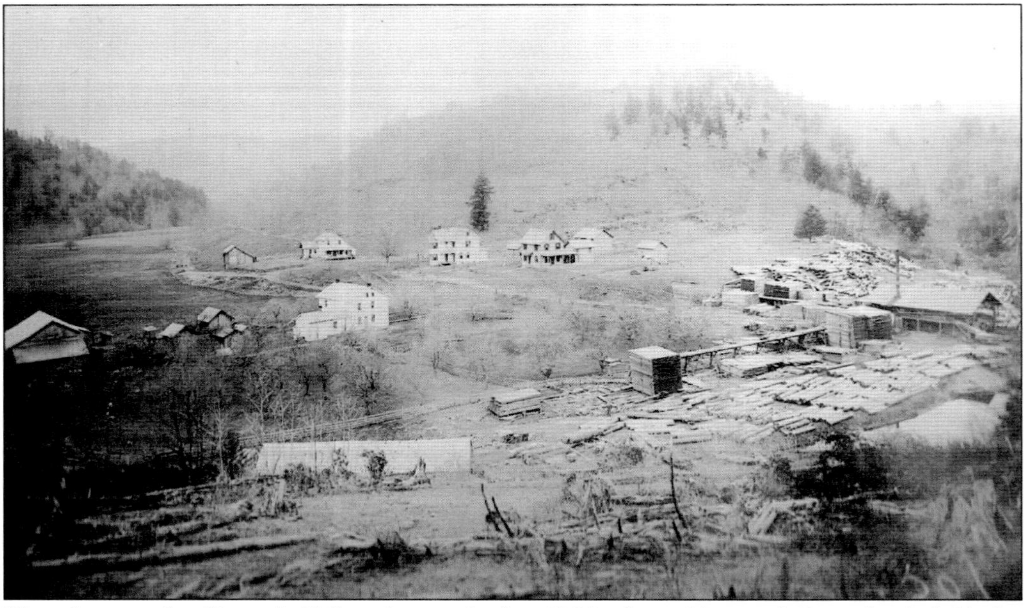

This photograph of Lincoln Falls, taken in the late 1800s, shows Hartung's Store (back, left); the John Morgan farm (center, left); and the Jonathan Rogers and Sons mill for wagon wheel hubs, shingles, and broom handles (right). The long roof (foreground) is the gristmill. Route 154 is now located where the photographer is standing. The first settlement was made at Lincoln Falls by Joseph Reeves prior to 1800. (Courtesy of Linda Faye Florentine.)

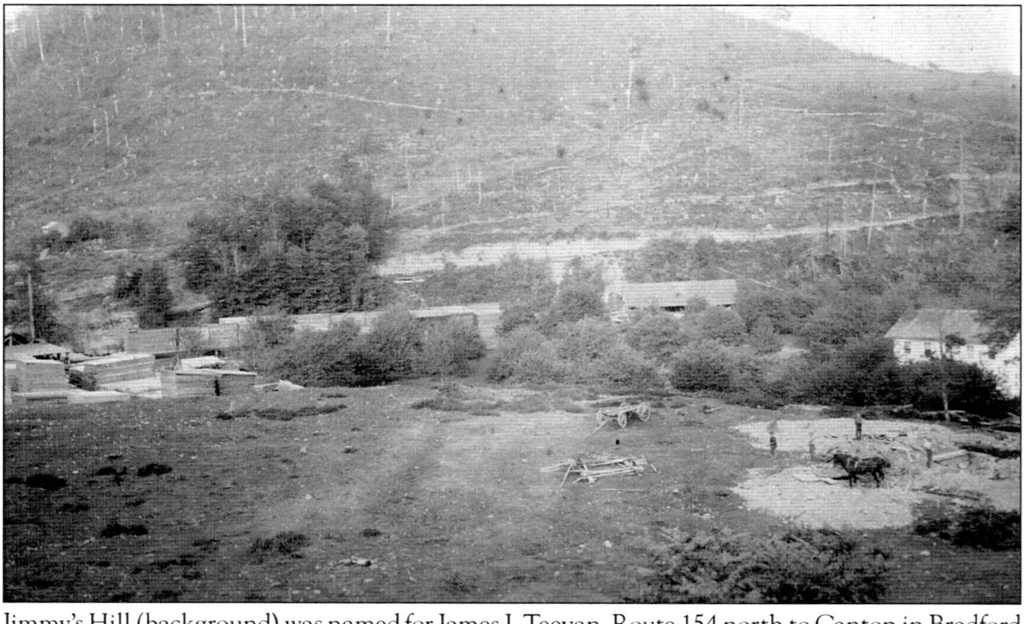

Jimmy's Hill (background) was named for James J. Teevan. Route 154 north to Canton in Bradford County is now located just in front of and below the photographer. The construction was for Sumner Rogers, son of Jonathan Rogers, and in 2009, it is the home of Elizabeth McFarland. John Morgan's Century Farm is just beyond the trees. The long roof (right from center) is the gristmill. (Courtesy of Linda Faye Florentine.)

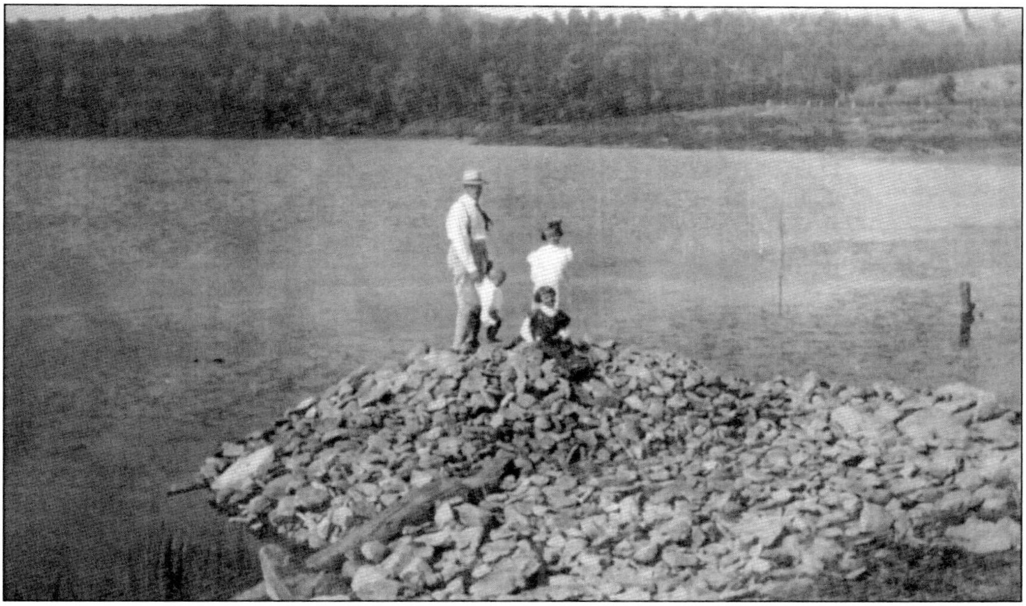

Victor Pilot Chaapel (1865–1921), a Williamsport physician, owned a summer place on the south side of Elk Lake (called Thomas Lake in the early 1800s) in the north part of the township. Pictured are Chaapel and his daughters Helen, Victoria (standing), and Eloise (sitting). The family summered here in the early 1900s. After Victor's death, his wife, Jennie Campbell (1864–1931), sold their land. (Courtesy of Ruth Rode.)

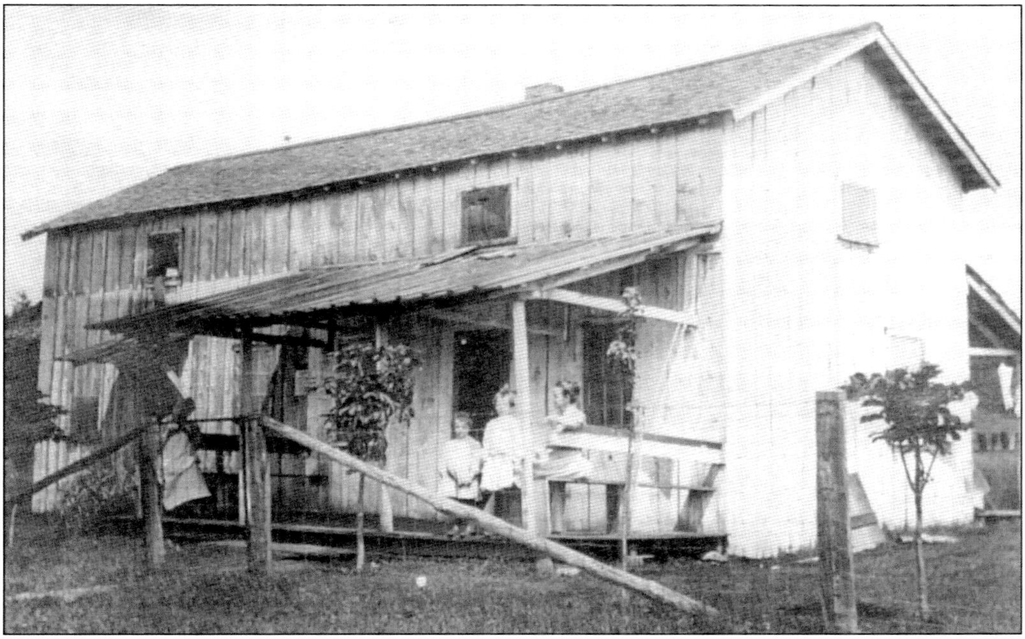

Jennie (Campbell) Chaapel poses with her two oldest daughters (on porch, right) at the farmhouse. Built in 1890, it was torn down and replaced with a cottage. The Nichols family owned land on the west side (Ranger's residence) where they ran a sawmill, made birch oil, and manufactured wagon wheel hubs of yellow birch wood for many years. (Courtesy of Ruth Rode.)

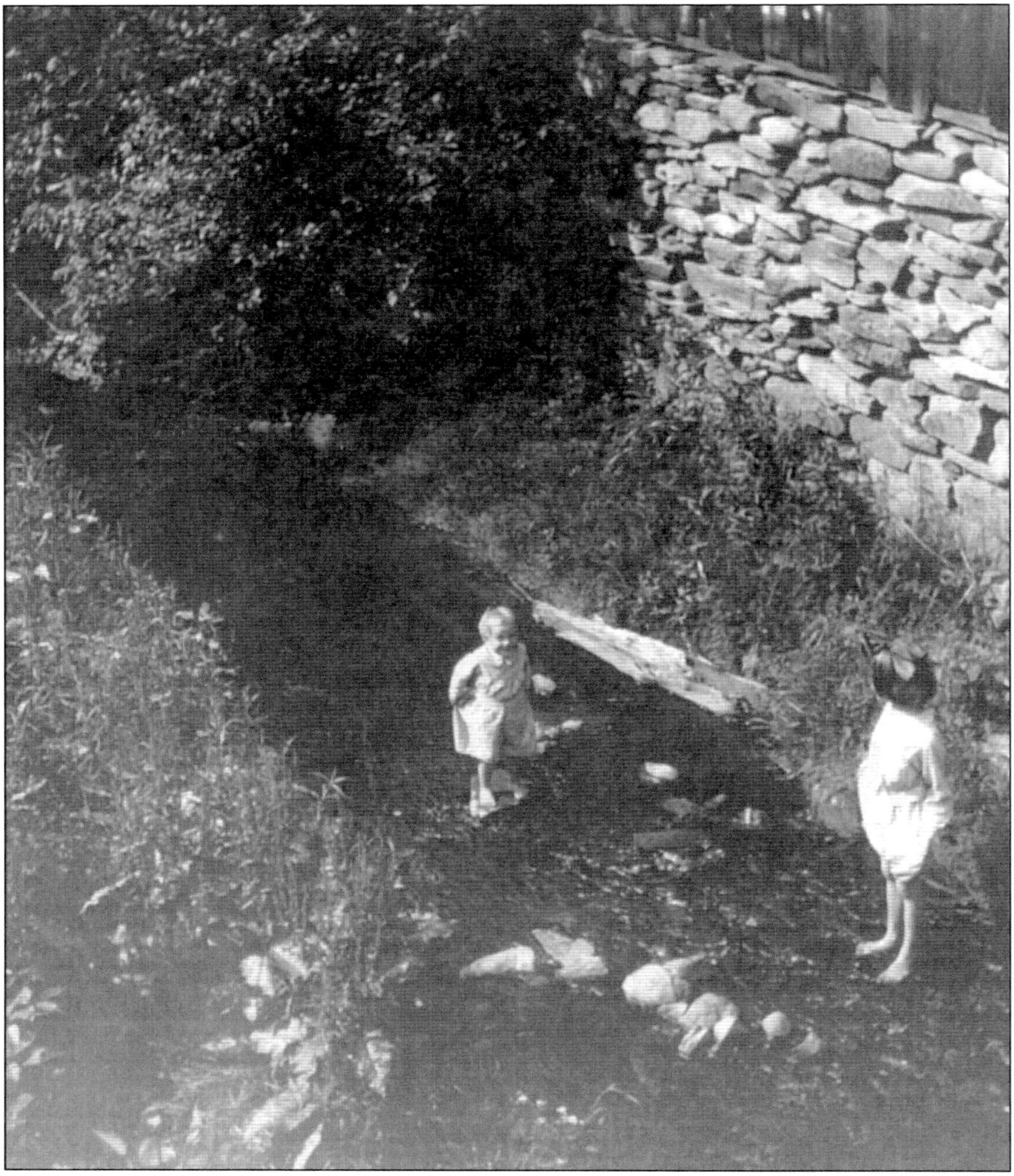

Two of the Chaapel girls wade in the outlet stream from the lake. The building seen at upper right was the old sawmill. There were four farms around the lake. The one on the east side belonged to Arthur Dickens, the one on the south side was Victor Chaapel's, on the west side was Hugh Nichols's place (currently the Ranger's residence), and John Veitengruber's and John Kamm's homestead was in the southwest corner. (Courtesy of Ruth Rode.)

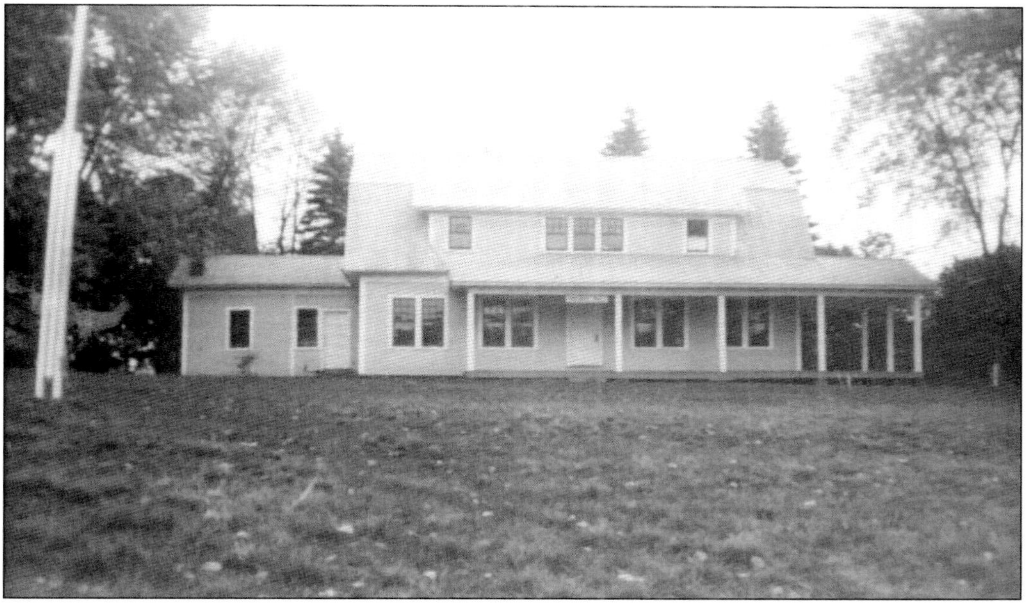

The Chaapel cottage replaced the old farmhouse. After the General Sullivan Council Boy Scouts of America purchased the property in 1928, the cottage was renamed Pancoast Hall for chief scout executive and founder Alfred H. Pancoast.

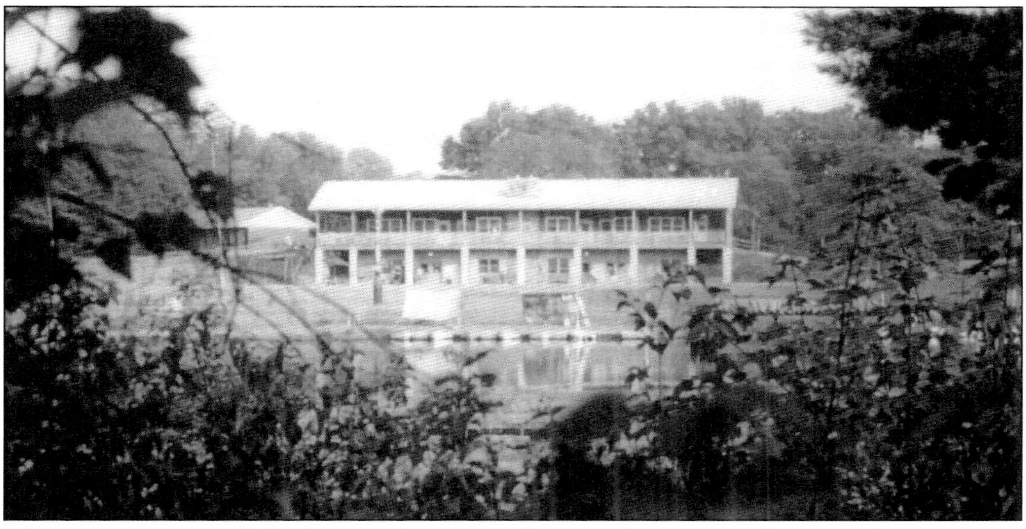

The new Pancoast Hall (built in 1999) is pictured as seen from across Elk Lake. The Boy Scouts renamed the land Camp Brule after Etienne Brule, who was thought to be the first white man to pass through the west or north Branch Valley area of the Susquehanna River in 1615.

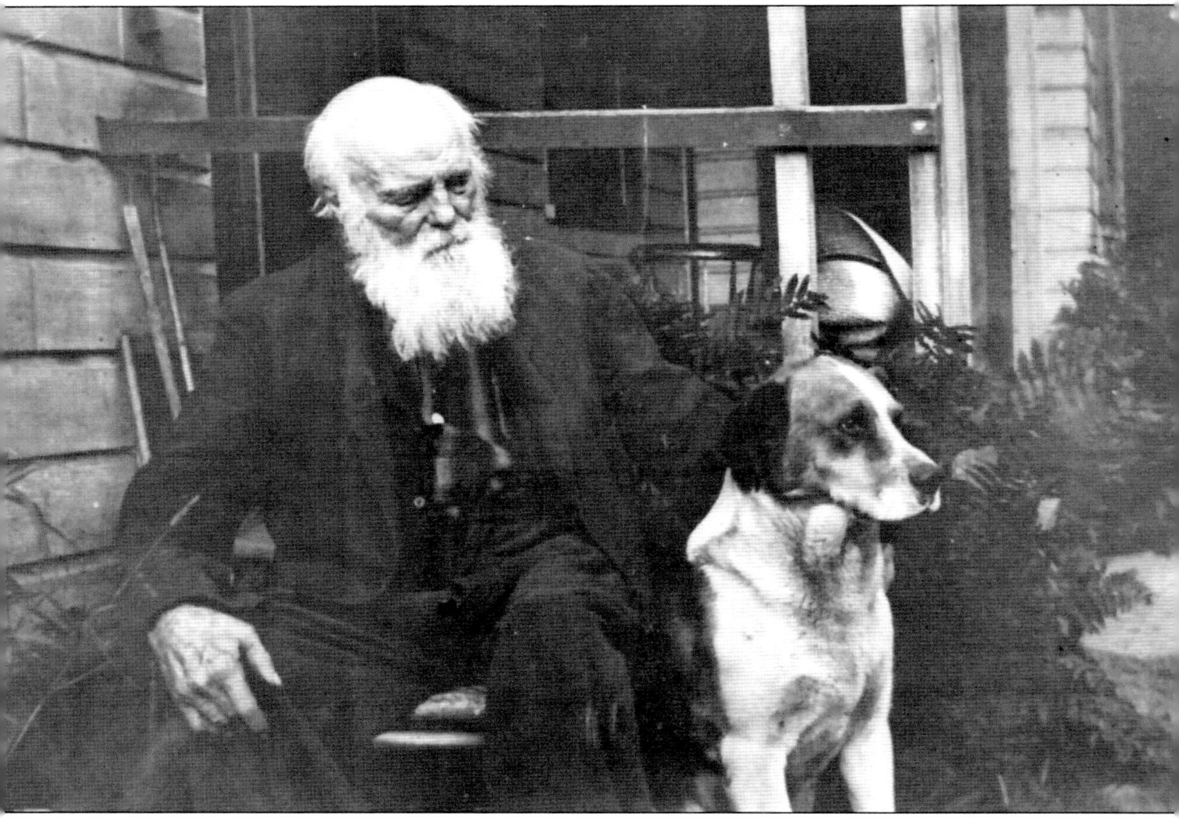

George Copeland Bird (1829- 1917) was descended from early settlers in Elkland Township, served in several township offices, and was an avid hunter for most of his long life until arthritis affected his health. His son Ulysses Bird (1856-1917) was one of the organizers behind the Sullivan County Telephone Company as well as involved in township and county politics. George's home is a private residence occupied by his great-granddaughter.

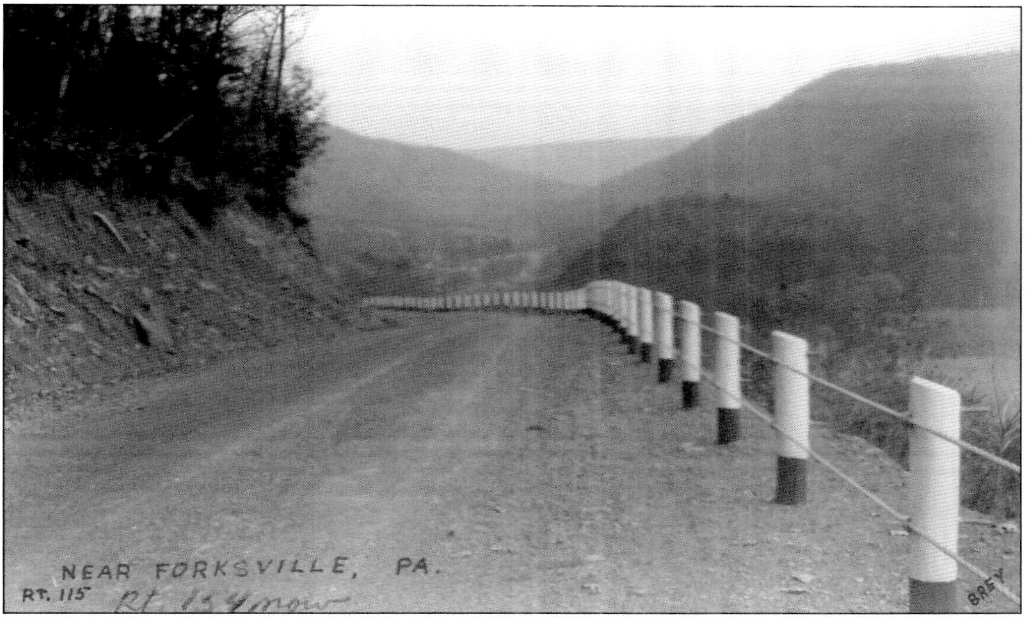

Higley Park (Almost Heaven Campground) and the Loyalsock Creek are seen down to the right of old Route 115 (now Route 154) as it heads down Forks Mountain from Estella. Forksville can be seen in the background.

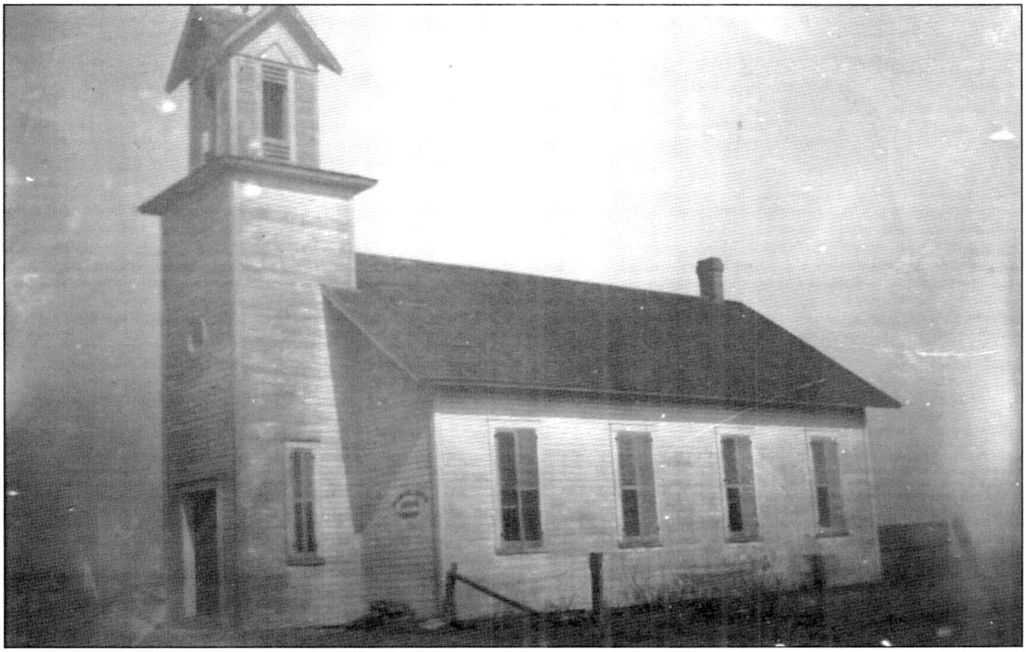

A log structure was built in 1805 at Hugo Corners where a German minister held services for local German immigrants. By the late 1800s, services were still held in and minutes were written in German. The new church (pictured) was built in 1874. By the 1950s, this building was inadequate for the growing congregation, and a newer building was constructed across the road in 1955.

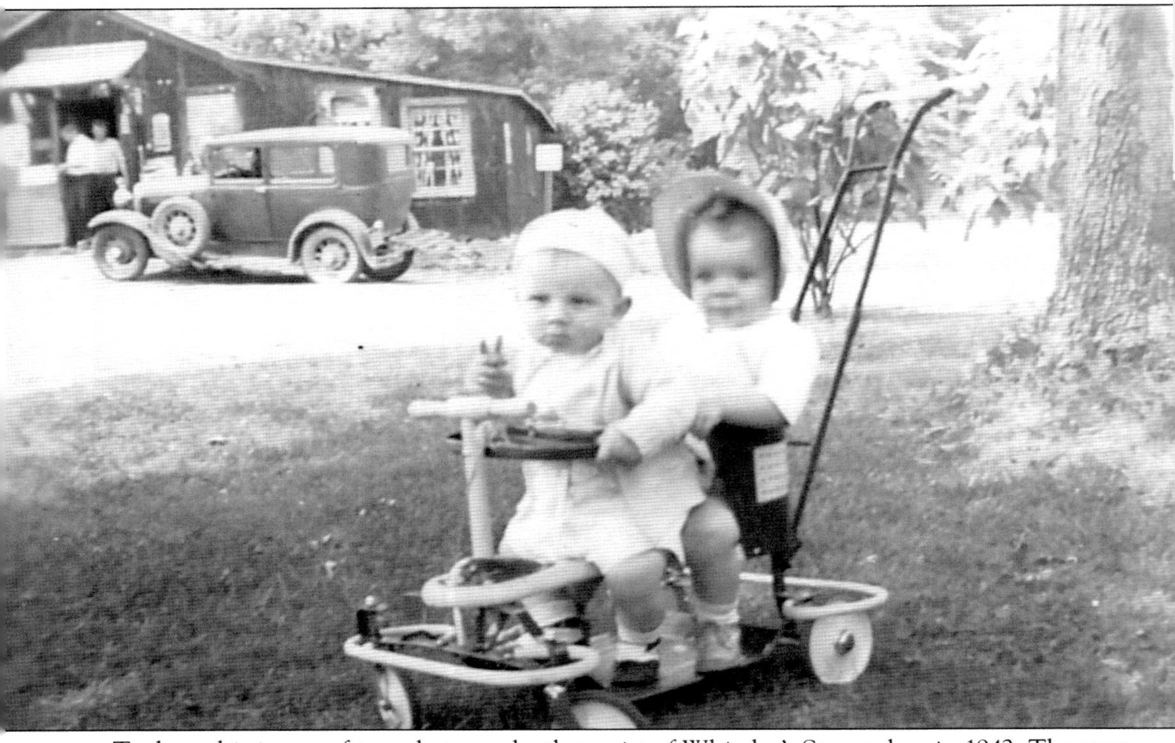

To date, this is one of two photographs that exist of Whiteley's Store taken in 1942. The store was located about a mile north-northwest of Bedford's Corners. John Roy and Fannie McCarty Whiteley operated it from the early 1920s to about 1950. The toddlers are cousins Sondra Burgess Thomas and Dale Bennett. (Courtesy of Doris McCarty Whiteley Stephens.)

Five

Forks Township

Forks Township was established by the court of quarter sessions of Lycoming County in 1833. The territory was taken from Shrewsbury Township. Bradford County borders Forks Township to the north with Cherry and Laporte Townships to the east, Shrewsbury Township to the south, and Hillsgrove and Elkland Townships to the west. The name Forks was derived from the settlement made at the forks of the Big Loyalsock and Little Loyalsock Creeks.

The first permanent settlers reached the Forks area by the Courson Road (1793), Genesee Road (1800), and Susquehanna and Tioga Turnpike (1810). A road leading up the Loyalsock from Hilllsgrove to Millview made it necessary to ford the creek many times. The English, first to locate in the township, came in by way of Muncy. The Germans came by way of the turnpike, and the Irish followed later. The first white inhabitants, although not permanent, lived in the Forks area about 1789 or 1790. They included a Mr. Miller; a Captain Brown, who lived near Forksville; and a Mr. Strong, who lived at what is now Millview.

Samuel Sadler Rogers Sr. (great-grandfather of Sadler Rogers) and his sons Samuel, William, and Jonathan built a large woolen mill on the Loyalsock Creek near Forksville (Forks Township) that they operated until it was destroyed in the 1816 flood. The Rogers were woolen weavers in England and operated the first power looms in Pennsylvania, making kersey cloth, which was worn by the American army in the War of 1812. Forksville was the shipping center for the glass manufactured at Lewis Lake (Eagles Mere) and is one of the two oldest towns in the county. At least 100 families lived within the Forksville Borough limits during its lumber and coal heydays in the late 19th century. Millview's town plot was surveyed about 1850, and the town prospered for several years into the early 20th century.

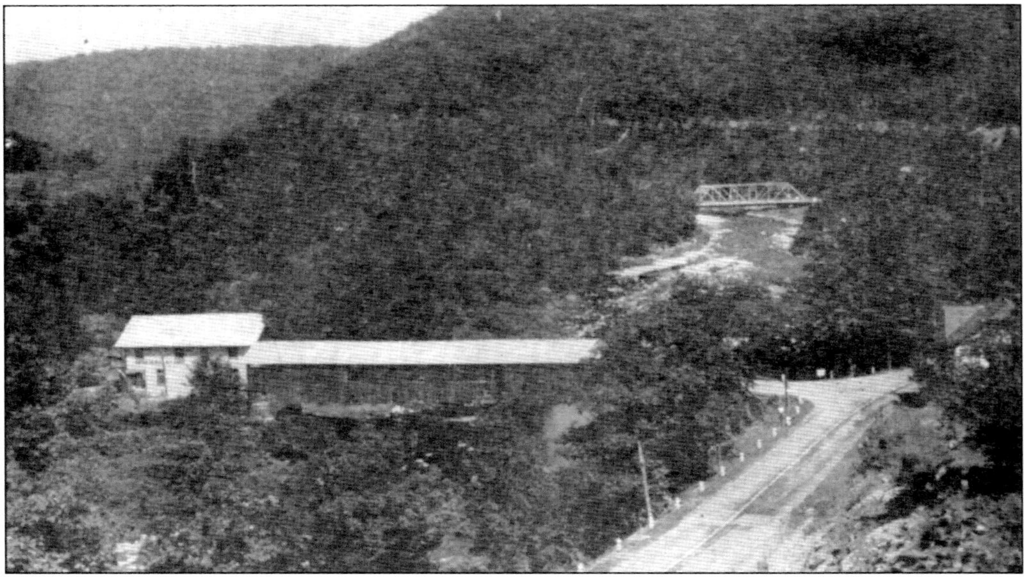

The Forksville covered bridge was built in 1850 by Sadler Rogers of Hillsgrove and renovated by Corbin Lewis 120 years later. Rogers also built the Forksville General Store (left) in 1851. The iron bridge (right, background) is Route 87 spanning the Big Loyalsock Creek. The Methodist church is to the right, out of the picture. Route 154 is seen at right and across the mountain (background).

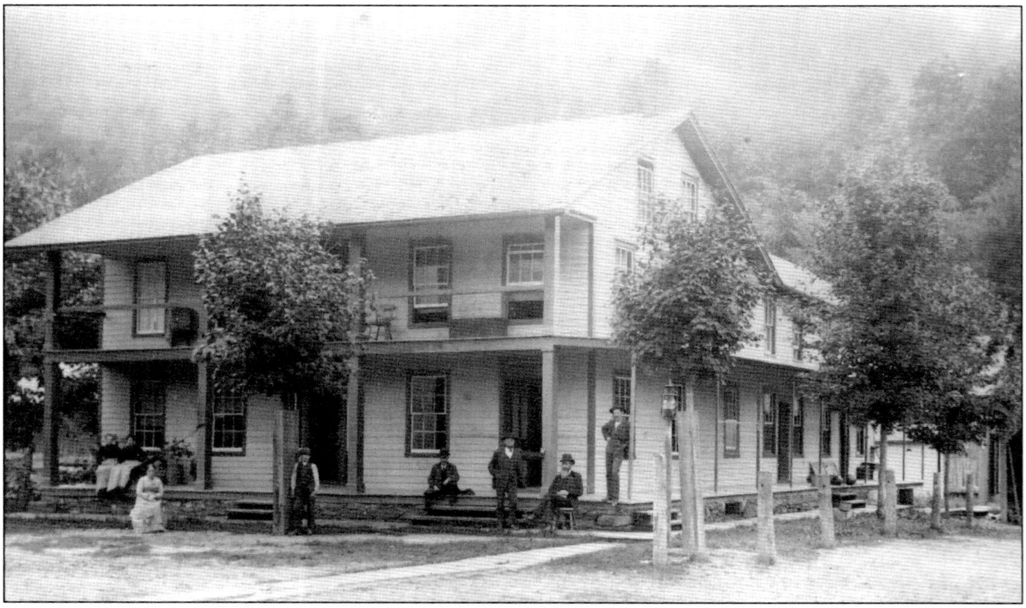

Charles H. Seeley owned the Forksville Hotel from 1893 to 1898. The gable-end windows were kept open to cool the unpartitioned third story of the hotel. Seeley died from injuries in an 1899 explosion, as he inspected a new gas machine installed in the hotel's cellar. The youth (standing and wearing a hat) is Fred Fawcett. The hotel burned down in 1906. The Forksville Fire Hall is located there.

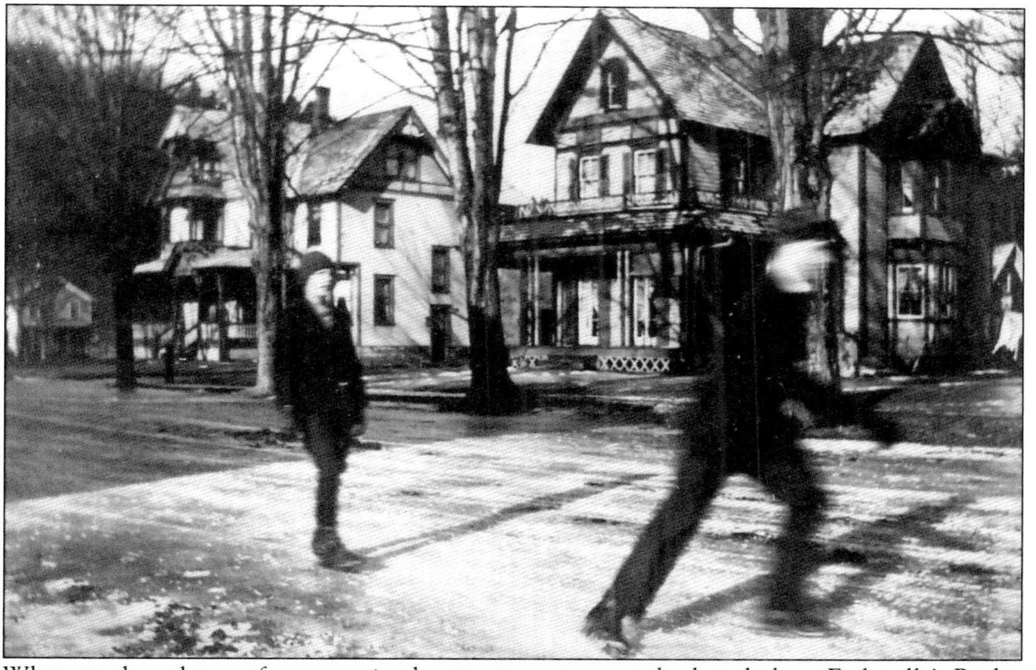

When mush and snow froze over in the streets, young people skated along Forksville's Bridge Street. Dr. William Randell built the house on the left about 1900. The house on the right was built by George "Artie" Rogers in the 1890s.

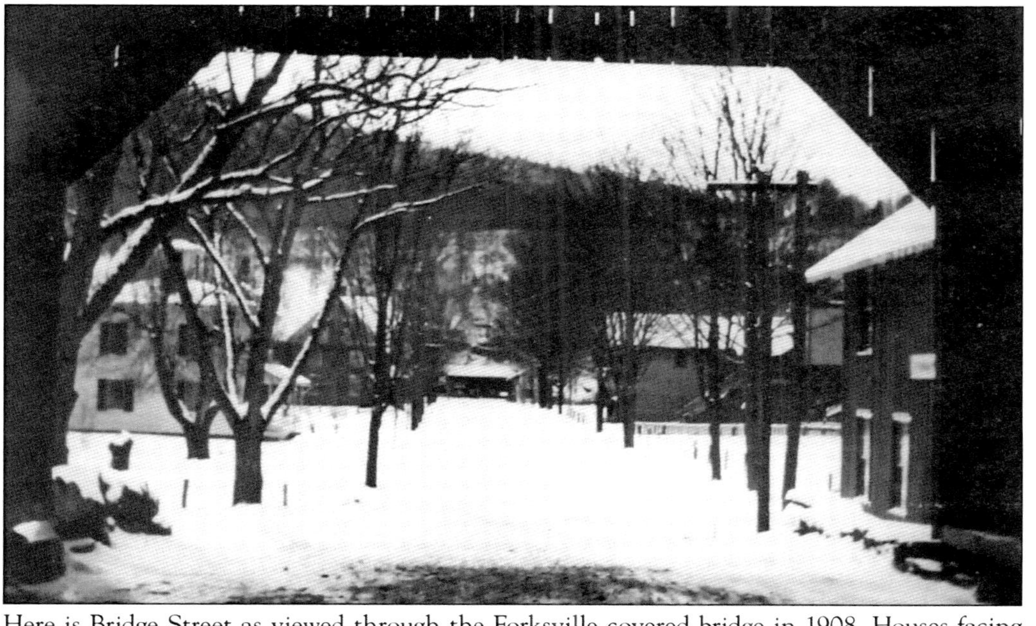

Here is Bridge Street as viewed through the Forksville covered bridge in 1908. Houses facing the street were the Fred Rogers house (far left) and Ben Wright house (second from left), Rogers General Store with post office and apartments (second from right), and Forksville General Store (far right). Ice cut from the frozen creek dammed downstream of the bridge was stored in an icehouse on the other side of the store.

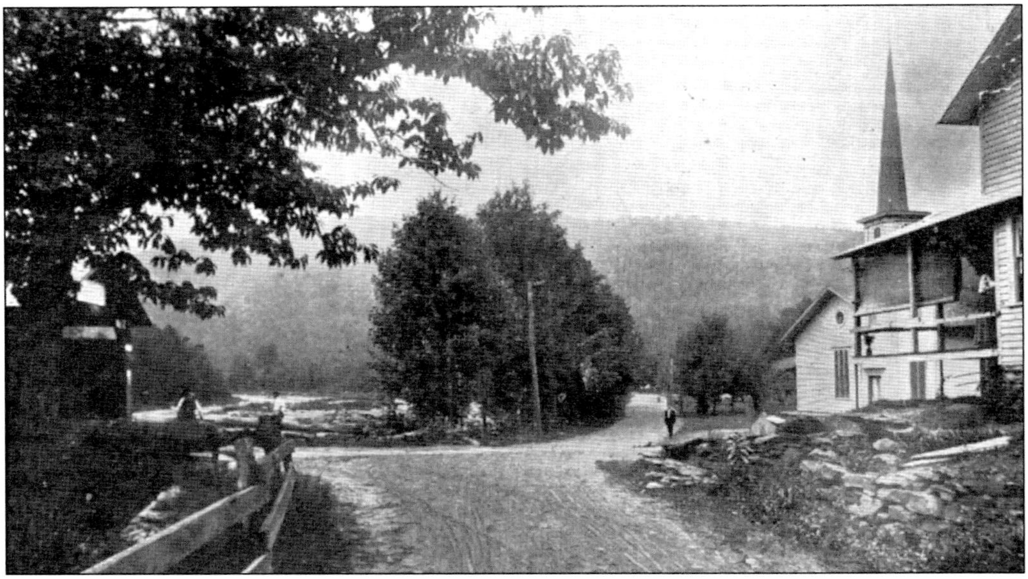

Across from the covered bridge (left, out of picture) is the Forksville Methodist Church (right). The road (foreground), now Highway 154, led to Forksville's second covered bridge (background), long since dismantled, where only a stone embankment remains. This area was called Brooklyn by the locals. Maud Hunter's residence (porch, far right), later the home of Howard Bennett, no longer stands.

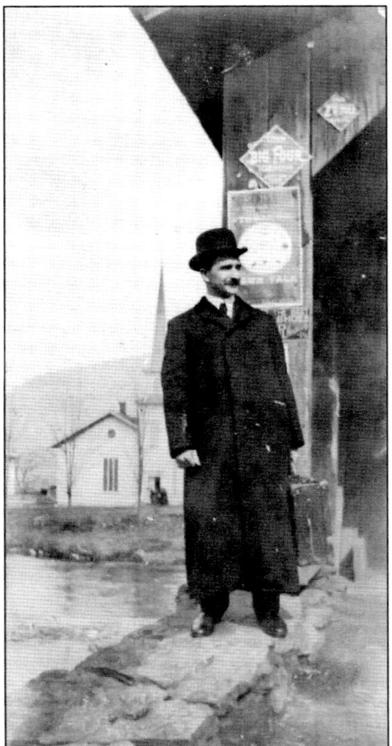

Prof. O. C. Gortner, with the local teachers' institute, is pictured standing by the Forksville covered bridge about 1909. Covered bridges were frequently posted with advertisements. The old Forksville Methodist Church, with its 100-foot steeple, is in the background. Originally the Forksville Methodists met in a log schoolhouse but then built a better building, which grew too small to conduct services in by 1870.

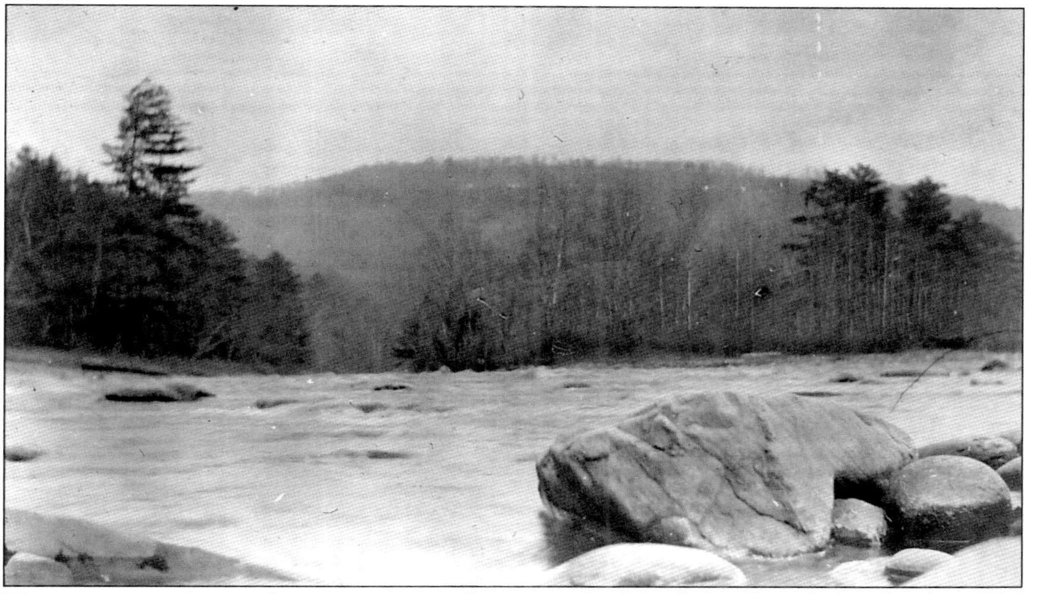

This view was taken looking upstream at the junction of the Big and Little Loyalsock Creeks about 1909. The Little Loyalsock is straight ahead, and the Big Loyalsock is to the right where Forksville is located. According to Thomas Ingham, who arrived in Sullivan County in 1850, many of the older settlers said they found an "Indian meadow on the flats above the forks of the Loyalsock."

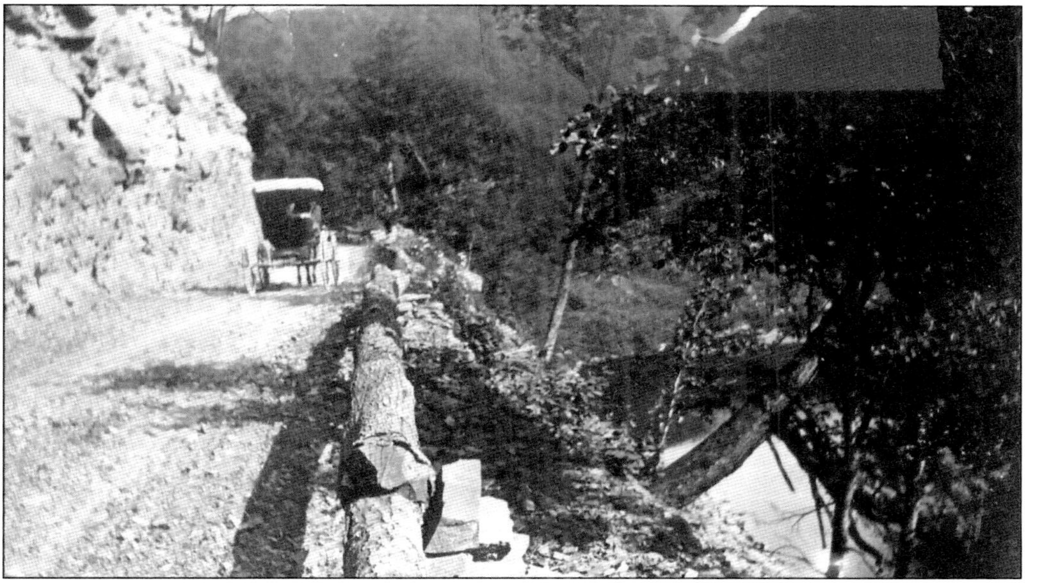

This spot in the road west of Forksville shows an area below Shelley's Turn in 1909. Around the bend to the left, Gardner's Inn (now Forksville Inn) was constructed in 1947. The Rogers' second woolen mill was located near the Loyalsock Creek (right, out of picture). The Loyalsock Creek is down to the right. This area is called the Gulf.

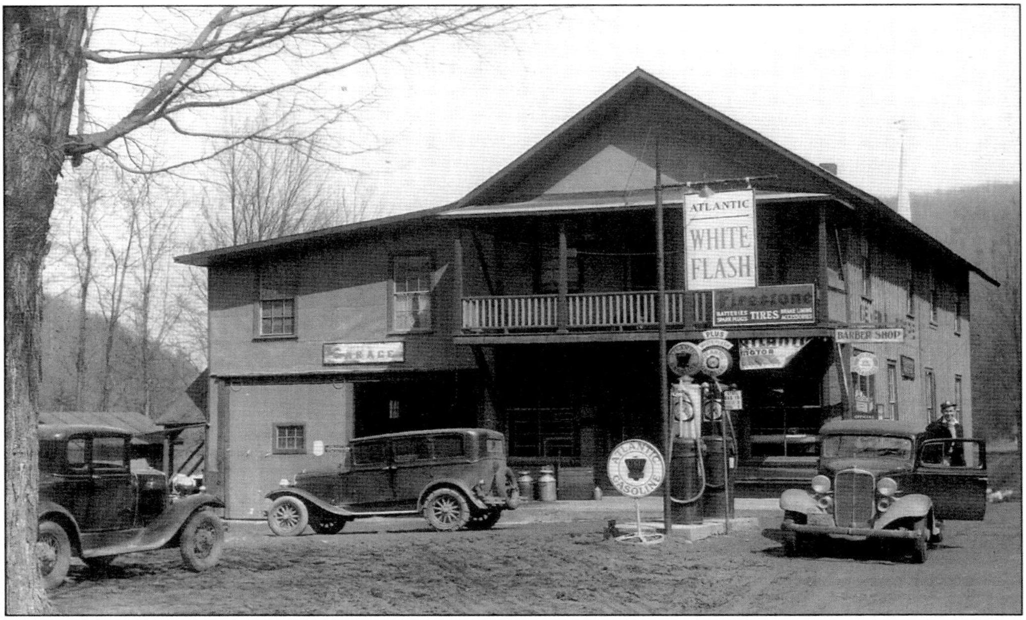

The Forksville General Store is shown in 1939, and Wayne Shelley, who was killed in World War II, is standing at the car (right). At the time, the store was owned by Harry and Irene McCarty. Note the Methodist church steeple. The covered bridge is to the right, out of the picture. (Courtesy of Michael Stasiunas.)

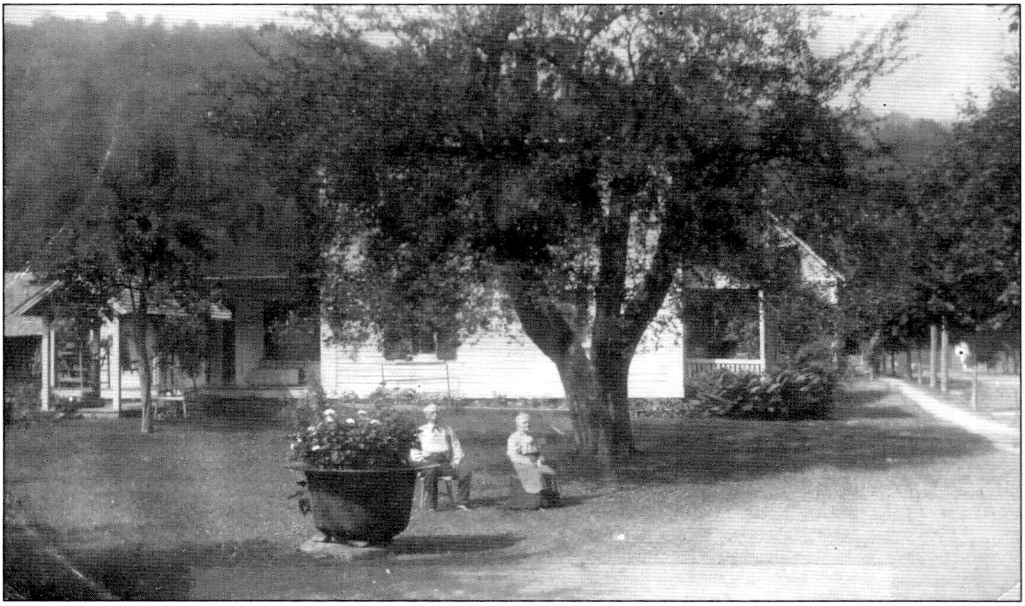

John Wesley and Anna Videan Rogers are pictured at their Forksville home that was used as a stopping place for travelers, a tradition John's grandfather Samuel started. The huge dye kettle was used in woolen operations by Samuel and in a second Rogers woolen factory below Forksville. It was pushed downstream by a flood in 1816 and recovered years later from the creek, pulled out by a team of oxen.

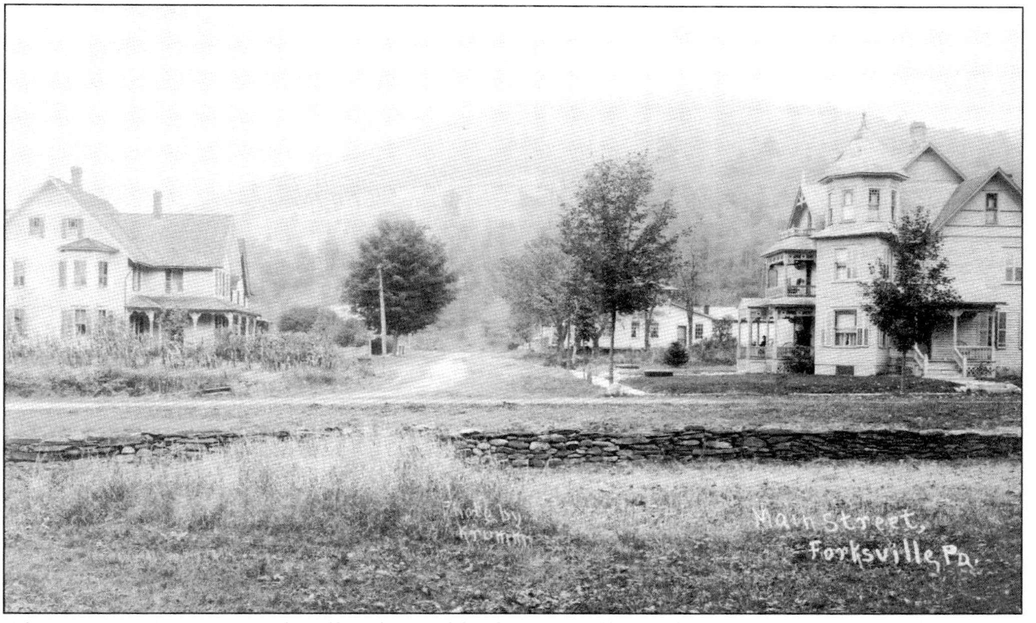

Along Main Street in Forksville where older houses still stand, Harry and Lena Snell lived to the left, and Benjamin Fawcett lived to the right. The Snells operated a small diner near World's End. Harry worked as a fireman for Edward Lee's sawmill. Fawcett was an undertaker. Bodies in caskets were placed for viewing in the first-floor square turret. (Courtesy of Kenneth Lee.)

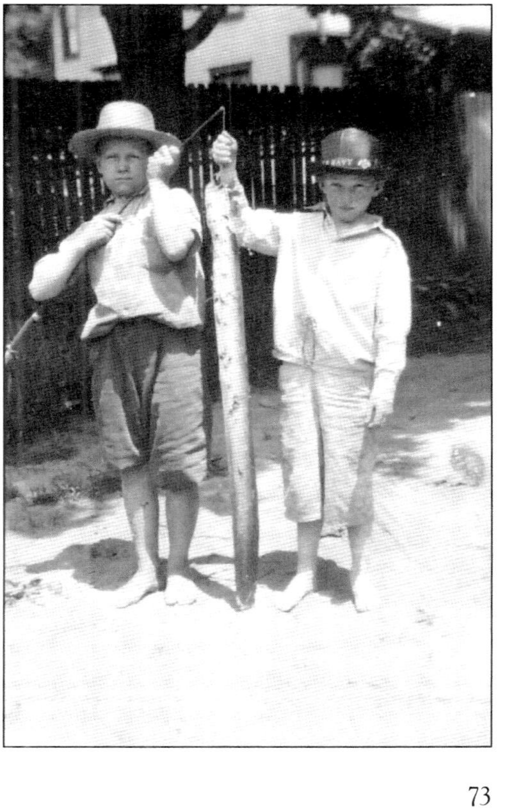

In the 1930s, brothers Charles, Richard, and Leon Gleockler caught eels on fishing line strung from poles laid out into the Big Loyalsock Creek with chub for bait. In the evenings, they put their catch in burlap bags and took them home where they cleaned and ate the eels for breakfast. Pictured with a 42-inch-long eel is Bruce Rosbach (right) with an unidentified friend about 1921.

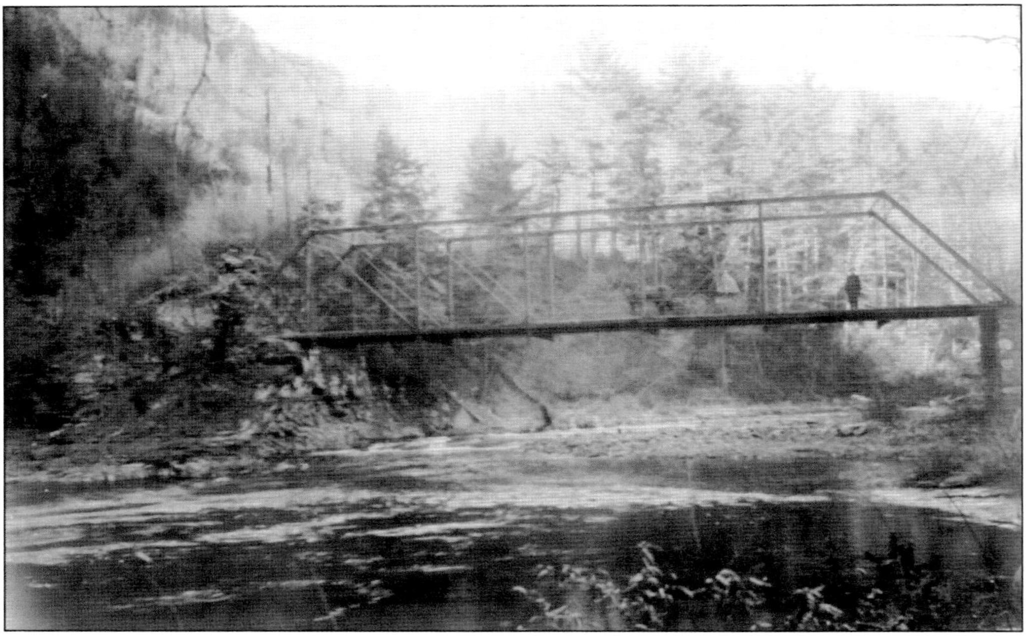

This iron bridge was built at World's End in 1897, dismantled in the early 1900s, and then moved upstream to Sones Pond Road just off Route 154. When constructed by Horseheads Bridge Company of Horseheads, New York, transportation consisted mostly of horse and buggy. The wooden deck has been replaced many times over the years that the bridge has been in use.

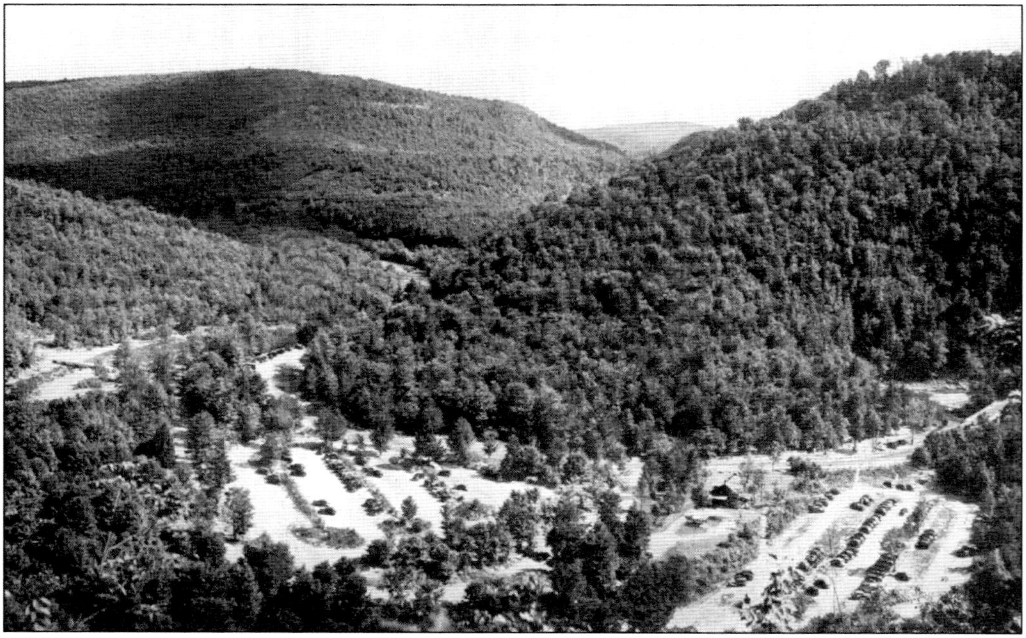

Construction was ongoing at World's End State Park through the years of Civilian Conservation Corps (CCC) existence from 1933 to 1941. Four camps operated in the county: Laporte (Camp S-95), Hillsgrove (Camp S-96), Emmons (Camp S-104), and Loyalsock or Mill Run (Camp S-128). CCC workers constructed World's End State Park.

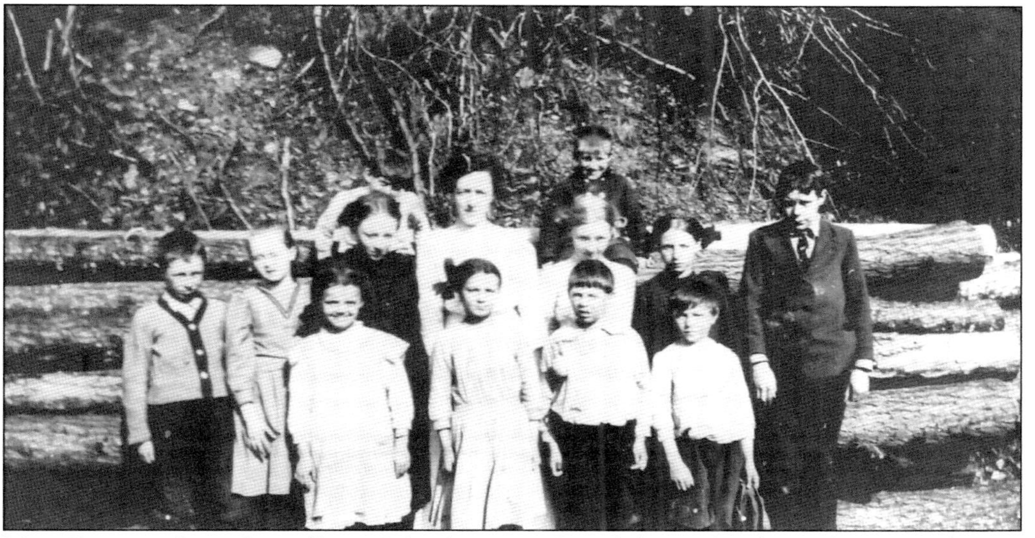

Mary Firon taught at the Millview School in 1918. From left to right, the students, standing on the Central Pennsylvania Railroad track between the schoolhouse and the mountain, are (first row) Laura and Mamie Sayman, Lyle Rumsey, and Lester Gilbert; (second row) Howard Rumsey, Grand and Alice Molyneux, Mary Firon, unidentified, Nellie McIntire, and Walter Gilbert. The boy on the log pile (left) is unidentified. The second boy is Carl D. Molyneux.

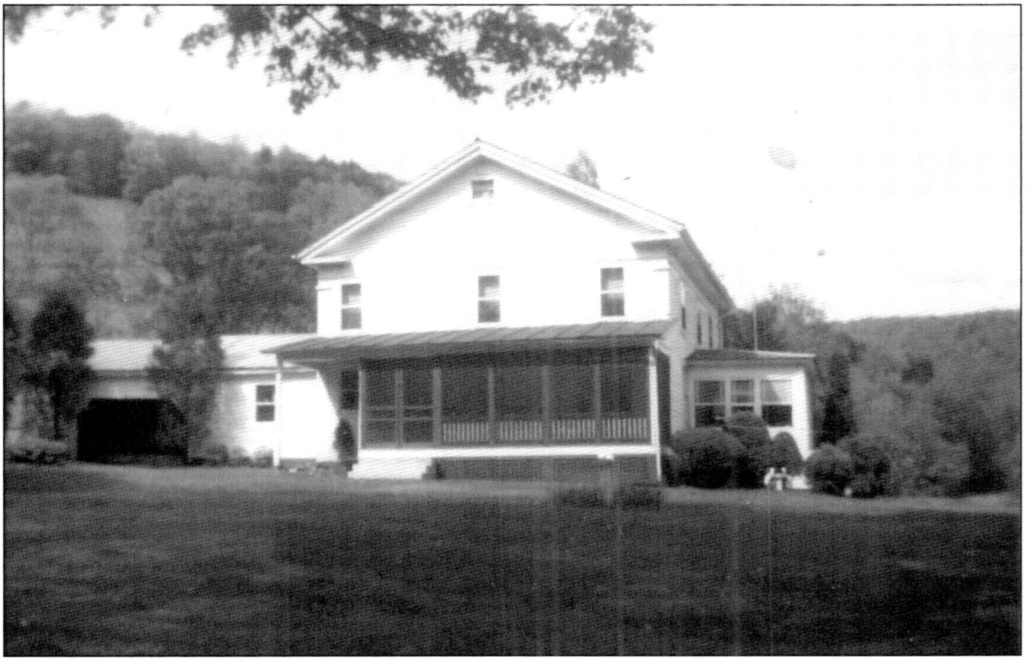

This was the fourth residence built in 1822 on the same spot by William Molyneux, one of the first settlers of the Forks area, and his son Thomas. The post office was where the screened-in porch is. A store was to the right, and a blacksmith shop was across the road. The Molyneux family reunion was held in a huge maple grove across from the homestead.

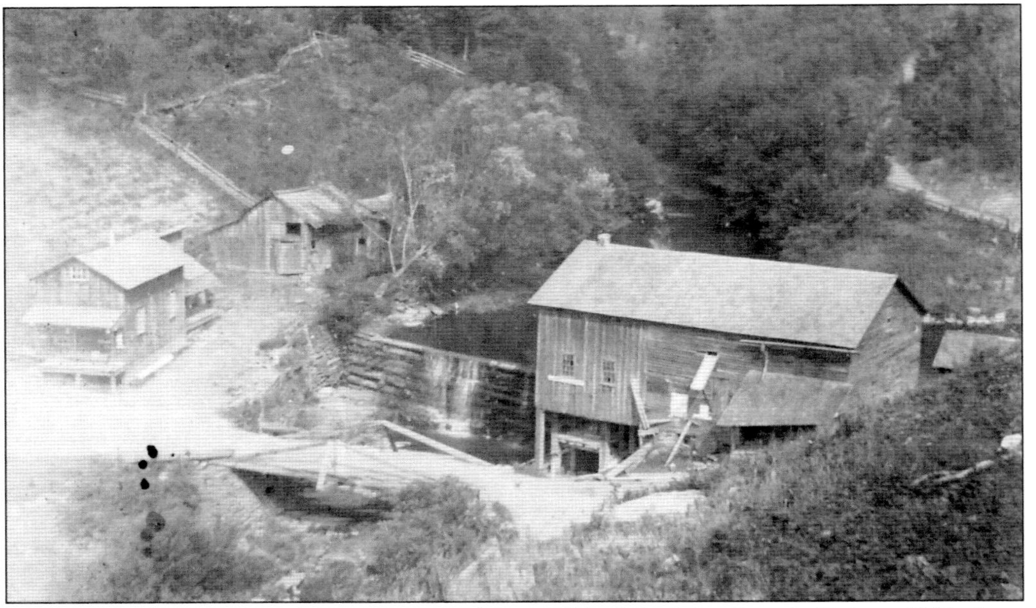

Campbellsville grew around a water-powered gristmill built by John Campbell about 1851 where Lick Creek and Level Branch meet. George Hunsinger built a sawmill nearby. The gristmill (center, right) and general store/post office (far left) served people for miles around. A barn sat behind the store/post office. Burke Road is seen to the upper right. The flood of 1901 took out both mills and damaged the covered bridge.

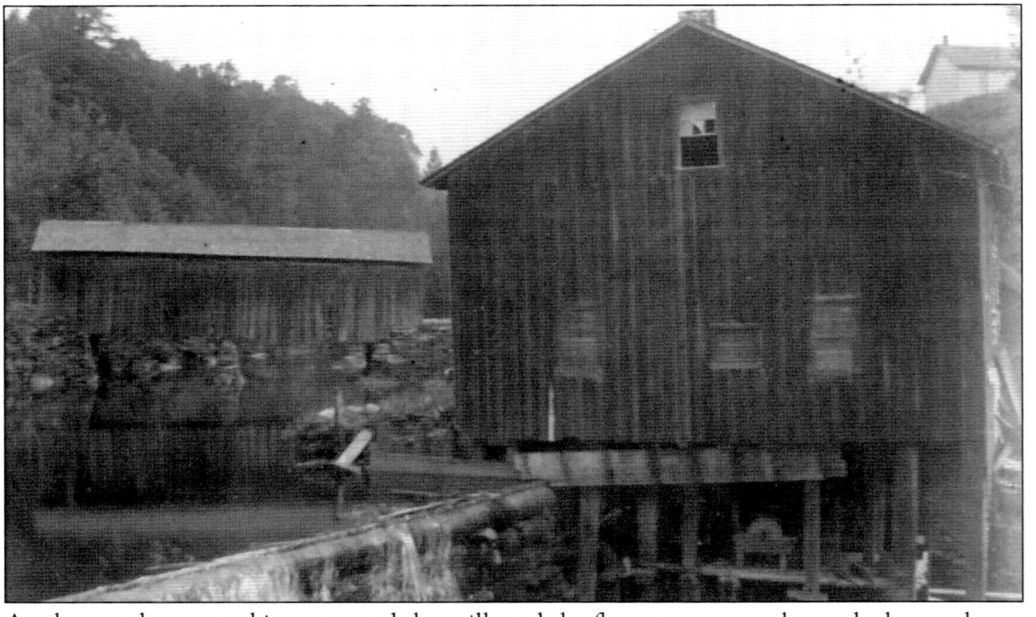

A submerged water turbine operated the mill, and the flume stream ran beneath the overhang. The first schoolhouse burned in 1853. Powell Norton was granted an indenture in 1884 from the school board for a new schoolhouse lot (upper right). Access was on Kelly Hill Road. Children walked barefoot to school in snow as early as March. Only the covered bridge abutment (back left) and a barn foundation remain in Campbellville.

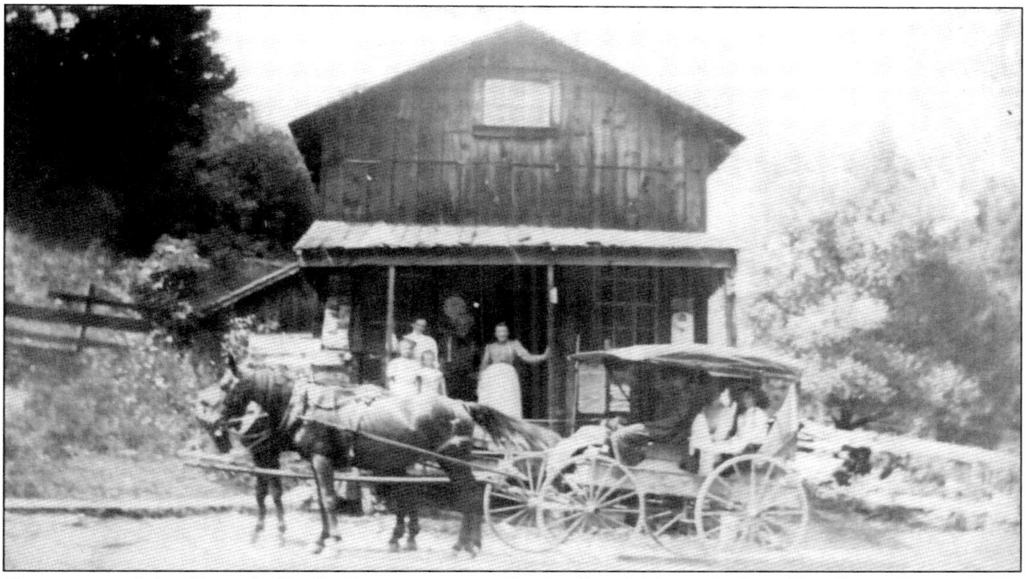

Operation of the Campbellville Store continued into the 1930s with Otis Hatch as manager. He was also the barber and postmaster. He and his wife, Florence (Molyneux), lived across the road from the store, which is behind the photographer. People on the porch are identified only as the Norton family.

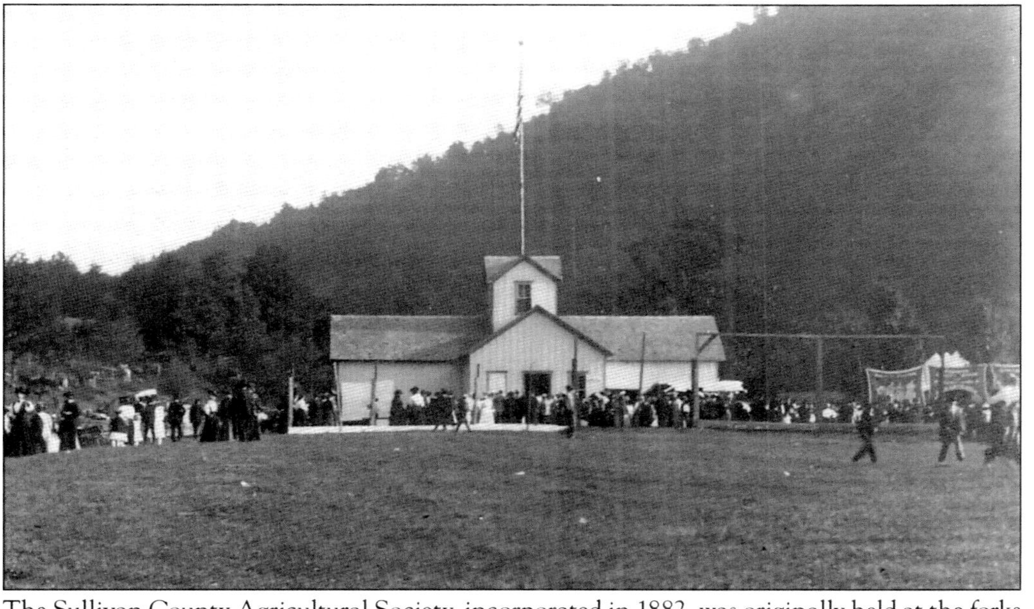

The Sullivan County Agricultural Society, incorporated in 1882, was originally held at the forks of the Big and Little Loyalsock Creeks and then later moved to its present location upstream from Forksville along Route 87. Before its permanent location near the village in 1891, it was moved about the county each year. The Flag Building (pictured) still remains in the center of the fairgrounds. This image was taken in 1907.

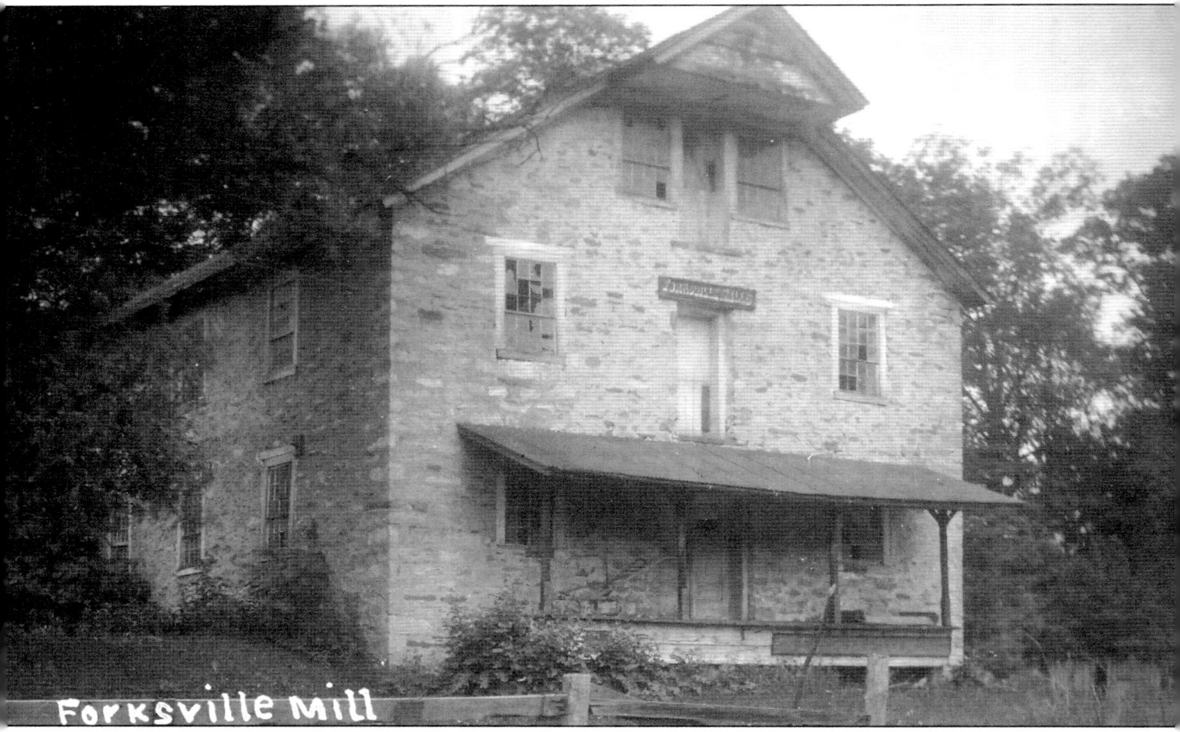

Built about 1856, the Forksville gristmill was owned and operated by James Black. Feeding the millpond, a raceway started just above a log dam that once spanned the Big Loyalsock Creek below the Forksville covered bridge. Remains of the mill, which is on private property, can be seen from Highway 87. Other owners and operators were Robert Mathews, Edward Miller, and a Mr. Allen.

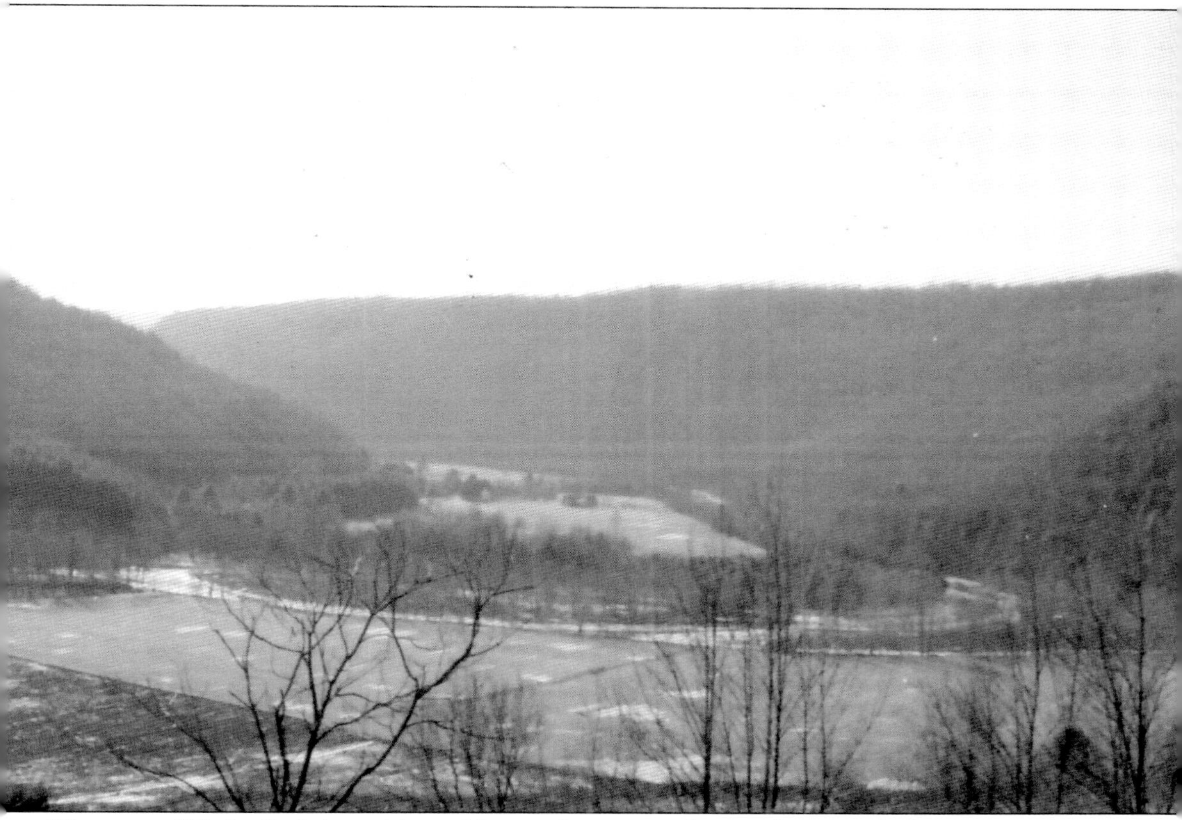

This view of Higley Park (now Almost Heaven Campground) was taken in 1959 from Route 154 on Forks Mountain. Donald Ralph Higley (1920–1971) bought it between 1945 and 1947 and farmed it until 1954. He married Evelyn Vough (1930–2002) in 1948. The park was started in 1968, and Evelyn sold it in 1984. (Courtesy of Vernon Hatch.)

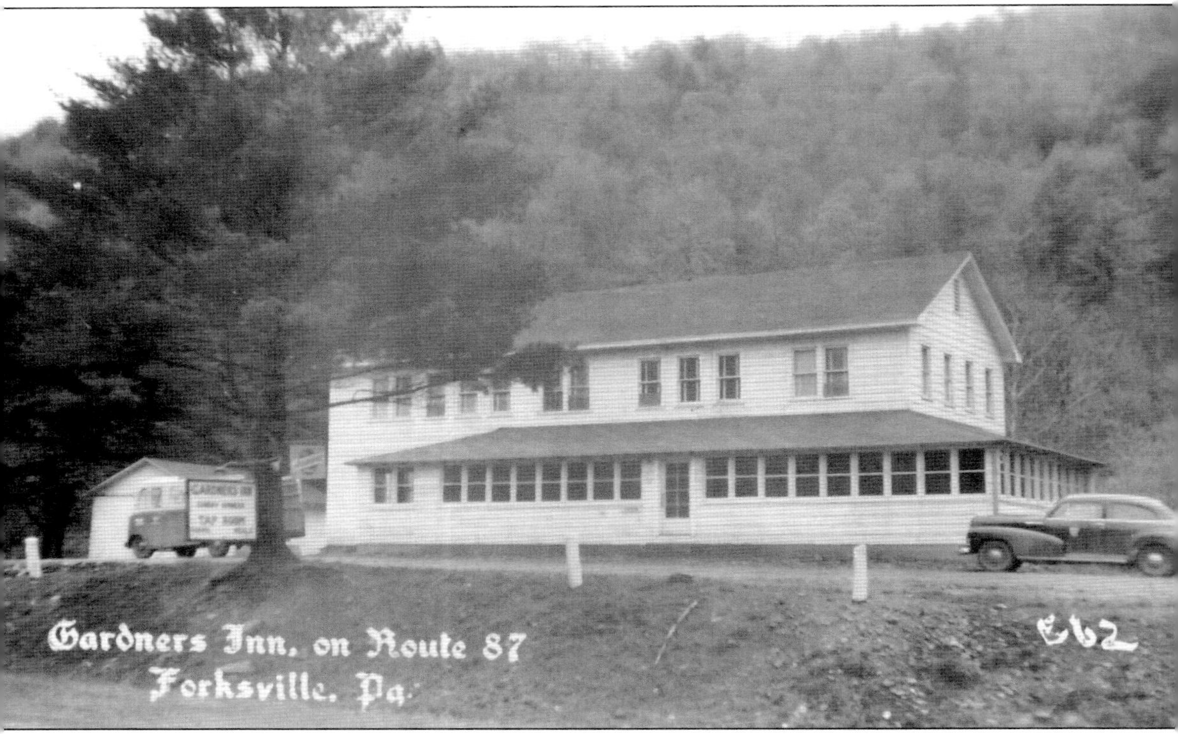

Ralph and Harold Gardner (father and son) built Gardner's Inn and Motel (now Forksville Inn) in 1947. Located on Route 87 one and a half miles from Forksville, it was constructed near where the Rogers woolen mill made cloth for uniforms during the War of 1812. At one time, the inn could accommodate 40 guests.

Six

Fox Township

Fox Township was established by the court of quarter sessions of Lycoming County in 1839. The territory was taken from Elkland Township. It was named in honor of Samuel M. Fox, a descendant of George Fox, the founder of the Society of Friends (Quakers). The township is located in the extreme northwestern corner of the county. It is bounded to the north by Bradford County, to the east by Elkland Township, to the south by Hillsgrove Township, and to the west by Lycoming County.

About 1800, Englishman Phineas Bond acquired substantial land holdings and offered 100 acres to the first 12 families to settle in the area. As an incentive, Bond offered an additional 300 acres to anyone who built a gristmill. After a road was cut past Elk Lake to Fox Center, the Hoagland and Battin families settled in. According to a deed on file in Williamsport, Joseph Hoagland and his sons were deeded 300 acres of land and built the gristmill just below the bridge crossing the Hoagland Branch in Fox Center. The mill had to be maintained for at least 10 years. People from as far away as Canton in Bradford County brought in grains to be ground. Fox Center became Shunk in 1847 after the village acquired a post office. It was named for Gov. Francis Rawn Shunk (1845–1848).

The village of Piatt, just east of Shunk, was named for William Piatt, associate judge of Lycoming County, and John Piatt, a sheriff of Lycoming County. This village once had a post office, several residences and businesses, two garages, a store, and a gas station.

Wheelerville, located in the northwest corner of the township, was started in the 1890s when the Susquehanna and New York Railroad was constructed through the area. There were two sawmills, a turning mill, three stores, a creamery, and several houses by the dawn of the 20th century. Wheelerville was the shipping point for Shunk at that time.

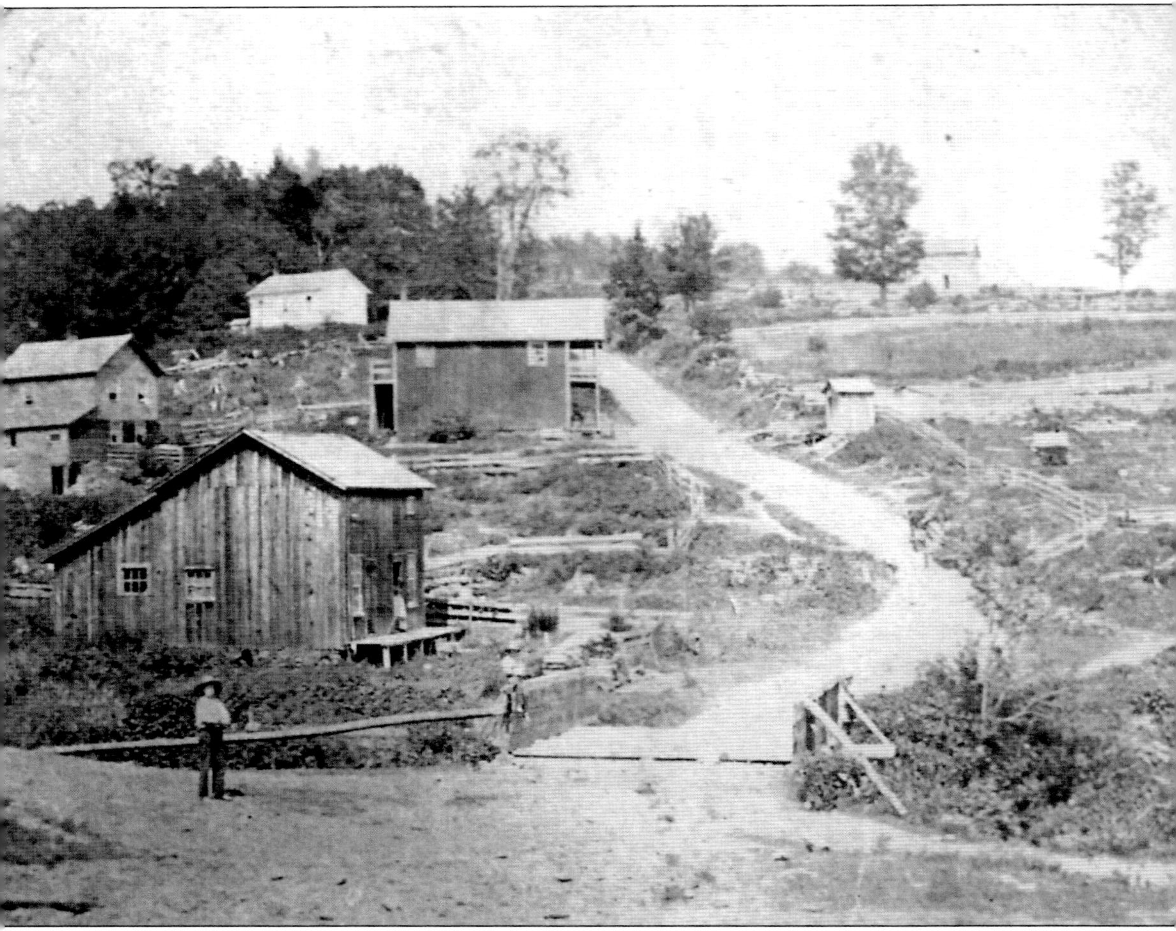

This picture was taken before 1887, the year the Shunk Church was built (background), from Shunk's Middle Road looking east with West Cemetery behind the photographer. Current Route 154 leads down from the background and cuts left where the unidentified boy stands. The old Williams mill is to the right. Charles Shaddock's home was later built on the spot behind the boy.

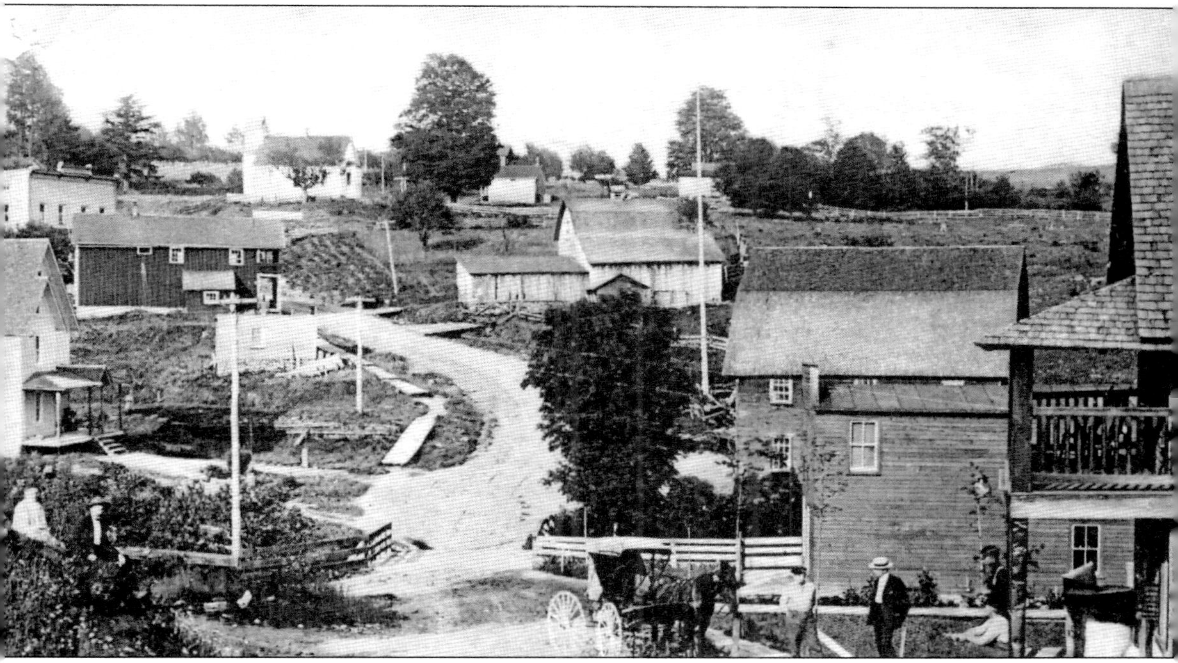

This view of Shunk was taken about 20 years later and shows changes that include the Shunk Church (background, left), election hall (back, center), Campbell Store (back, left), Shaddock home (front, left), and the W. H. Fanning general store (far right). Soon after building the Shunk Church, the congregation ordered seats. Since there was no money to pay for them, the church and property were sold to Benjamin Tripp, who deeded it to the Union Church Association of Shunk.

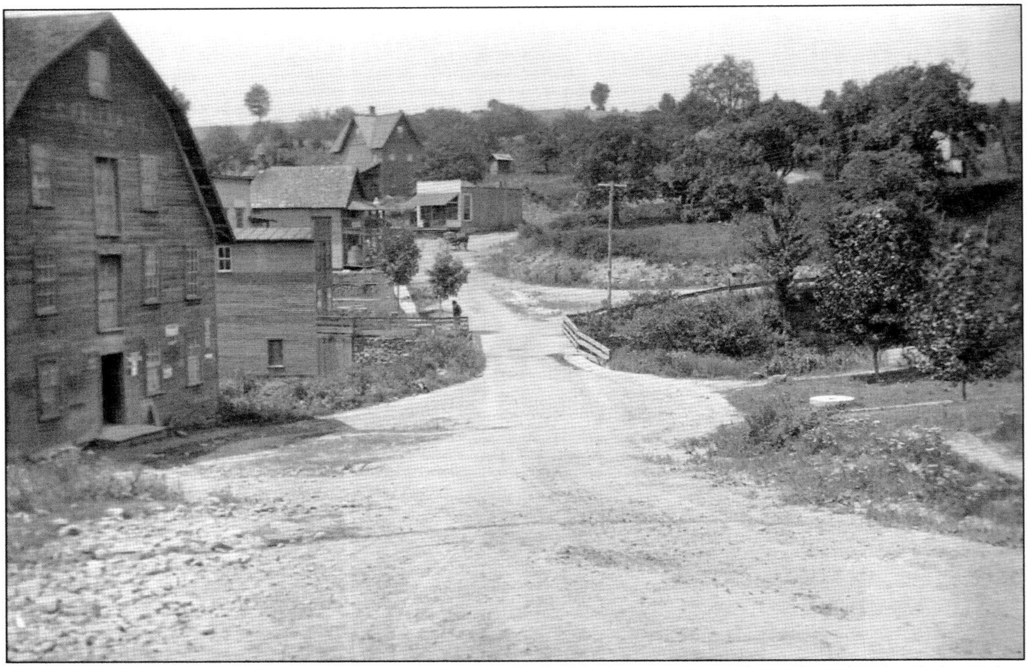

Shunk is pictured about 1900 with the gristmill (left) that was purchased and rebuilt by John Campbell in 1865. Joseph Hoagland built the original mill about 1803. There were different managements until the Great Depression hit and the mill was dismantled and razed. Middle Road is seen in the center to the upper right. Current Route 154 is at center and to the right, after the bridge. (Courtesy of Harry Earle Campbell.)

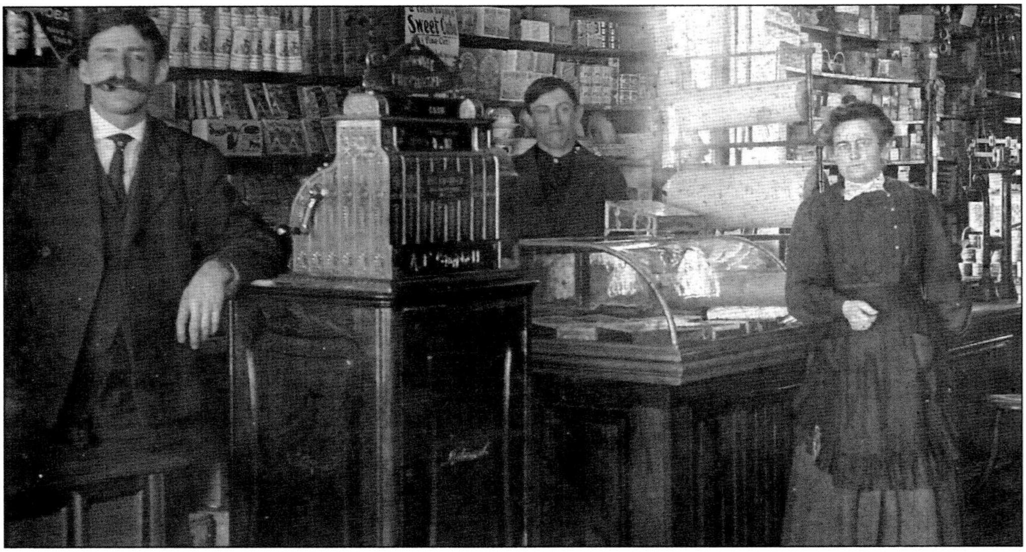

Ambrose Earl Campbell's general store was built in 1905. He was a grandson of John Campbell who moved from Campbellsville to Shunk in the 1860s. From left to right are Ambrose, son Edgar Carlton, wife Clara May (Ferguson). Ambrose was a postmaster, mercantile appraiser, township clerk, and school director. Edgar was a graduate from Bucknell University and a hunting buddy of Burke Campbell's father, Kenneth Haughey Campbell.

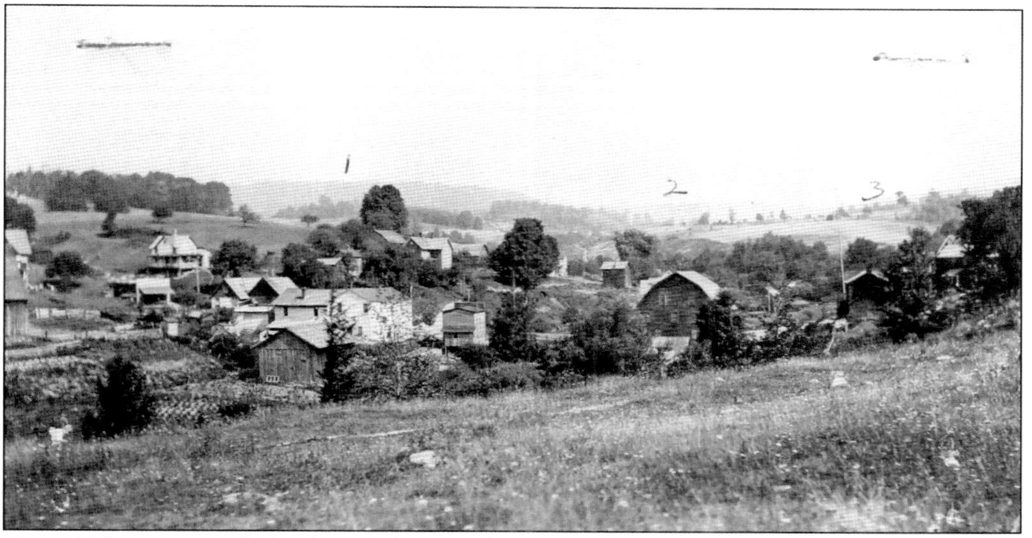

This 1908 overview of Shunk and the Hoagland Branch Valley shows the location of the old hotel building (1), the Williams gristmill (2), and the Patriotic Order of the Sons of America Hall (3). (Courtesy of Harry Earle Campbell.)

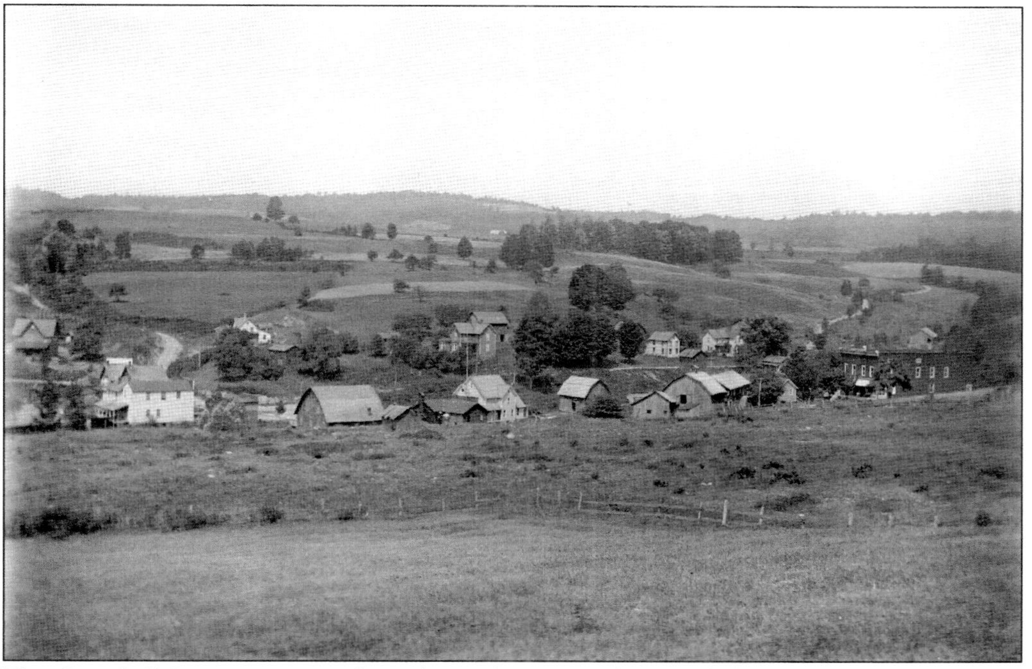

The Campbell Store is seen to the right in this 1890s photograph looking north. Subsequent owners of the store were James and Nancy Parrish, Rozelle Porter, and the Baumunk family. Middle Road is to the left, and present-day Route 154 is at center winding to the right background. The mill roof is left of center.

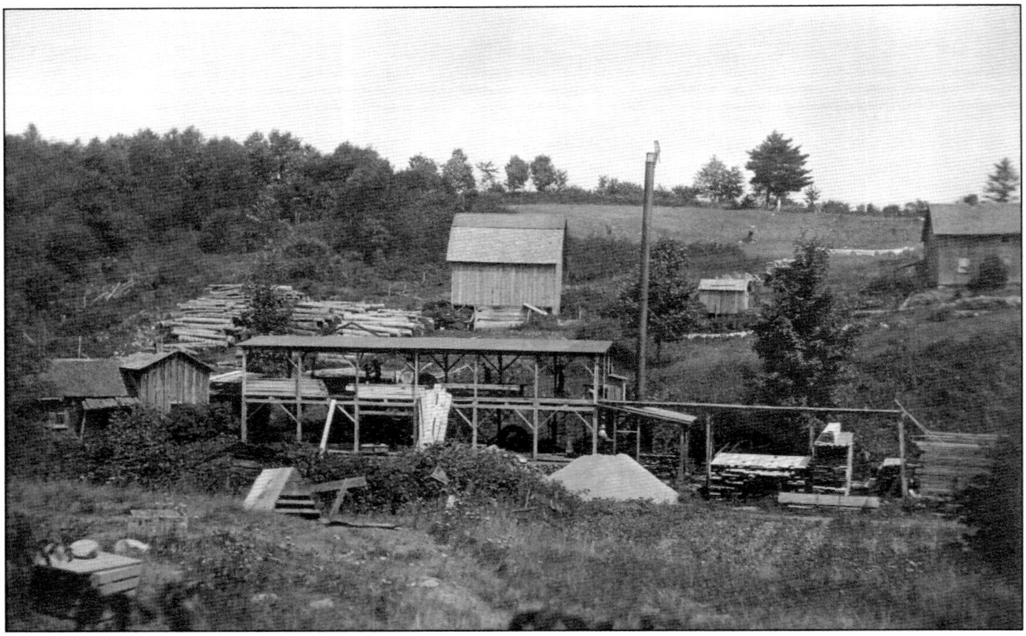

The John P. Kilmer and Son steam-powered sawmill was built in 1892. Kilmer also served as "overseer of the poor" and a school director. Kilmer's son Francis (born in 1871) ran the mill, was a sawyer and carpenter, and also served as a casket maker and undertaker. (Courtesy of Harry Earle Campbell.)

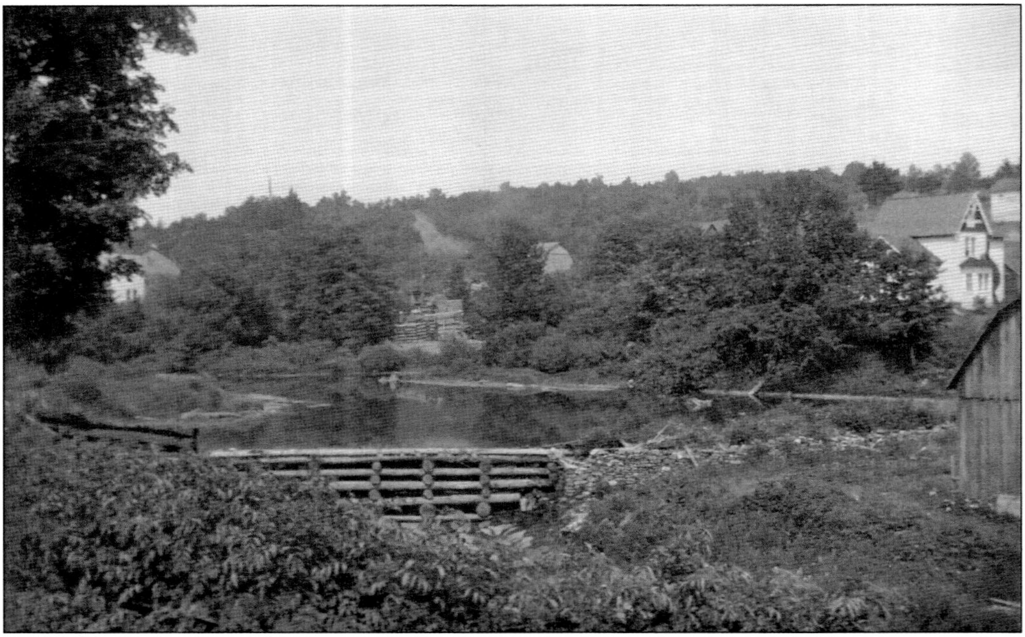

Charles Shaddock cut ice from this millpond, which furnished waterpower for the gristmill. The icehouse was close to the barn (right, foreground). The house (right, background) was built by Ambrose Earl Campbell in 1895 and was home for his son, teacher and photographer Harry Earle Campbell. Kilmer's house was on the opposite side.

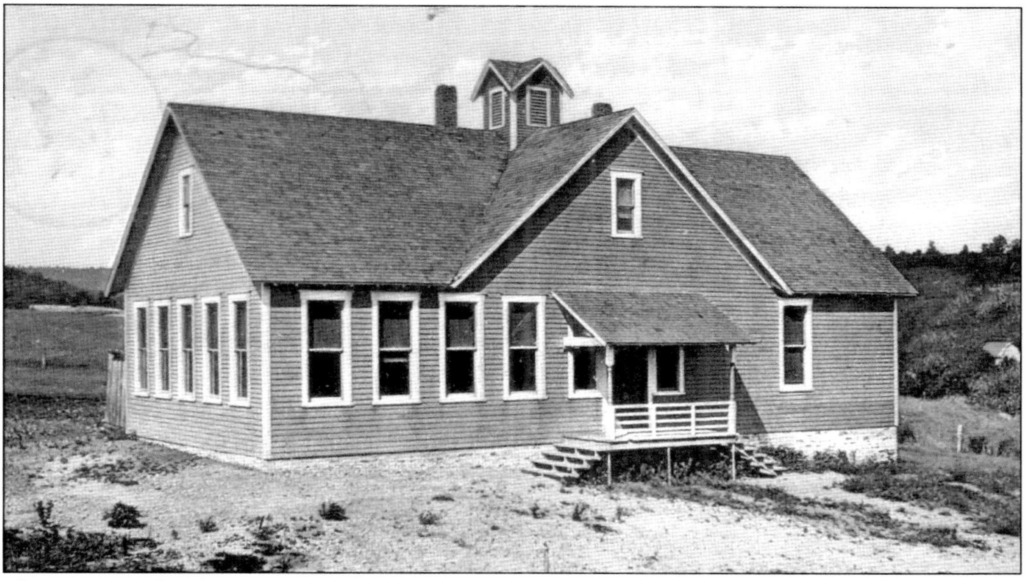

Elementary school was taught on the left half, and the high school was on the right. The outhouses were on the back side. The old Shunk schoolhouse now serves as the community hall. Lois Morgan Norton took her first two years of high school in the 1930s here. She completed college and taught in area county schools for 35 years.

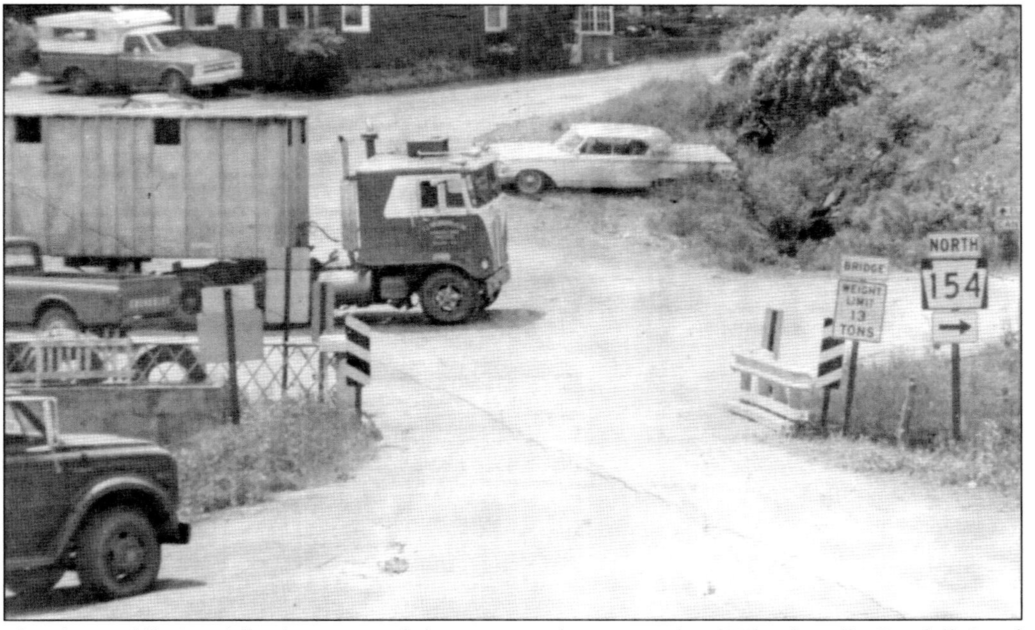

Shunk's Middle Road (back, upper right) went to within one mile of Wheelerville. Burdell Quail purchased the garage (left, out of photograph) in the 1950s from Alex Morgan, who also drove a school bus during that time. Current Route 154 north leads to Canton in Bradford County. Ellenton Road leads up to the left.

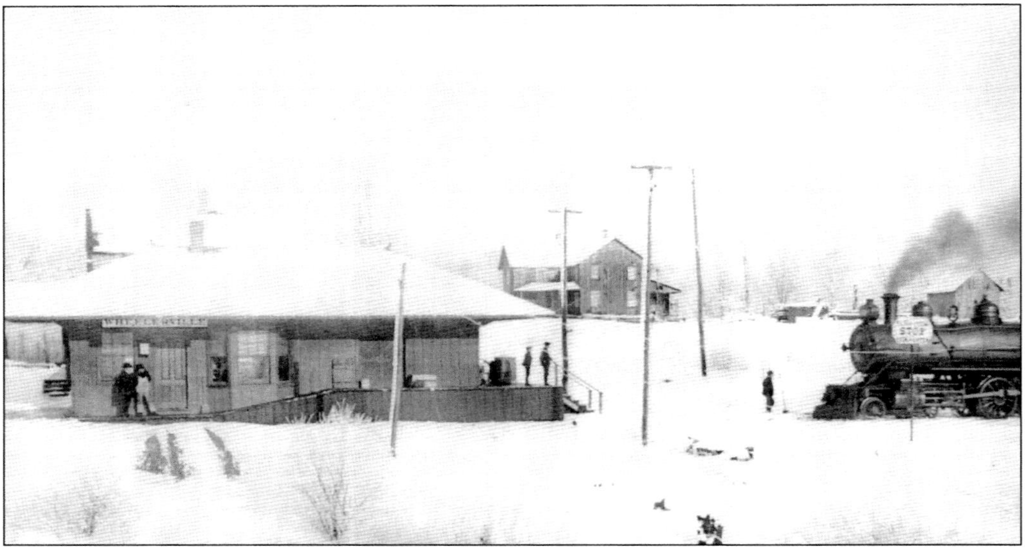

When the Susquehanna and New York Railroad was constructed through Wheelerville, the village outgrew Shunk. Its three grocery stores over the years were owned by Mary Kilmer, Preston Raub (with the post office), and Charles Kaseman.

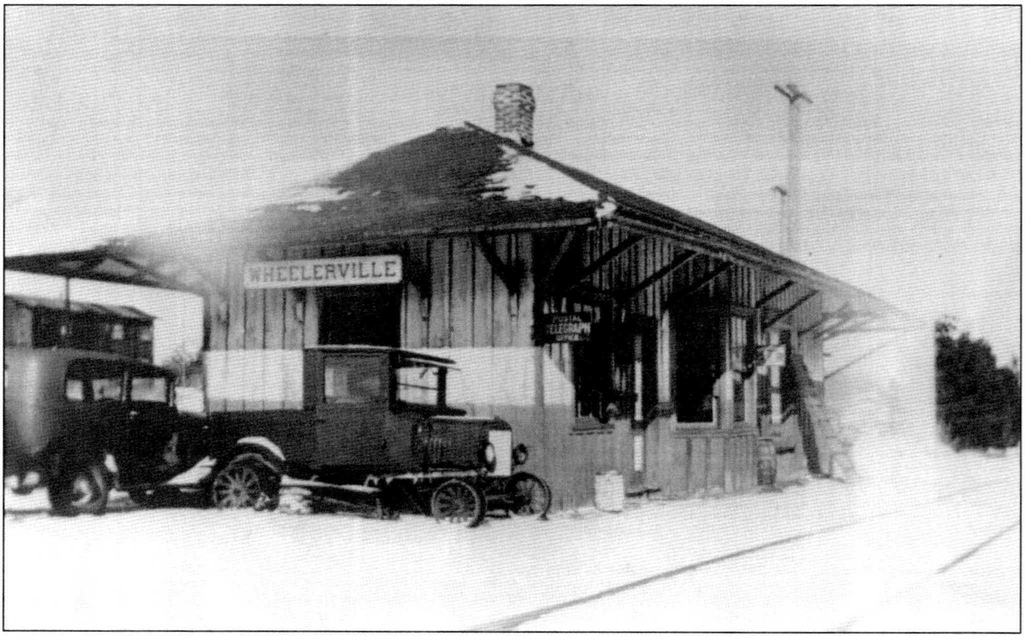

This picture of the Wheelerville station (along Route 154) on the Susquehanna and New York Railroad was taken sometime during the 1920s. This station was along the railroad that ran between Ralston, Ellenton, and Towanda. The rails were later scrapped during World War II.

Seven

Hillsgrove Township

Hillsgrove Township was taken from a part of Shrewsbury Township in Lycoming County. At the time Sullivan County was organized, the township was a part of Plunkett's Creek Township (Lycoming County) and retained that name until 1856 when an act of the legislature was passed changing the name from Plunkett's Creek to Hillsgrove to save confusion. Both the village and post office were called Hillsgrove during this time. The village was named for John Hill, an early settler. Lycoming County is to the south and west of the township, with Fox and Elkland Townships to the north and Forks and Shrewsbury Townships to the east.

The first road in Hillsgrove Township was made by Samuel Wallis of Muncy after he purchased a large number of tracts of land along the Loyalsock Creek in the 1790s. Needing a way to get supplies to his surveying crews, the Courson Road was cut about 1793 from Muncy to the summit of the Allegheny, down the mountain to Hillsgrove, and then up the creek to Forksville. The Genesee Road, opened about 1800, was an emigrant route from Muncy (Pennsburg) to Monroeton.

Daniel Ogden was the first white man to settle in what is now Sullivan County. He lived at the mouth of Ogdonia Creek below Hillsgrove about 1786. James Ecroyd (Ecroid), an Englishman, lived at Hillsgrove and later moved to Elkland Township about 1800. Charles Felix Rui Boulogne (also spelled Roulogne), an agent of the French Asylum Land Company, drowned in the Loyalsock Creek while on an inspection tour of the 200,000 acres on his return from Lycoming County. His was the first burial at Hillsgrove in 1796.

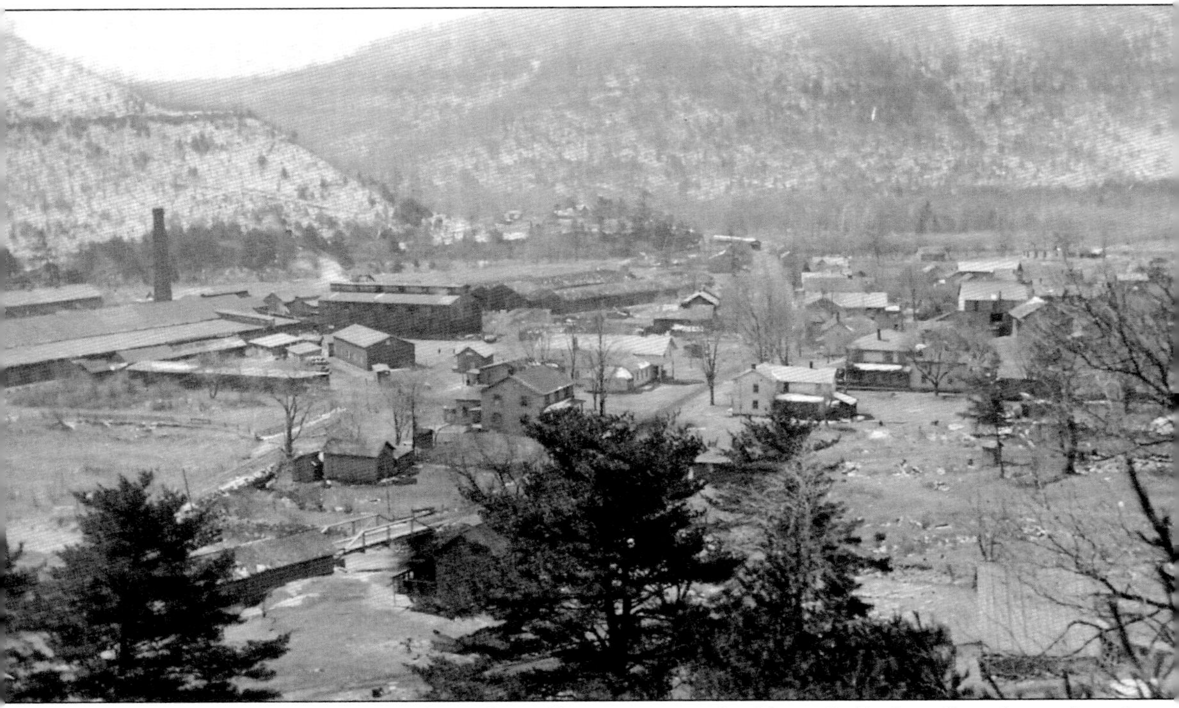

This view, taken about 1900, shows the Hillsgrove tannery buildings (left), the village (center), and the covered "spook" bridges (background, center). Mill Creek (foreground) joins the Loyalsock Creek (left, out of picture) that loops around the valley to the left toward the bridges.

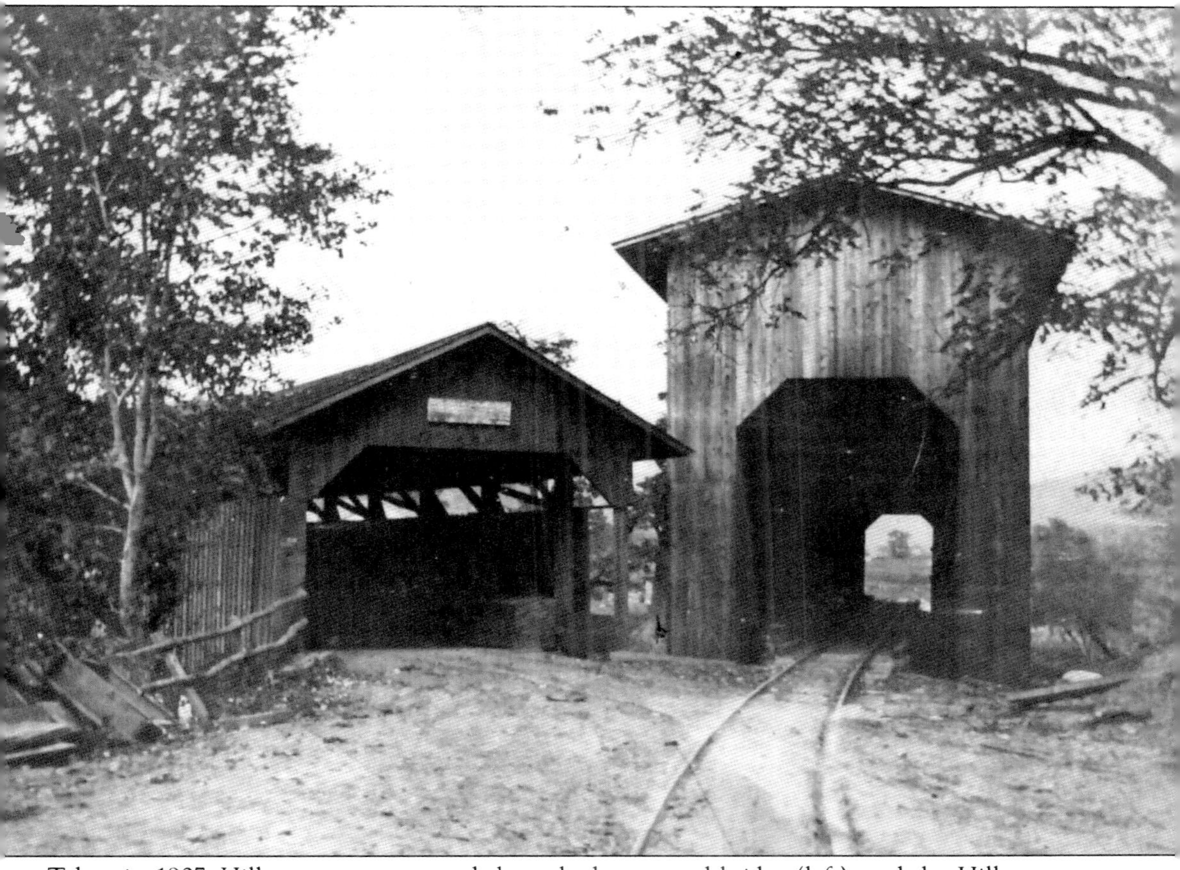

Taken in 1907, Hillsgrove was accessed through the covered bridge (left), and the Hillsgrove tannery was accessed through the Susquehanna and Eagles Mere Railroad bridge (right). Known as the "Bridge of Spooks," the small covered bridge is approximately where the Route 87 (formerly U.S. Route 115 and Route 291) bridge crosses the Loyalsock Creek today. Covered bridges were built narrow but high for hay wagons. And since horses were often afraid of rushing water, the barnlike interior of covered bridges calmed them. In winter, snow was shoveled into these bridges so horses could pull sleighs across. Covered bridges are dark and eerie at night, and sightings of ghosts have been recorded. Charles Felix Rui Boulogne, an agent for the Asylum Land Company, drowned downstream in this area in 1796. It has been said that his spirit still walks the bridge. Now a steel bridge crosses there. It is called the "jumping bridge" since many young people jumped from this bridge into the Loyalsock Creek from May to August. The depth of the water along here is about 40 feet.

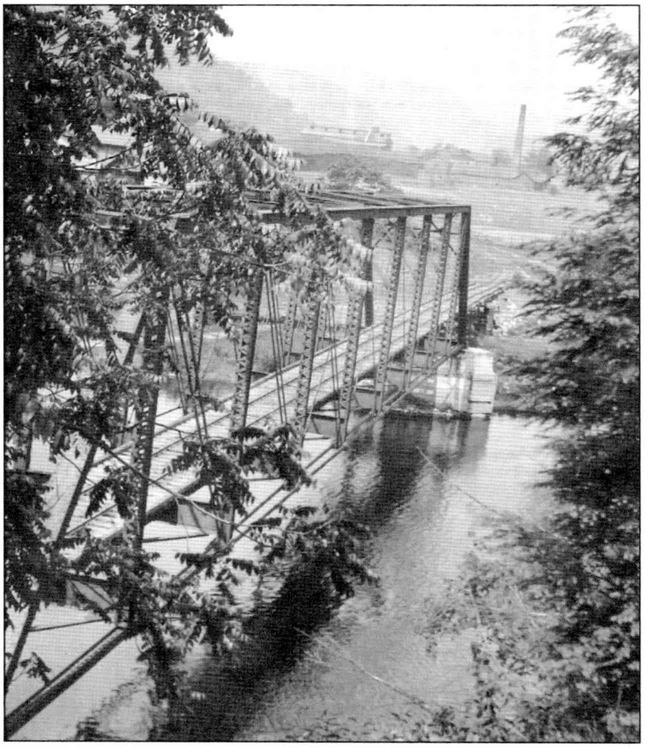

Nelson Caulkins, documentary photographer of many early-20th-century communities and industries in central Pennsylvania, took this picture of the Susquehanna and Eagles Mere trestle at Hillsgrove about 1920. The tannery is in the background, and Hillsgrove is to the left. The steel bridge replaced the covered railroad bridge after it collapsed under the weight of a logging locomotive.

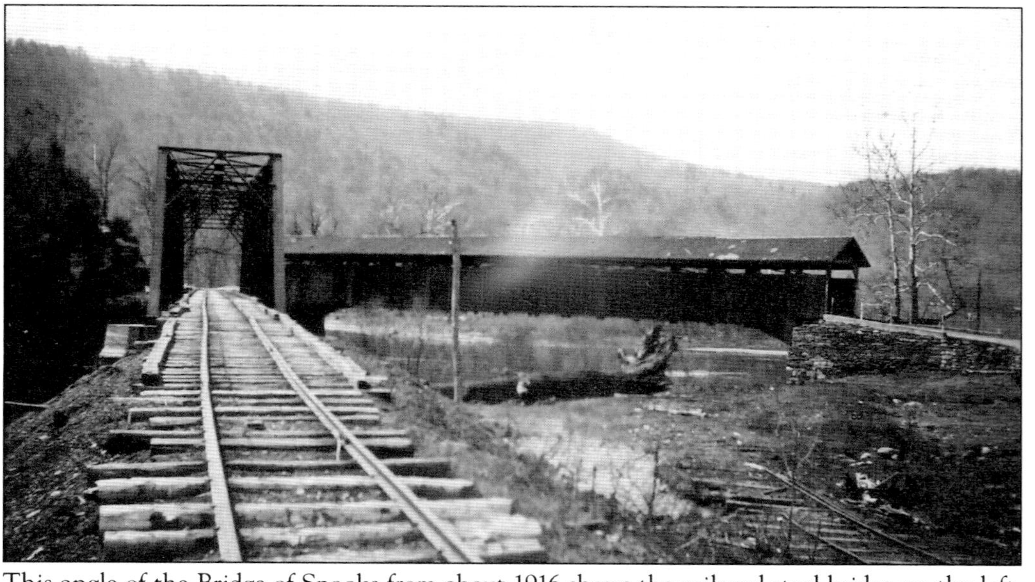

This angle of the Bridge of Spooks from about 1916 shows the railroad steel bridge on the left. Hillsgrove is behind the photographer to the right. John and Henry Hill built the old wooden bridge in 1876, the third one using the same foundations. The horse-and-buggy covered bridge (right) was condemned in 1934.

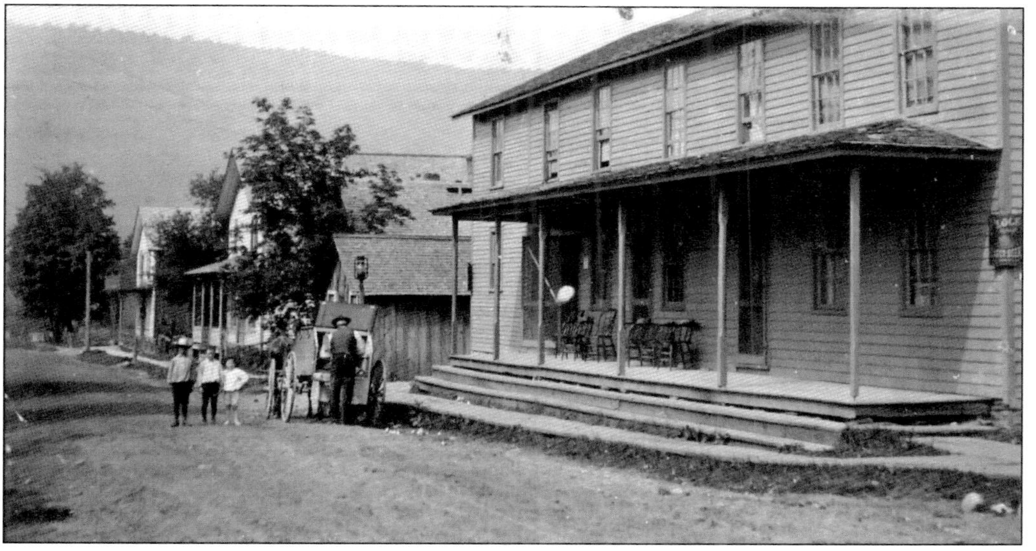

Seen around 1909 on Main Street, the Hillsgrove (Sadler's) Hotel was built in 1878 as a temperance house by a Colonel Biddle. The Bridge of Spooks is to the left out of the picture. Written on the back of the photograph was, "Delivering meat, come out with dishpan."

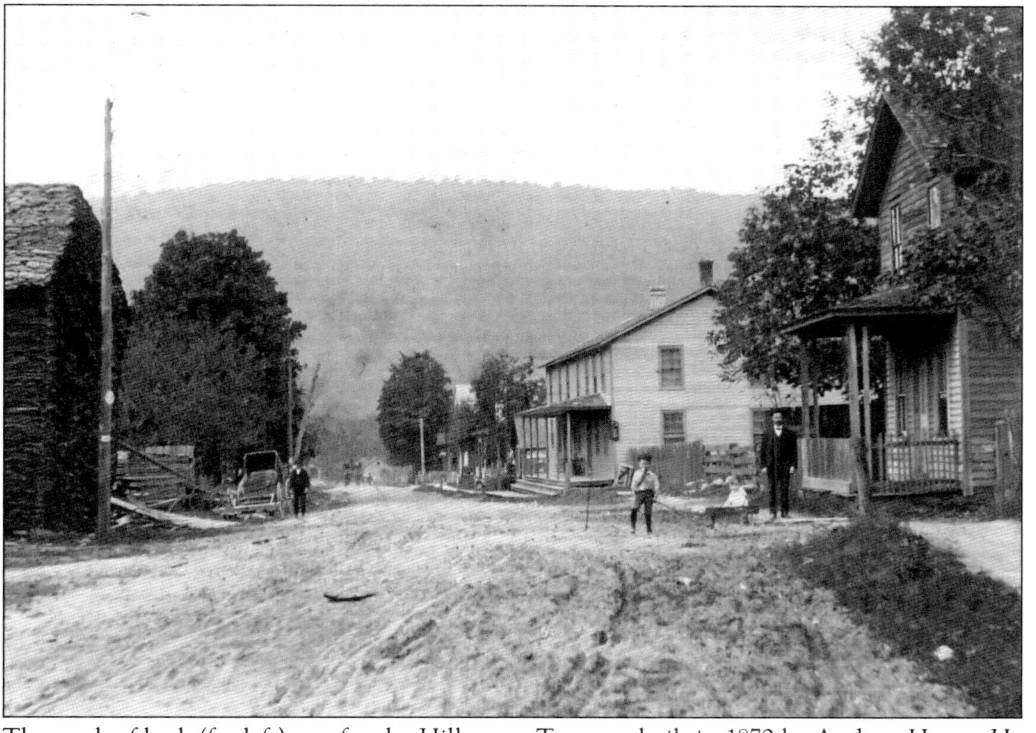

The stack of bark (far left) was for the Hillsgrove Tannery, built in 1870 by Andrew Hawer. He sold to Thorne, McFarlane and Company in 1874. McFarlane sold to Hoyt Brothers of Sanford, Connecticut, in 1878. The plants were sold again in 1892 to the United States Leather Trust but abandoned by 1922. The covered bridges are far left of center, and Hillsgrove Hotel is the second building from the right.

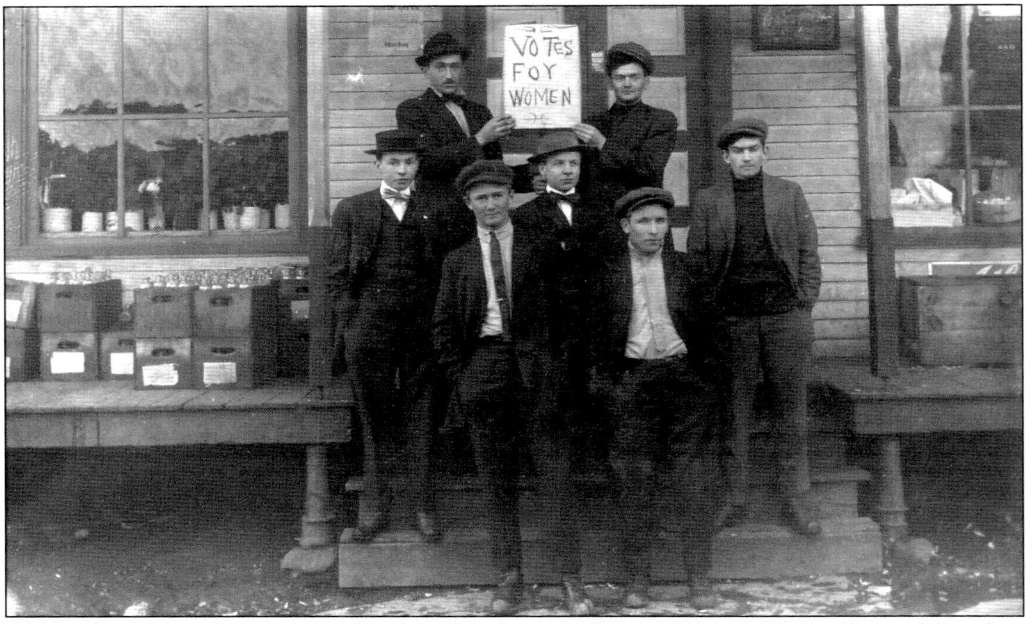

Although it is not known exactly why this photograph was taken, it shows Howard Speaker, Harry Harrison, Hieb Barrath, Ransom Byles, Trueman Speaker, and Edward Ortlieb, all of Hillsgrove, holding a sign, "Votes for Women." This was taken sometime after 1907.

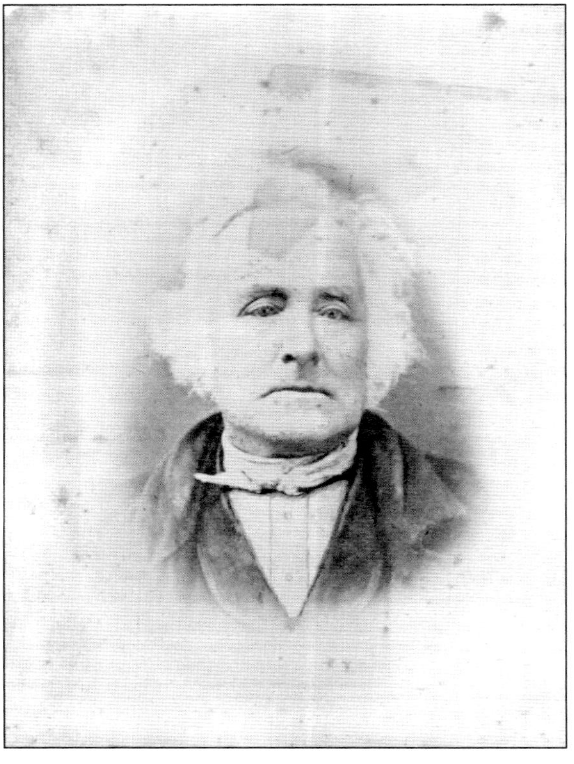

Sadler Rogers (1831–1913) was a veteran of the Civil War and one-term county commissioner who learned the carpenter's trade. He was reportedly 18 years old when he carved parts for the Forksville covered bridge model that he later supervised building in 1850 as well as the Hillsgrove covered bridge on Covered Bridge Road.

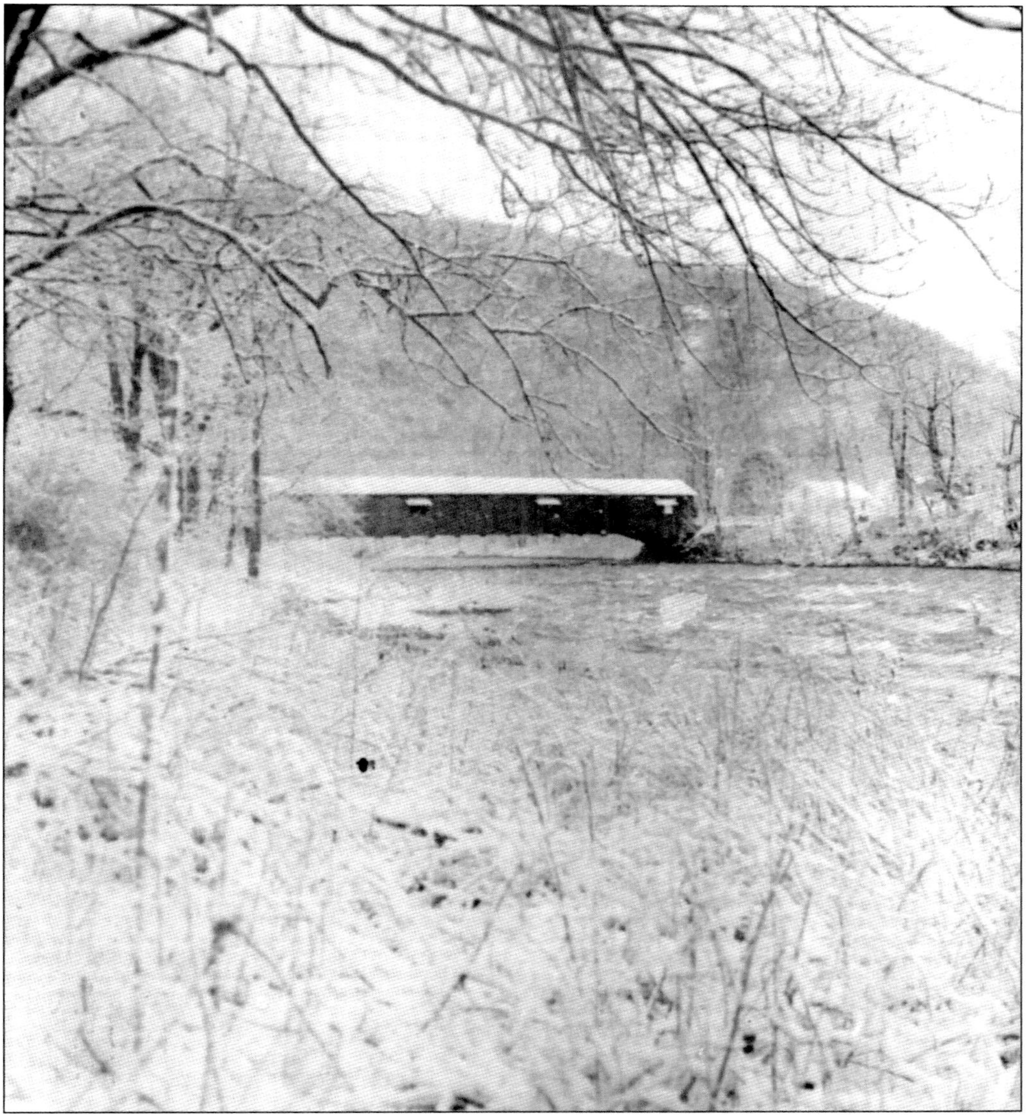

Built in 1850 by Sadler Rogers, this covered bridge is northwest of Hillsgrove on Covered Bridge Road off Route 87. It was placed on the National Register of Historic Places on February 2, 1973. Restorations and repairs were primarily made by Corbin Lewis. His constant attention saved the bridge.

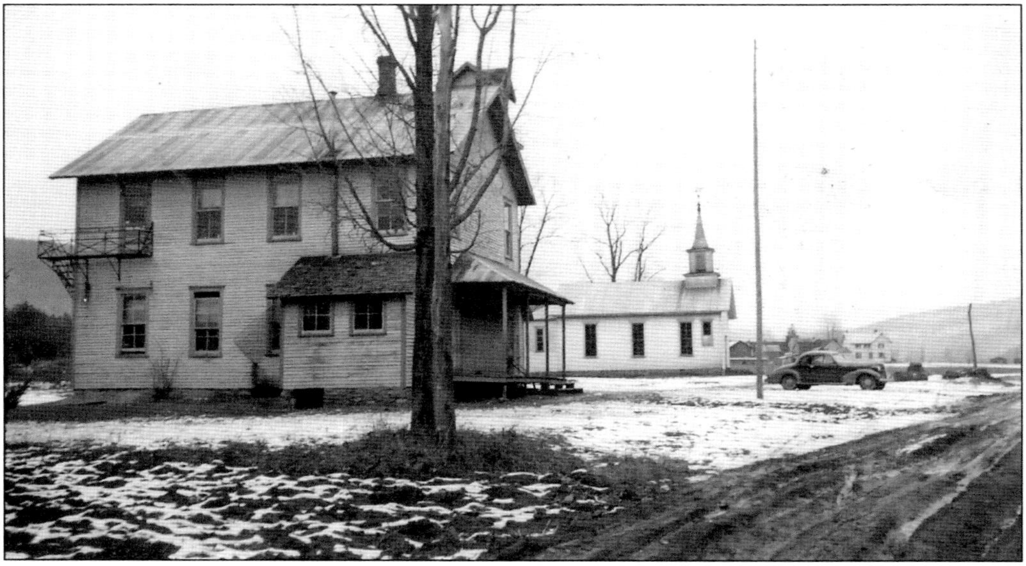

Early settler John Hill donated land for a school, a church, and a cemetery about 1800. The Hillsgrove high school (above, left) was built about 1900 and is shown with the Methodist church (background and below). The high school and library were on the second floor, while intermediate grades were on the first floor. Primary grades attended in a building (torn down) between the high school and church. The Hillsgrove Union Church was built in 1871 with two separate entrances for men and women. The church is presently used by the Methodists and is served by the Forksville circuit pastor. Hillsgrove's old Church of Christ, located in the center of the village, was erected in 1895 but fell into disuse by the 1920s. There are no photographs of this church.

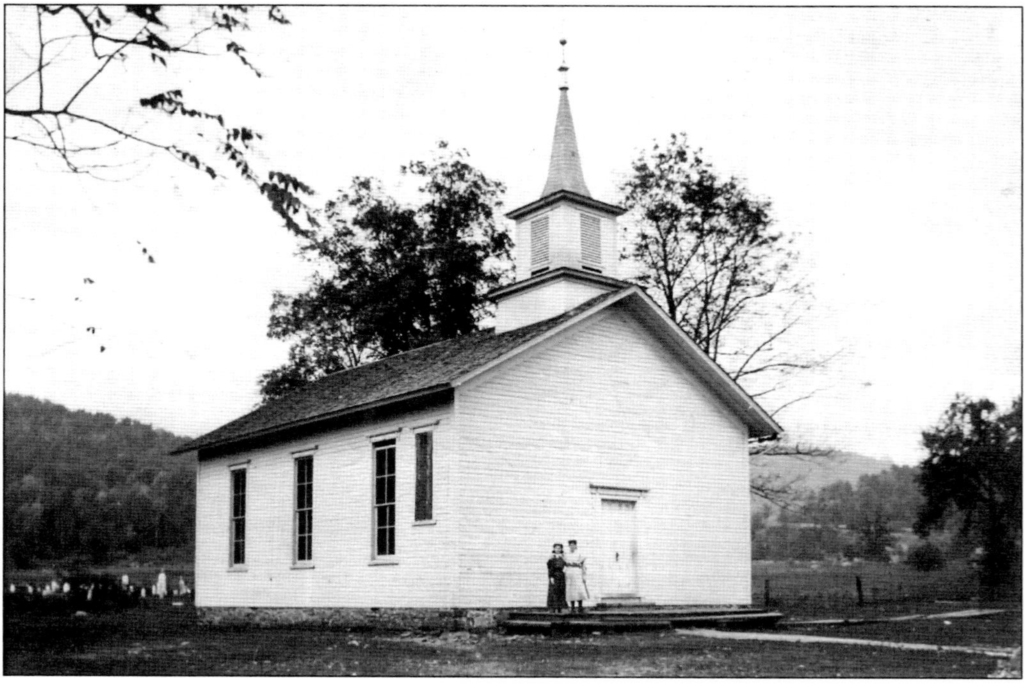

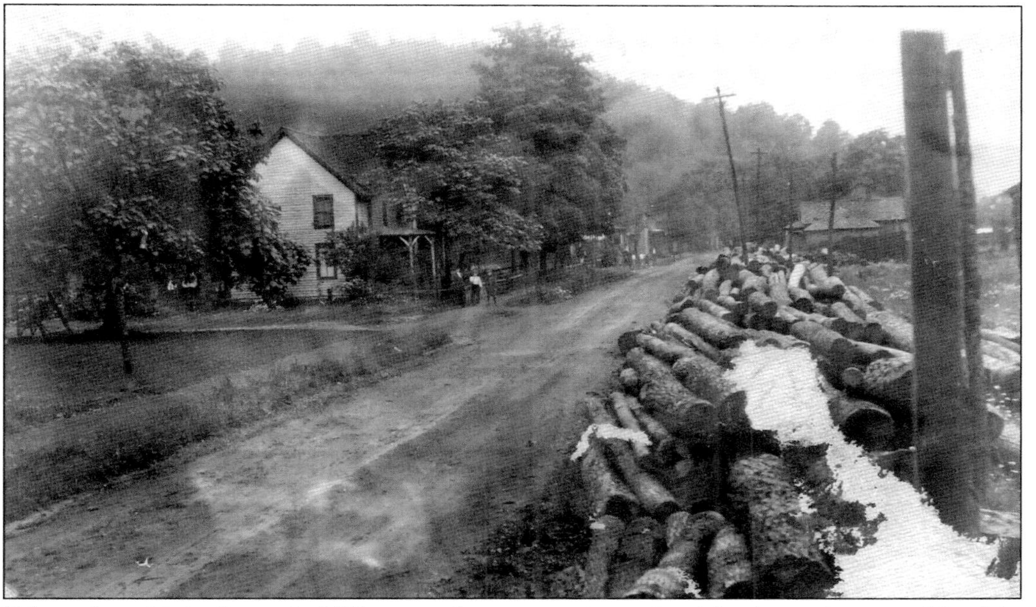

Taken along Main Street in Hillsgrove, the tannery is to the right (note the row of logs) in the field between the street and the Loyalsock Creek. The covered bridges are behind the photographer. No one is identified. Underneath the old bark mill, bodies were kept in a pine icebox until the undertaker arrived to ready the bodies for burial.

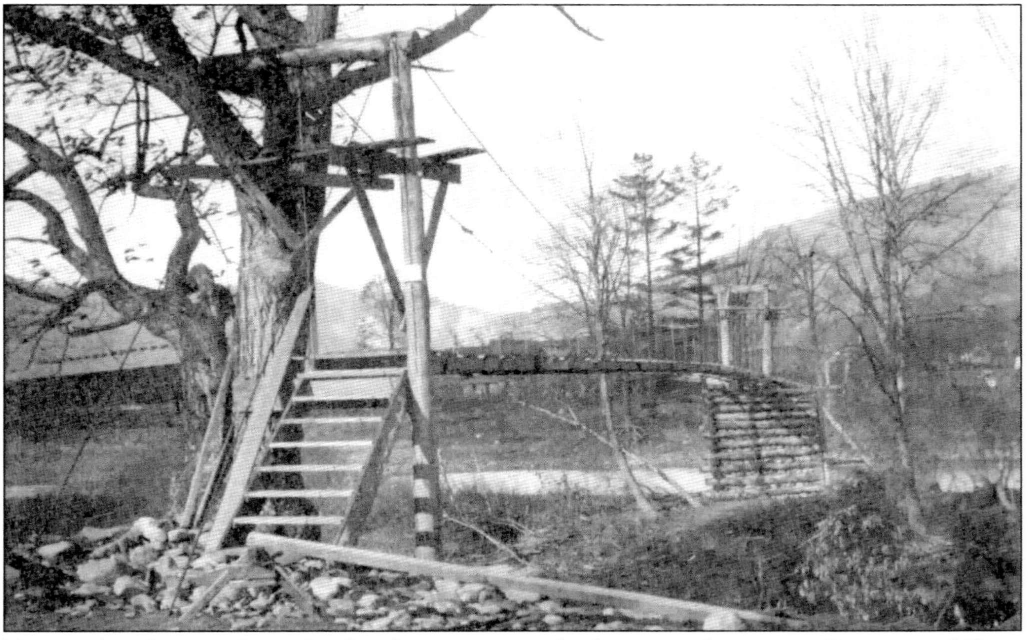

Not much is known about the Speaker suspension bridge near what is now Buttonwood Farm outside Hillsgrove village. It was likely built in the 1880s after Ida McBride Speaker and her two sons, Fred and Raymond, drowned while crossing in a boat on Christmas Eve in 1881. This photograph was taken about 1907. The bridge was damaged during a flood in the 1930s.

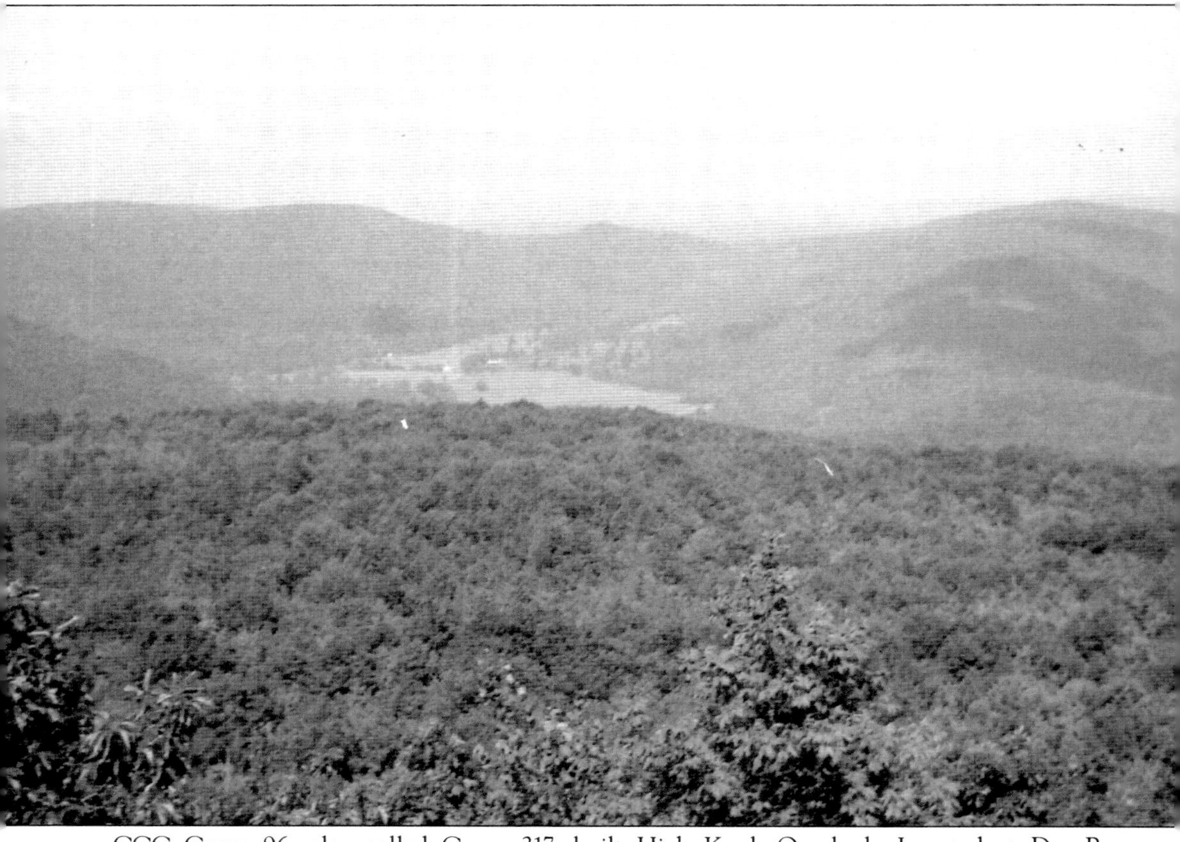

CCC Camp 96, also called Camp 317, built High Knob Overlook. Located at Dry Run near Hillsgrove, now the Hillsgrove Ranger Station, some 6,723 workdays were put into the construction of the Skyline Drive in 1937. High Knob is just east of Hillsgrove in the Loyalsock State Forest. This view extends out over seven counties. (Courtesy of Vernon Hatch.)

Eight

Laporte Township

Laporte Township was organized by the court of quarter sessions of Sullivan County in 1850 and formed from parts of Cherry, Davidson, and Shrewsbury Townships. Laporte Borough was organized in 1853 and laid out by landowner Michael Meylert (1823–1883), who named both the township and the village for his friend John Laporte. Laporte was speaker of the Pennsylvania General Assembly in 1832, a congressman from 1832 to 1836, and the last surveyor-general of the state from 1845 to 1851. He helped Sen. Charles Sullivan of Butler County to push the petition creating Sullivan County from Lycoming County through the legislature. The Laporte family was French exiles who settled in Asylum (now a ghost town) in Bradford County at the time of the French Revolution.

Seku Meylert (1784–1849), father of Laporte's founder, settled in Susquehanna County where he became a financial and landholding agent for Philadelphia's three powerful families: the Binghams, Merediths, and Clymers. In 1845, the Meylerts used Clymer and Meredith money to purchase 33,000 acres in northeastern Lycoming County. Seku died shortly after and left his son Michael in charge of business affairs. Michael was involved in various public works and surveyed several railroad routes. As a member of the state legislature, he was instrumental in passing the first railroad bill that allowed a railroad to be built between Catawissa and the state line.

When Laporte Borough (originally called the Center because of its central location in the county) was organized in 1851, three barely passable roads led into the small, stumpy clearing that was surrounded by miles of dense forests with six families living there. The nearest railroad was 28 miles away. The most prominent argument used for the county's formation was the long distance to Williamsport, the county seat of Lycoming County.

A square mile of land called Celestia was settled in 1864 by Millerites, a religious group who waited for the end of the world. Peter Armstrong, who owned the land, deeded it to God before he died. God did not pay taxes, and the land was sold by the county to Armstrong's descendants for back taxes.

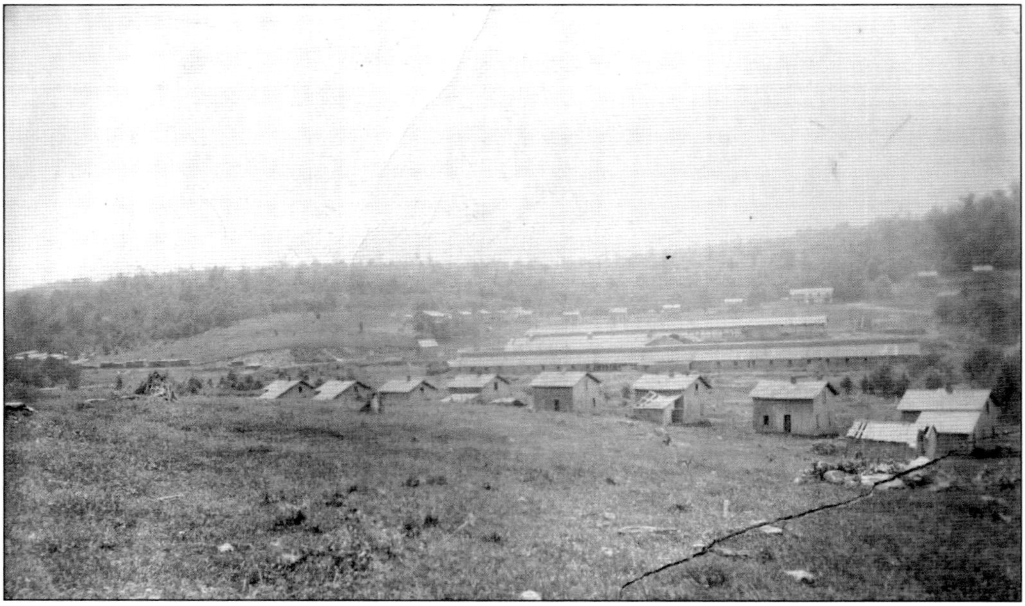

Thornedale tannery was built in 1868 by Jonathan Thorne and James McFarlane. Sullivan County's onetime largest tannery ran 40,000 hides per annum and consumed over 5,000 cords of bark. The tannery sheds (above and below) are the long buildings, and the company houses are in the foreground. In the latter days of the tannery, which closed in 1893, some of the hemlock bark and tanning materials were hauled over to the smaller Laporte tannery also owned by Thorne, McFarlane and Company. A new chemical method made the use of hemlock bark tanning obsolete. The Laporte tannery, four miles west of Thornedale, became one of the last to close in 1920. Older locals remember seeing stacks of hemlock bark at the old Laporte tannery site (where Routes 154 and 220 junction). A forest fire burned the Thornedale buildings in 1900. Pictured below is the weigh station at Thornedale.

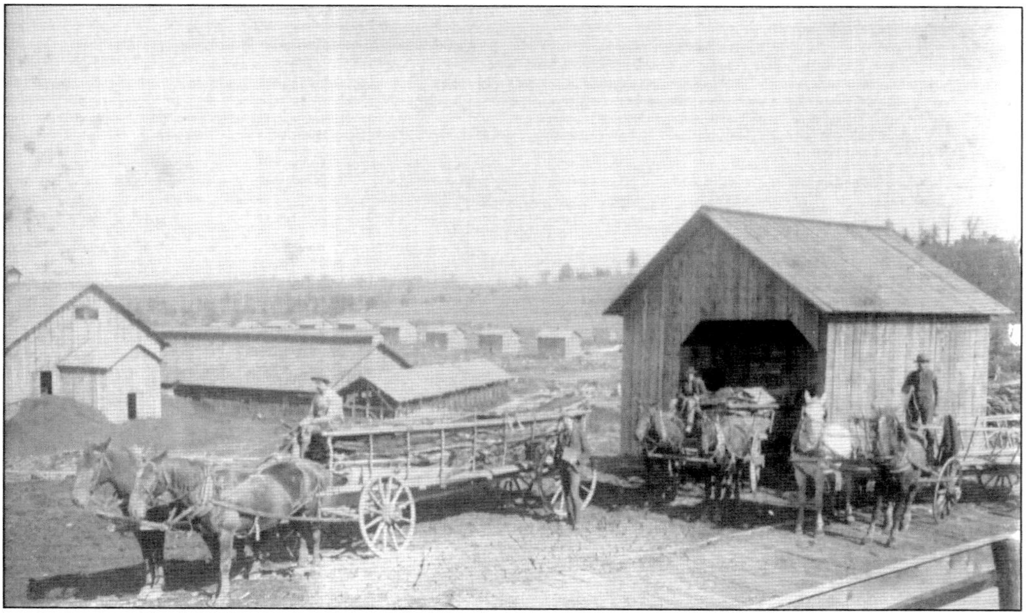

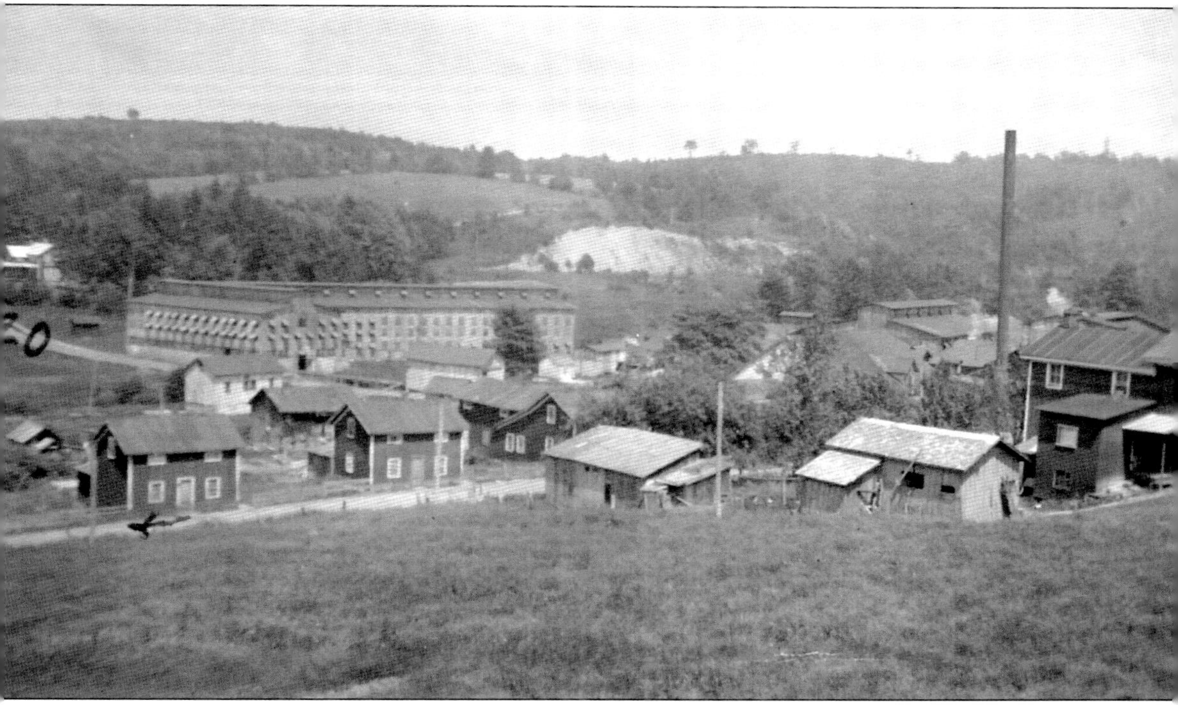

Laporte Tannery Town (closed in 1920) was located along Mill Creek at the junction of Routes 220 and 154. Michael Meylert started the Laporte Tanning Company in 1851, which later became Thorne, McFarlane and Company. The Williamsport and North Branch Railroad ran behind the tannery. Over 100 men worked in the business, and about 400 people lived in the town. The white building (center left) was the tannery school. It and the house at the upper left are the only remaining buildings.

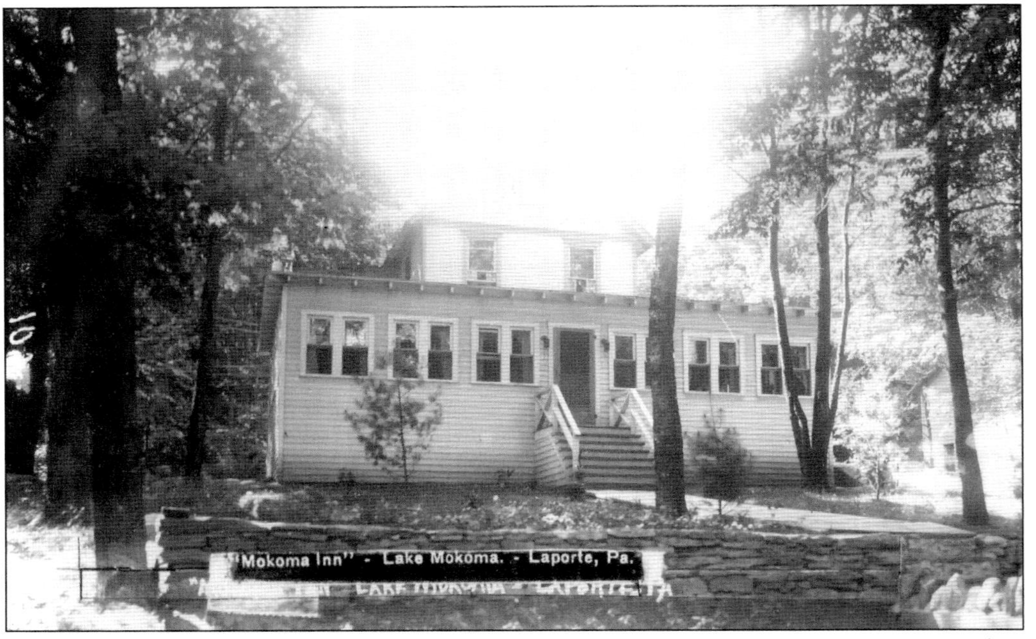

The second Mokoma Inn (above) was built in 1897 as the Karns Boarding House to accommodate Lake Mokoma vacationers. By 1930, it was called Mokoma Inn. Tea and lunches were served in the front enclosed room. In the 1950s, the front part was removed by Mac Mathe and used to construct a cottage on the hill in back. The remaining part is a private residence. The dance hall and theater (below) were built by the New Lake Mokoma Company that took over after the dam was reconstructed in 1928. It was torn down about 1940 by the Lake Mokoma Development Corporation. These photographs were taken during the 1930s.

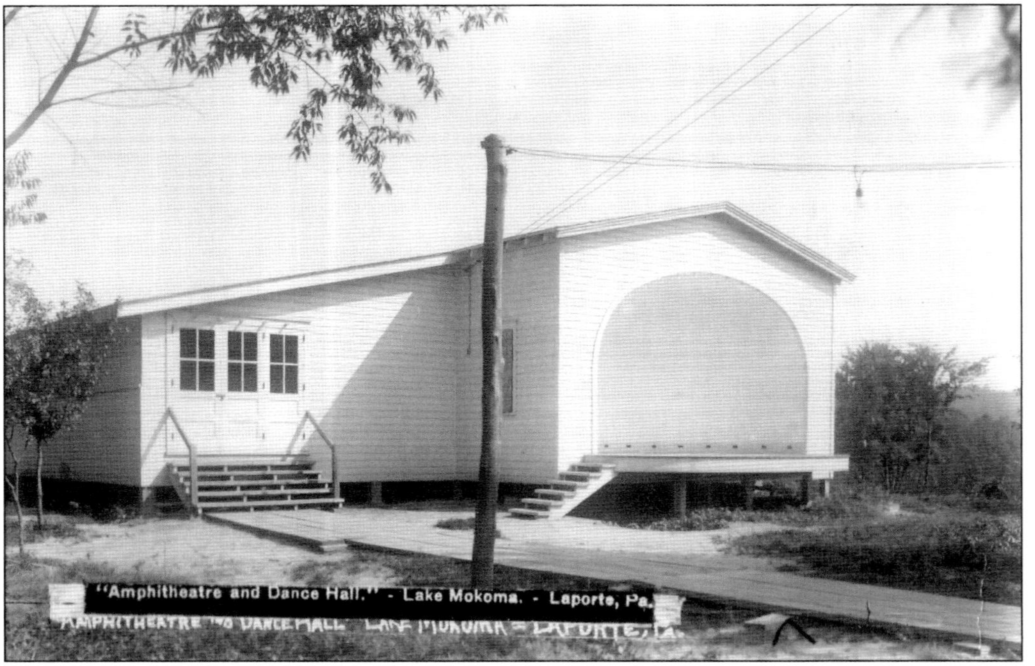

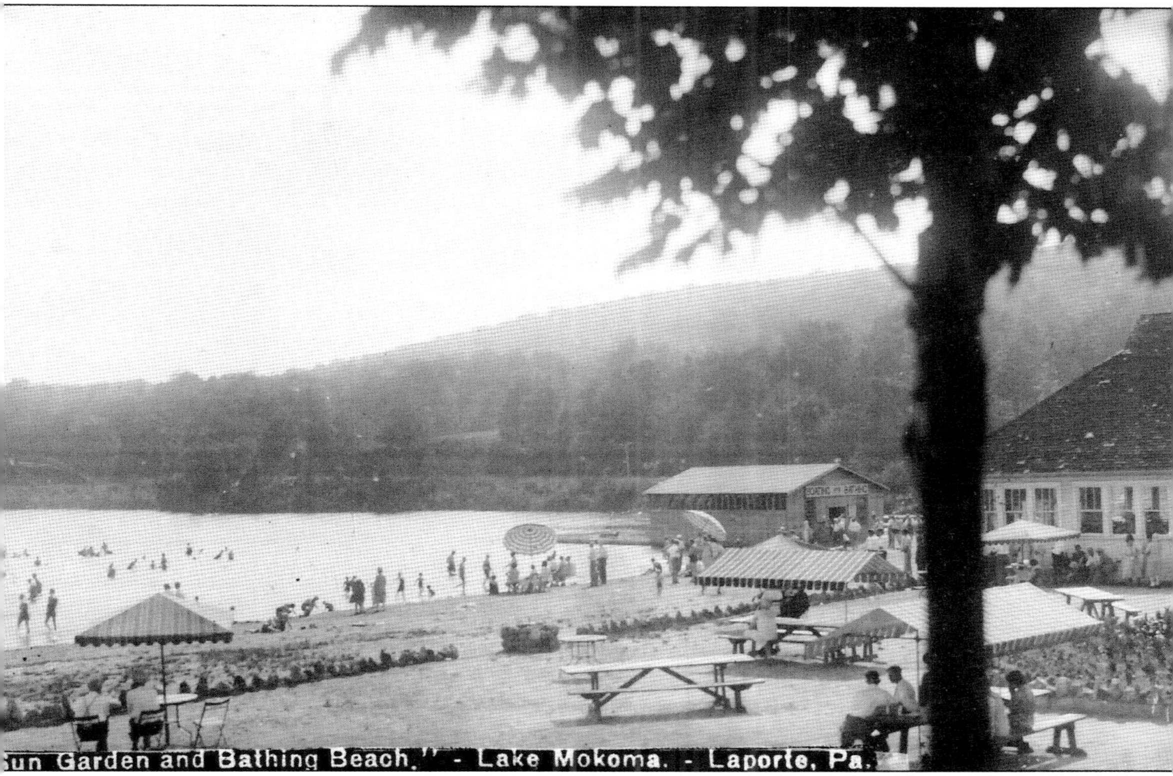

Originally a marsh at the headwaters of Mill Creek, Lake Mokoma was enlarged to its present size in 1888. The summer resort was built by people from Williamsport and Laporte. After 1894, the Williamsport and North Branch Railroad ran along the west shore of the lake. The hardwood floor from the dance hall and theater was placed inside the beach house around 1940 (far right), which was moved several times over the years.

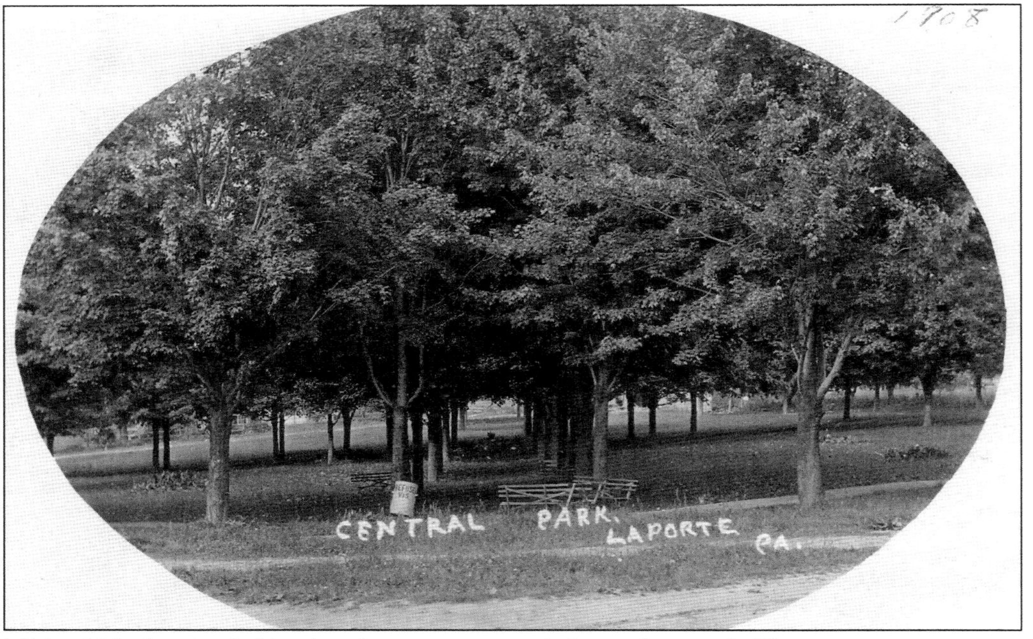

Michael Meylert deeded land to the county commissioners for a park. The area was an uneven, "stumpy clearing" covered in hay. Local women formed the Village Improvement Society (VIS) in 1906, and it was their major project until 1923 to keep the park clean. This photograph was taken in the 1920s (not 1908) after the maple seedlings lining the paths were grown.

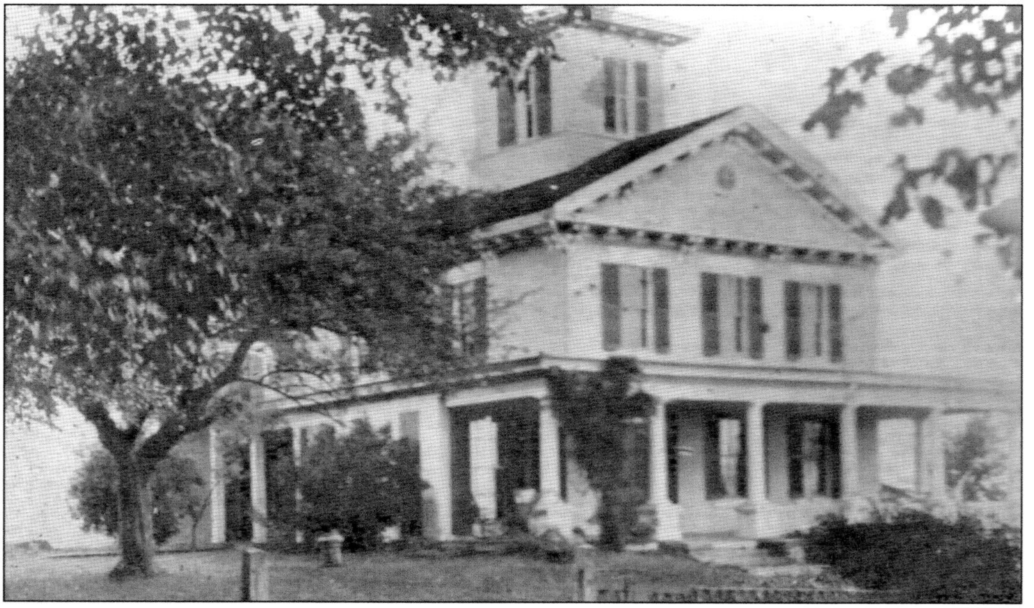

Meylert's three-story mansion, built with local brick and painted yellow, boasted 32 rooms and a watchtower (widow's walk) on top. He and his wife, Ann (Finch), lived in another home nearby while the mansion was constructed over the span of 20 years. Isaac Lamareau was the chief builder of Meylert's brick house.

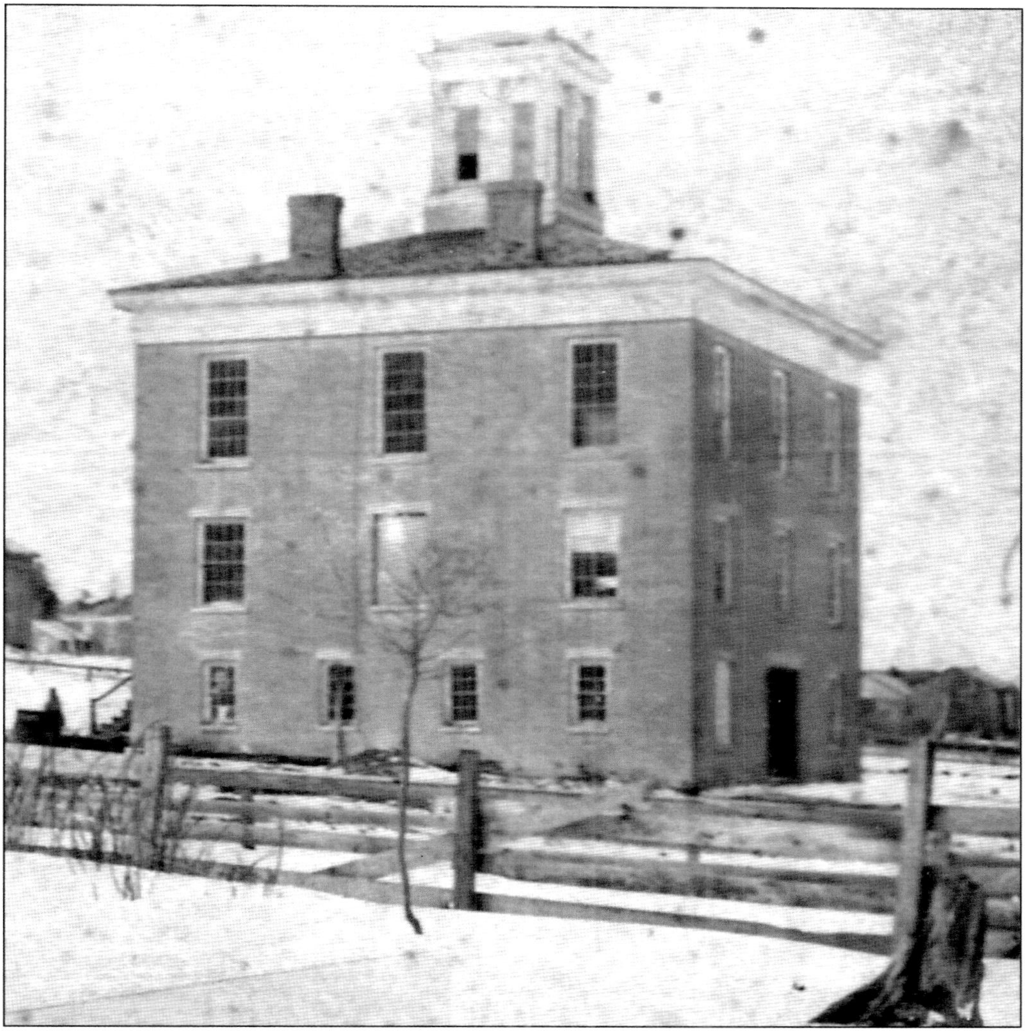

The first courthouse, completed in 1852, sat on the north side of the courthouse square. Made using locally manufactured brick, the building was 41 feet square and three stories high with a jail, sheriff's dwelling (three rooms), and public offices. By 1890, the bricks had deteriorated so badly that the building was torn down and replaced by a new courthouse. A plank board fence surrounded the square. Plans for the courthouse were drawn up by architect Stephen V. Shipman from New York.

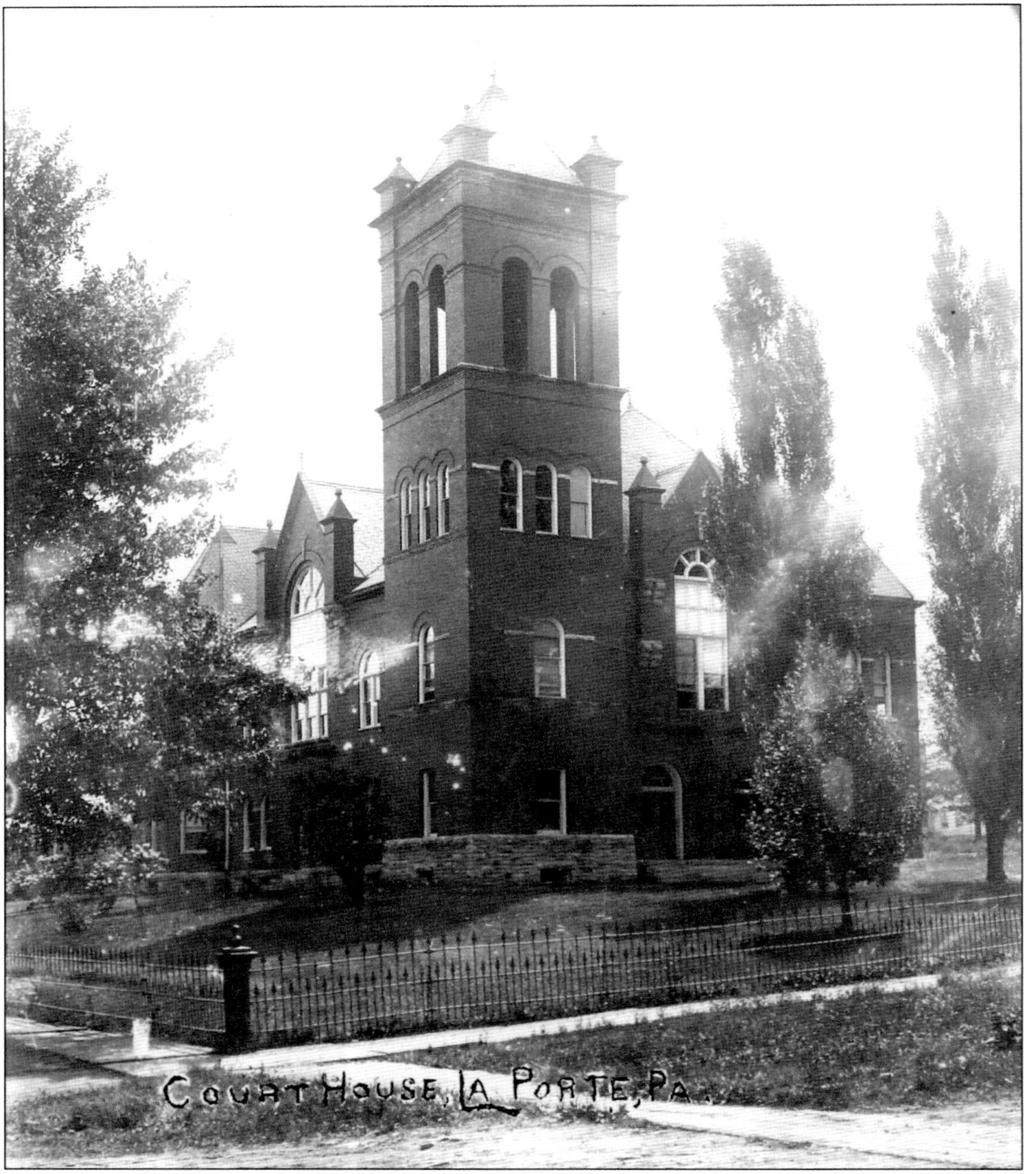

Sullivan County's second courthouse was built in 1894 by the Lawrence Brothers in the center of the square. It contained a courtroom on the second floor, county offices, jail cells, and an apartment for the sheriff and his family. The sheriff's wife cooked for any prisoners housed there. During the interval between the demolition of the old courthouse and the completion of the new one, county business was conducted in a brick building on the south edge of the square. This building now houses the Sullivan County Historical Society and Museum.

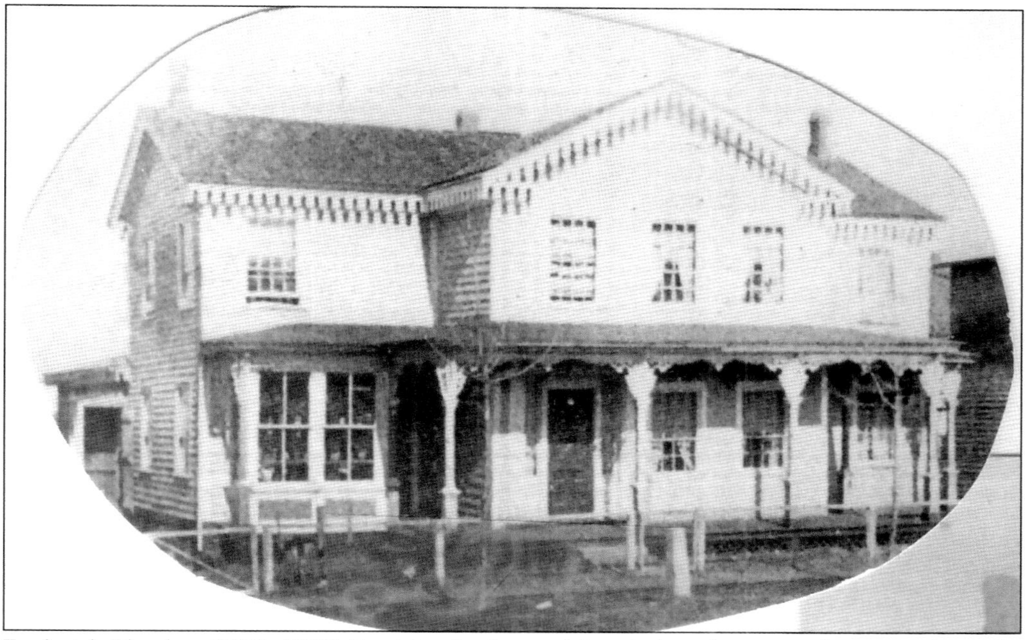

Frederick Fleschut (1818–1888) lived in the house (above) directly across the street from the old Mokoma Inn in Laporte. Here he made and sold stomach bitters reputed to cure dyspepsia, costiveness, cholera morbus, dysentery, fever, and ague. Needing more water, he built a stone house (below) along the present Thorne Street that leads down to the current Route 220. A few stone foundation walls are all that remain of his second home.

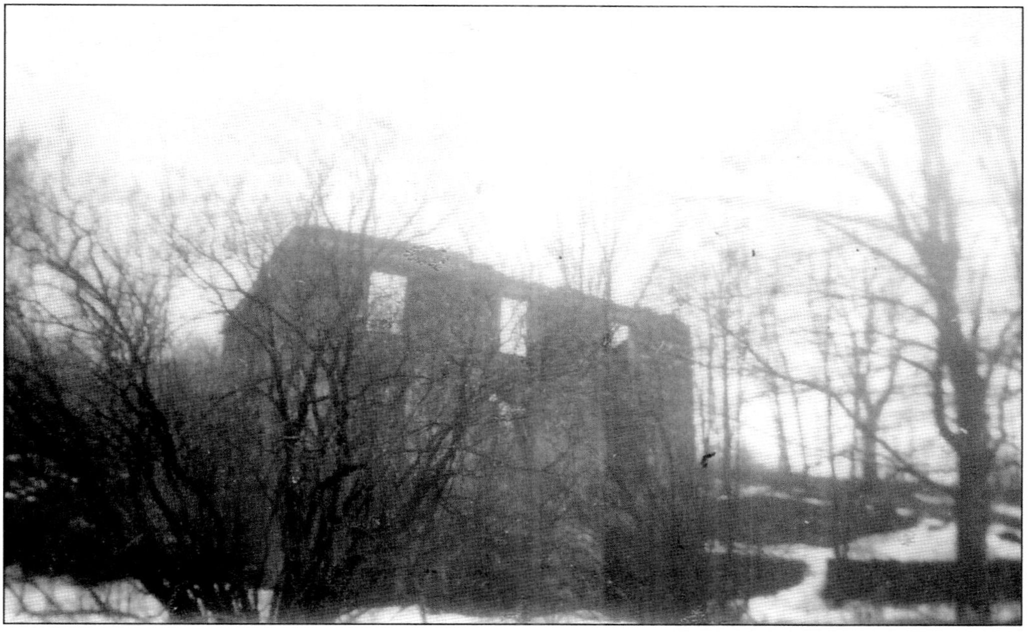

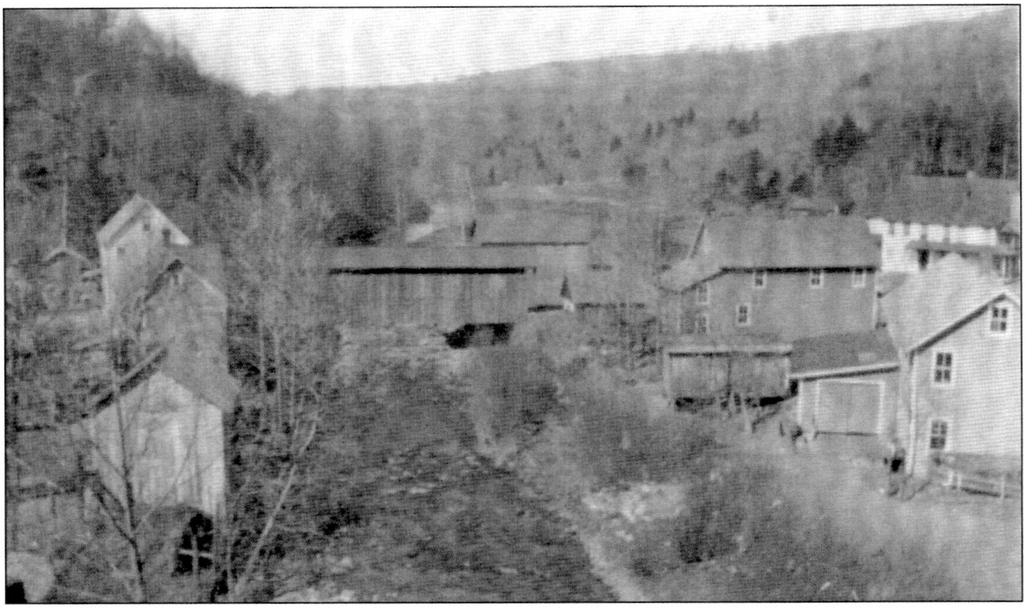

Williamsport and North Branch Railroad officials changed the name of Elk Lick to Nordmont. The photograph above, taken prior to 1938, shows the covered bridge over Muncy Creek and the boundary line of Davidson (left of creek) and Laporte (right of creek) Townships. Locals objected to their covered bridge being condemned in 1954. A concrete bridge was built in its place. Below (clockwise from left) are Lloyd Little's store, the Grange hall, the Nordmont Hotel (wraparound porch), Snider's barn (still standing), Nordmont school (background, right of center), Sones Company Store, the Bert Snider home, and the Phil Peterman home. The company store, now a community hall, was the site of a cigar factory in the 1890s organized by James Deininger. (Courtesy of Fairy M. Walters.)

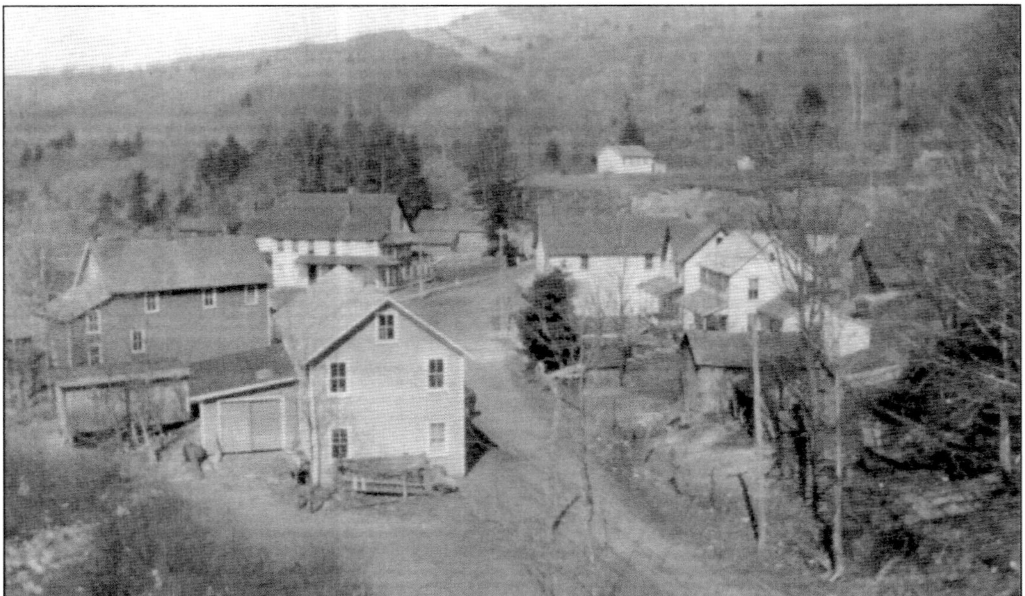

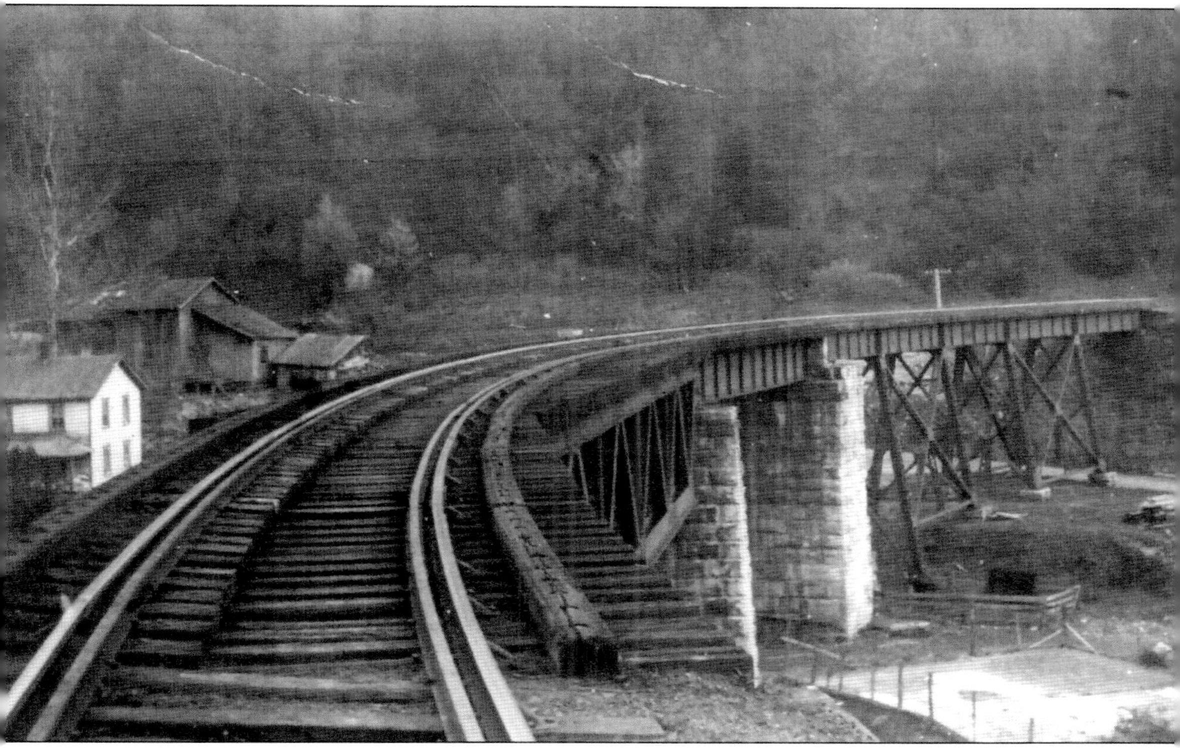

The Nordmont Williamsport and North Branch Railroad trestle is pictured about 1898 after the line to Sattersfield was completed. The railroad reached Nordmont in 1888. The Goose Neck line was a horseshoe curve with the village sitting directly in the center of the curve. The trestle was 40 feet high and 336 feet long. The tracks climbed 350 feet on a 1.5 percent grade following the creek to Lake Mokoma. Thomas J. Laird lived in the lower house (left). He was a blacksmith and one of the first settlers of Nordmont. The next house up was where some of the train people lived. At the time, a passenger coach was used as the depot and sat just above tracks (far right), and the engine house was in a barn (center, no longer standing). (Courtesy of Fairy M. Walters and Nancy Little Spencer.)

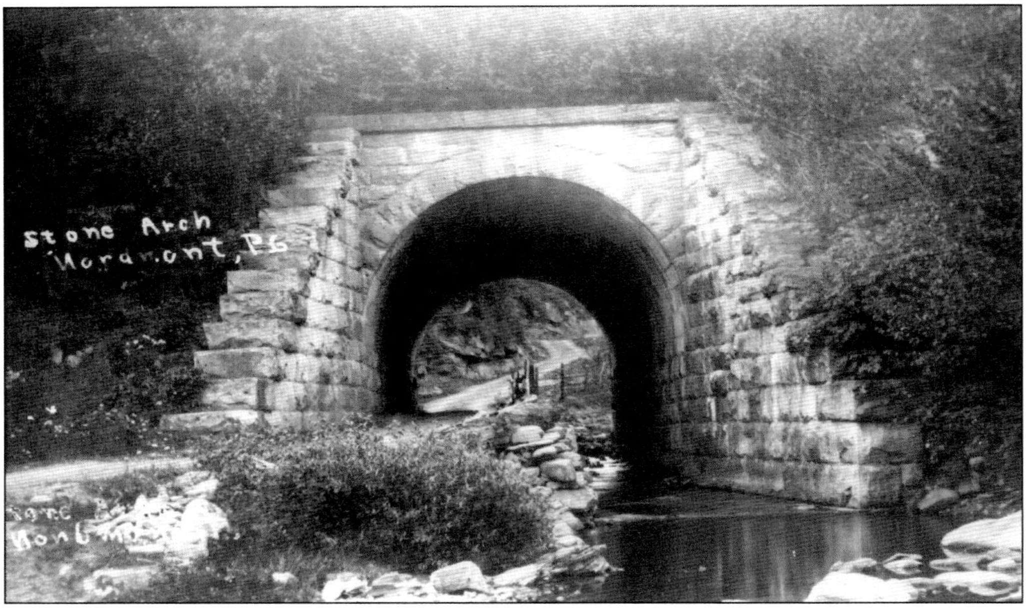

The stone arch at Nordmont is pictured in 1910 where the Williamsport and North Branch Railroad crossed the top and vehicles and the creek passed underneath. When the railroad was pulled out, State Road 2003 was built through the fill at left. The stone arch was saved from destruction in the 1970s. Today it is one of two remaining arches in Sullivan County from the railroad era.

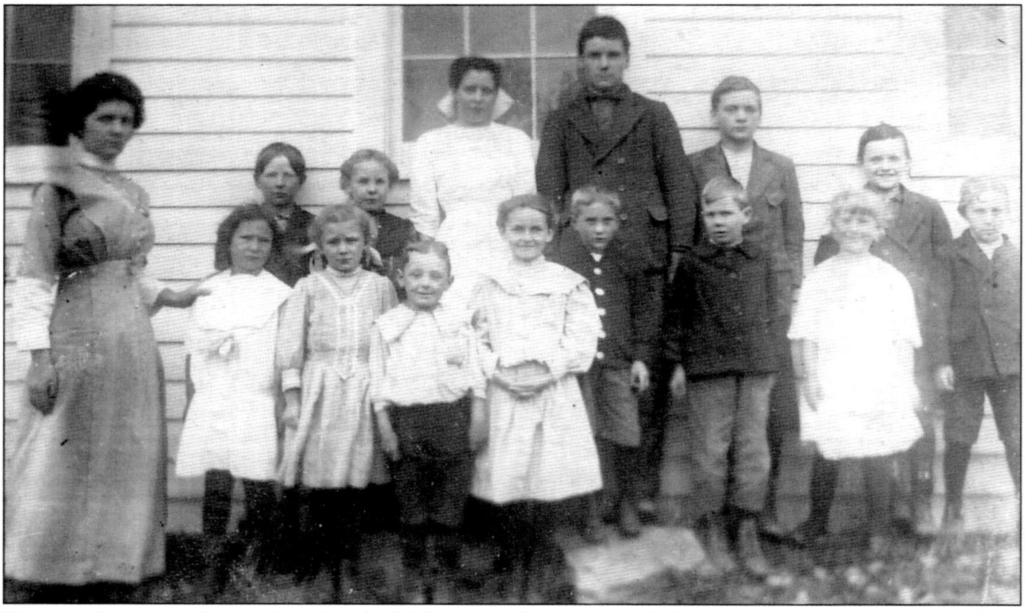

King's school was located on Little Hill at Nordmont. In 1912, Freda Armes was the teacher. Pictured from left to right are (first row) Della Shaffer Krause, Lena Shaffer, Howard Shaffer, Myrtle Hess, Raymond Reese, Lee Hess, and Mabel Little Kingston; (second row) Lloyd Little, Ocie Hess, Mag Rider, Dallas Hess, Robert Hess, Frank Hess, and Wesley "Jack" Little. (Courtesy of Fairy M. Walters.)

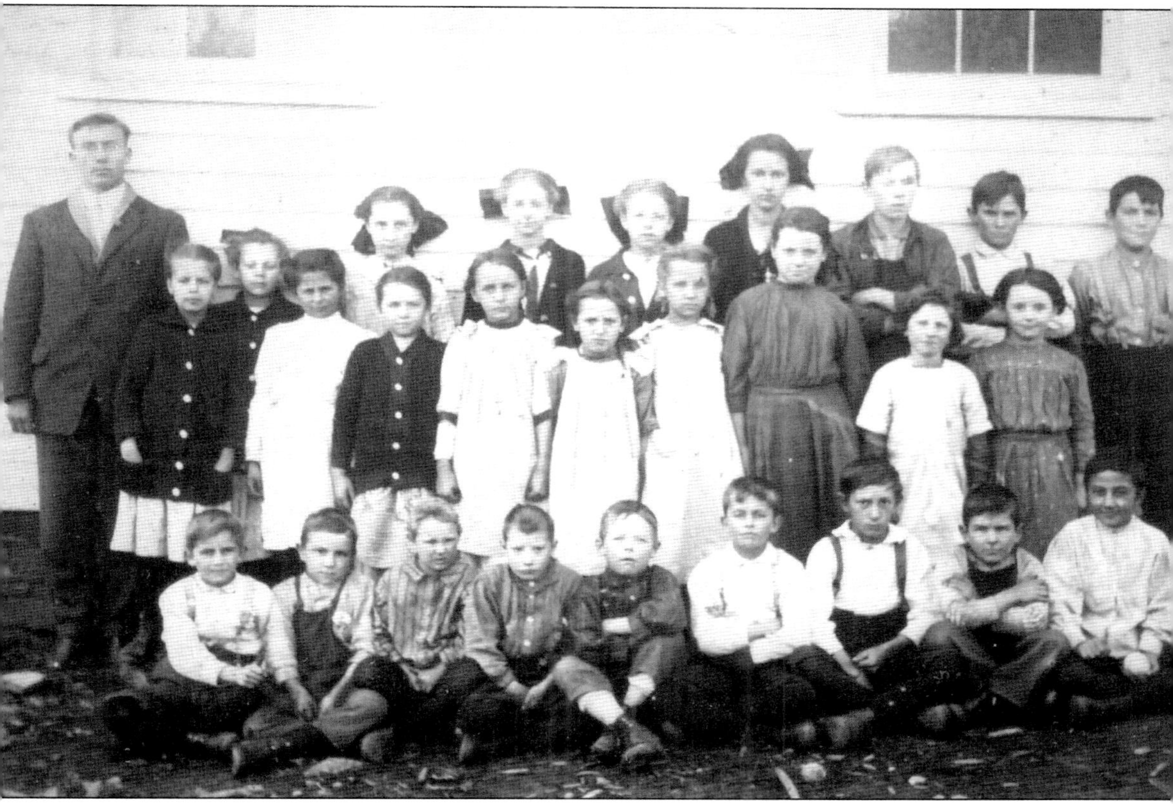

Blake Gavitt was the Sugar Point schoolteacher in 1914. Pictured from left to right are (first row) Charles Hunter, Jay Peterman, Elmer Hess, Ed Gorman, Howard Peterman, Harold Hunter, Ralph Sharrow, Harry Peterman, and Angelo Navarra; (second row) Edna Peters, Delia Peterman, Beulah Peterman, Ruth Sharrow, Alice Sharrow, Emma Hess, Pearl Mosteller, Mary Mosteller, and Pheobe Walter; (third row) Ethel Peters, Elsie Botsford, Mabel Traugh, Mary Peters, Anna Sharrow, Emory Botsford, Charles Faulkner, and Dewitt Gorman. The school was located east of Nordmont on Hunter Road. (Courtesy of Fairy M. Walters and Charles Hunter.)

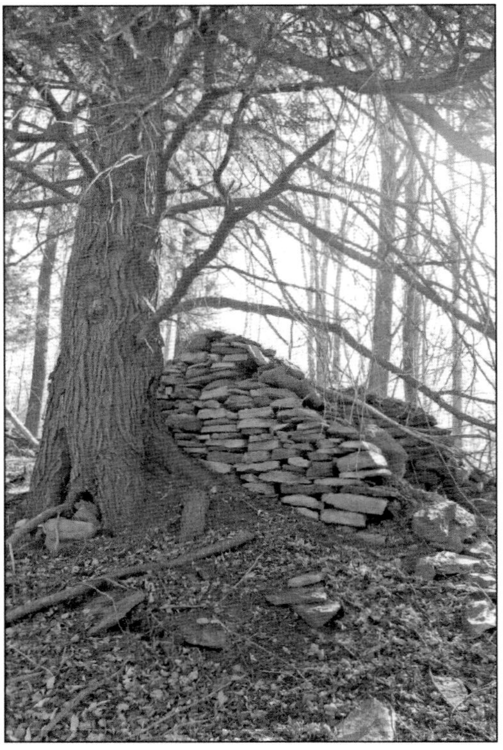

A limekiln outside Nordmont was used by locals in the mid-1800s. Limestone was burned into ash for fertilizer and for cement mortar. This kiln was built of sandstone and stacked without mortar, and perhaps this is the one listed on a F. W. Beers topographical map of Sullivan County (1872). It was near Tilly Road (now private property), which leads from the Nordmont community hall.

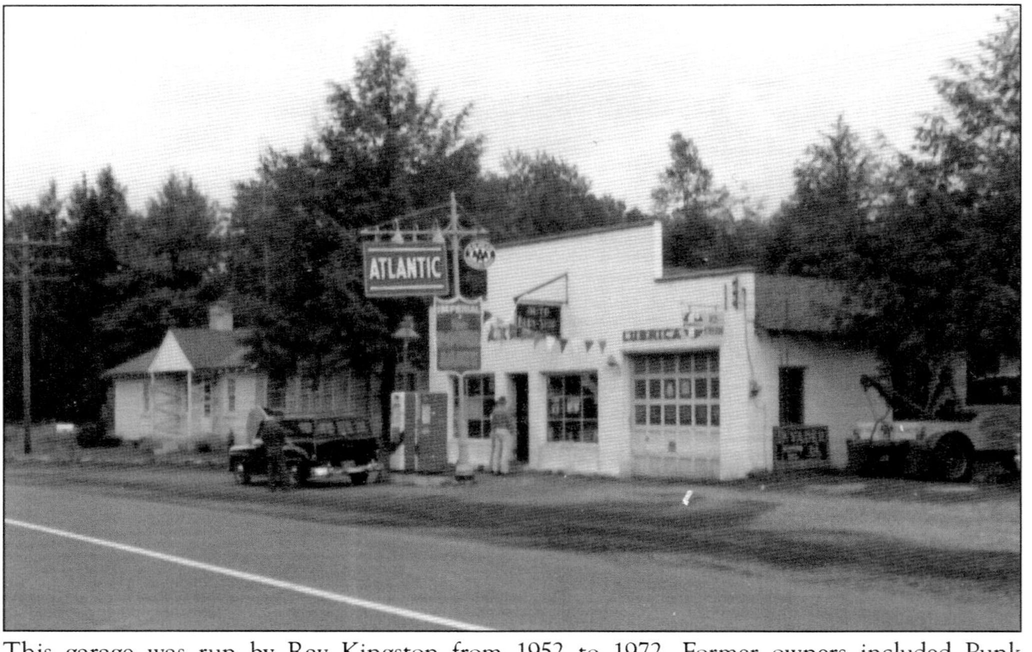

This garage was run by Ray Kingston from 1952 to 1972. Former owners included Punk Houseknecht and Bobby Gumble. Kingston and his wife, Mabel Little Kingston, lived in the house to the left. Located along Route 220, it is now the Laporte Township building. (Courtesy of Fairy M. Walters.)

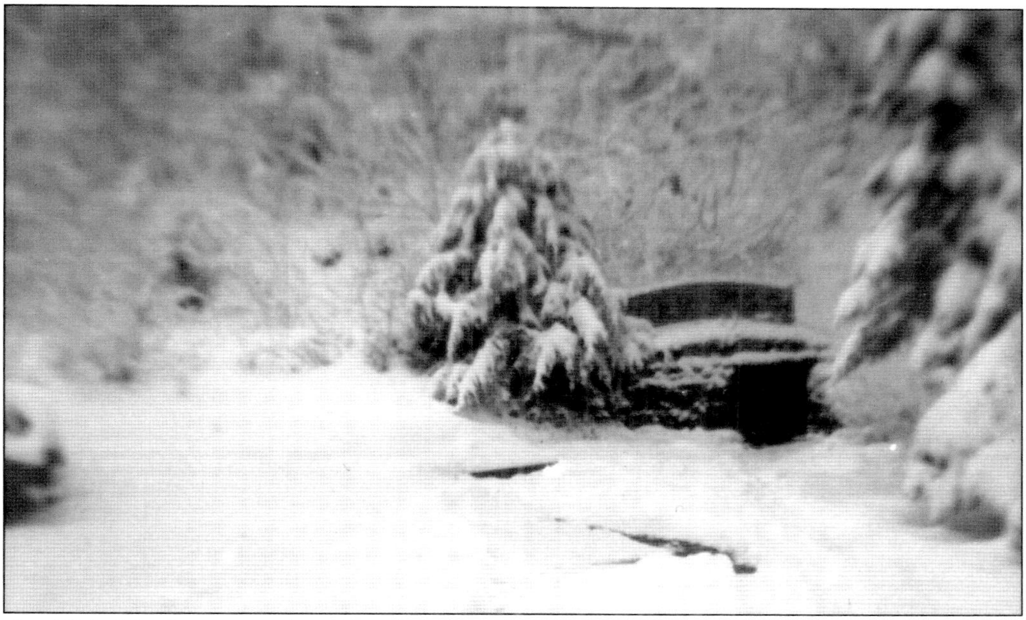

In 1893, Nordmont resident Sara Laird, wife of Thomas J. Laird, met with surveyor and Laporte judge William A. Mason to save the Nordmont cold springs, the only water source available to local residents. Her strong determination to have the railroad resurveyed saved the springs. When she returned to Nordmont, she was asked how she managed. Her reply was, "Grit, just grit."

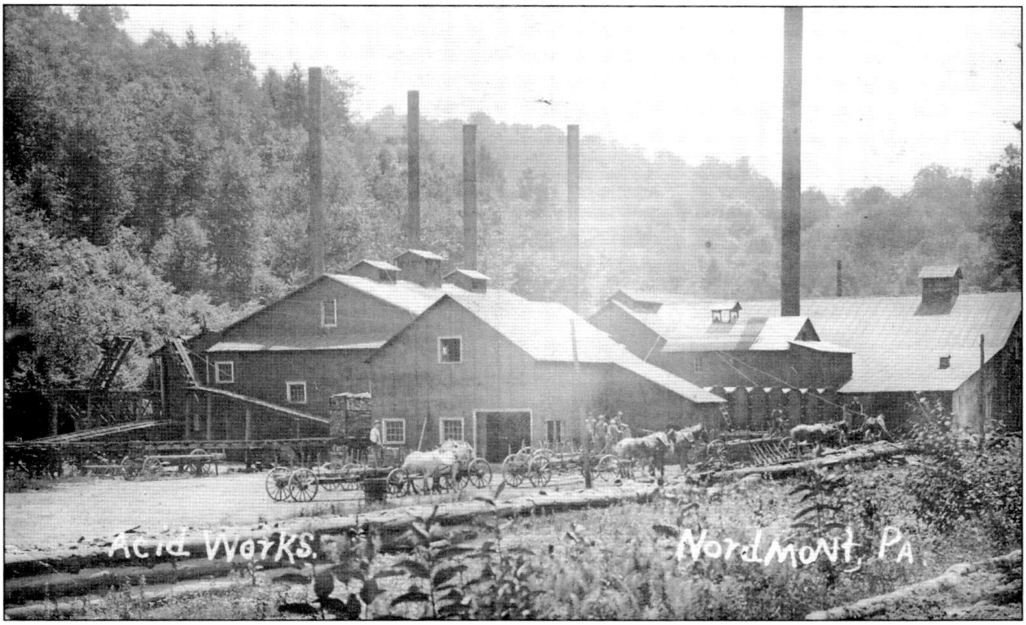

The Nordmont Chemical Company is pictured about 1900 when it produced tannic acid from hemlock bark. Bark was hauled in on wagons. The remains of this site are a short way up Muncy Creek from the village. Tannin was used to process rawhides into leather. In 1923, the holdings were sold to C. W. Sones, who converted it to a sawmill. The mill closed in the late 1930s.

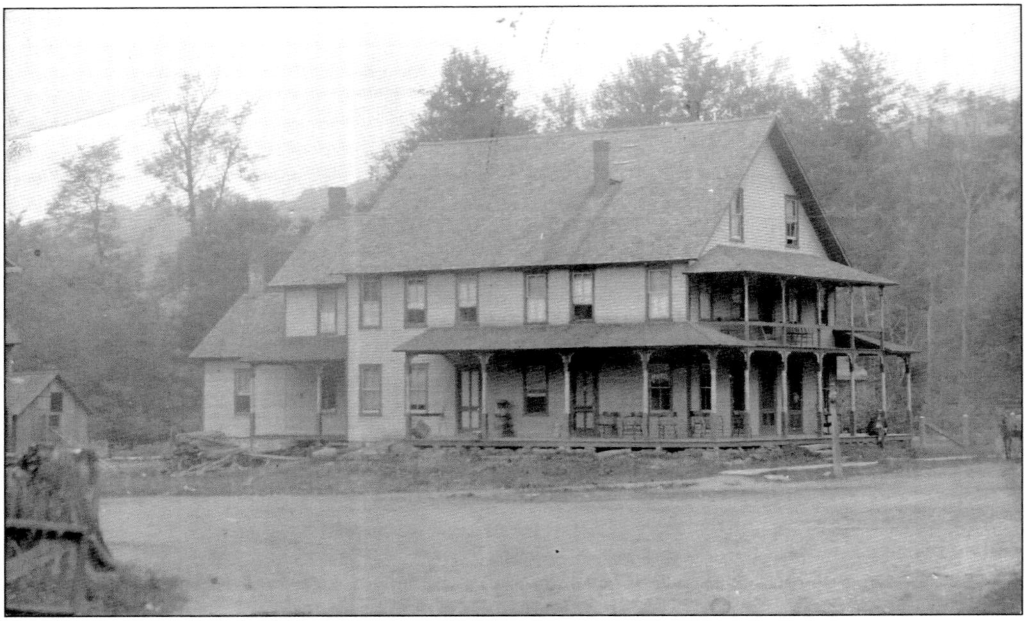

The Nordmont Hotel was built about 1900 and was first operated by George Fiester. Later owners Ben and Delia Peterman Stiger used the old hotel as a residence and rented rooms out to hunters and fishermen from the 1930s until about 1960. The old hotel is now a private residence. (Courtesy of Fairy M. Walters.)

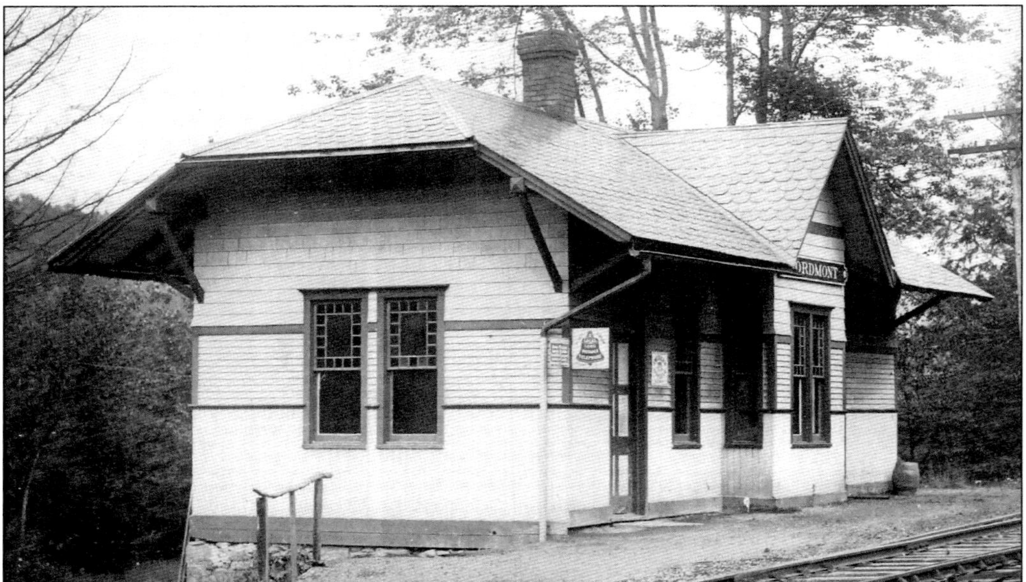

The Nordmont depot was built about 1890 along the Williamsport and North Branch Railroad. The first Williamsport and North Branch Railroad passenger train reached Laporte on August 26, 1893. The sign depicting a bell on the corner reads, "Public station—local long distance telephone." (Courtesy of Fairy M. Walters.)

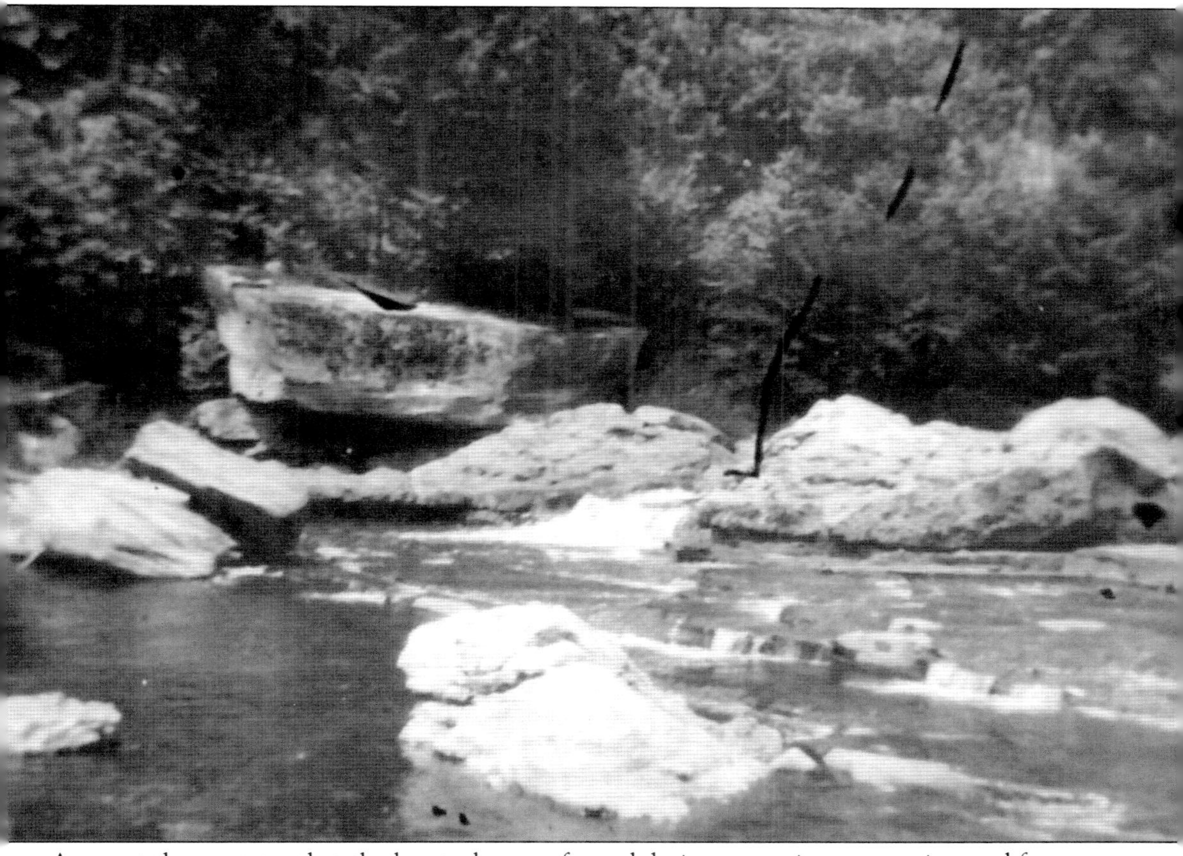

A recent theory states that the haystacks were formed during an ancient tsunami caused from a meteorite and not from the "Big Sock" eroding softer sandstone over the eons. During the lumbering era, two- and three-story-high logjams were frequent here. The natural formation is located about two miles west of Route 220 at the Big Loyalsock Creek. (Courtesy of Louise Molyneux Woodhead.)

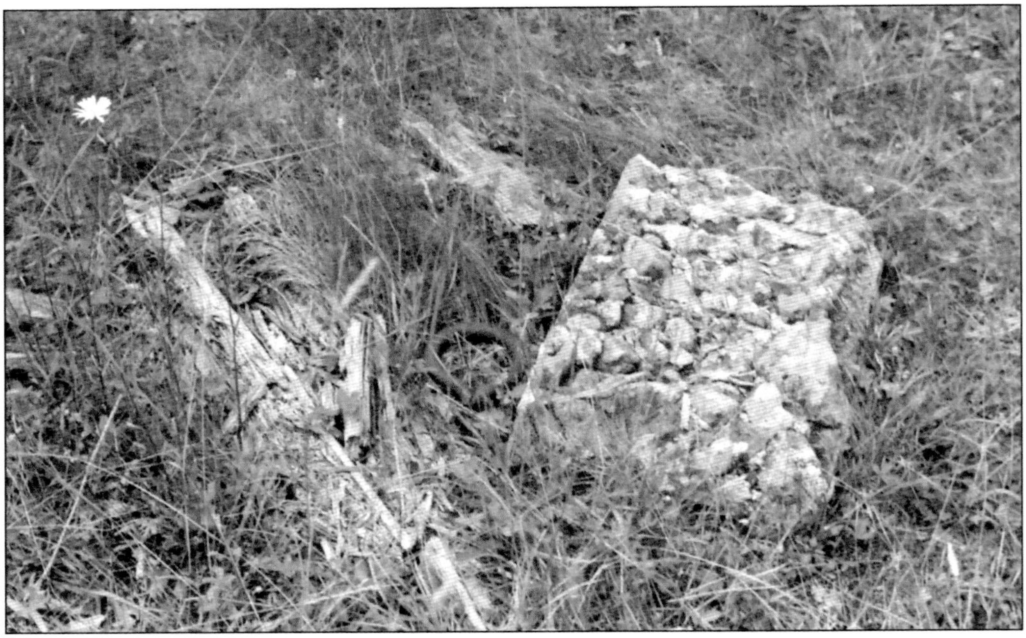

Purchased in 1850 by Millerite Peter Armstrong, the Celestia community was embarking on the sale of lots in 1853 for $10 each. Millenarian movements in the 1830s and 1840s included the Shakers, the Perfectionists, the Mormons, and the Millerites. In 1864, Armstrong deeded the property to God, declaring it free from taxation. His wife, Hannah, did not believe in the movement, but her business acumen kept the town surviving. After the predicted date of the Messiah's second Advent arrived and passed (1866), Celestia became a ghost town. In 1876, the county sheriff auctioned the property for back taxes ($30.10). Armstrong died in 1887. Only foundation stones and bricks (above and below) mark where Celestia was located between Laporte and Eagles Mere.

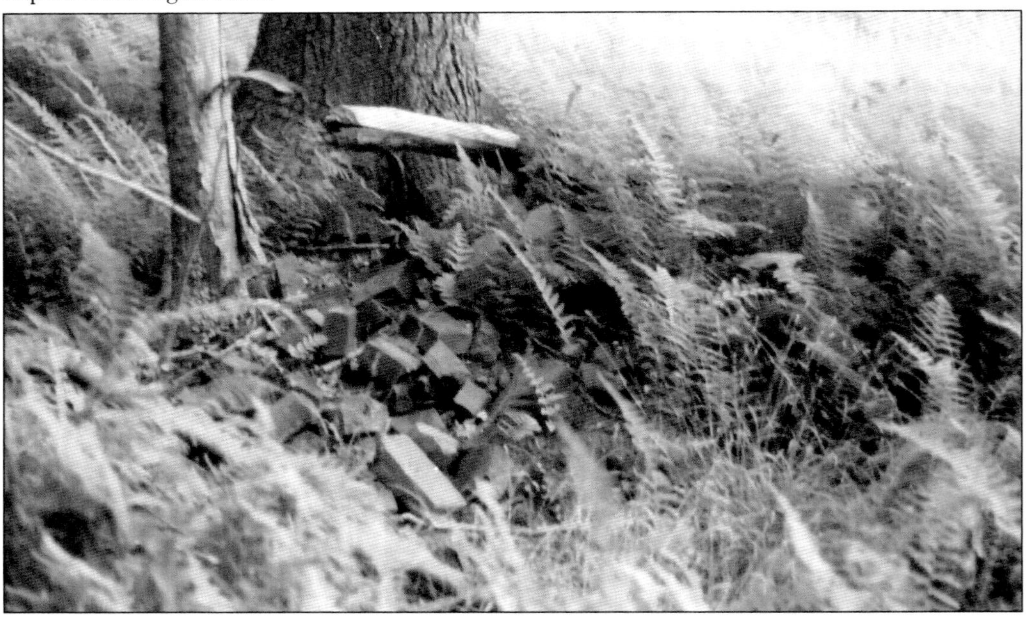

Nine

Shrewsbury Township

Shrewsbury Township was established by a decree of the court of Lycoming County in 1803. The rest of the county's townships were cut off from Shrewsbury, which was probably named after the township in Monmouth County, New Jersey, the original home of the Littles and Bennets who settled in Sullivan. Its boundaries are Davidson Township and Lycoming County to the south, Lycoming County and Hillsgrove Township to the west, Forks Township to the north, and Laporte Township to the east. Eagles Mere Lake and Hunter's Lake are the two large lakes in the central portion of Shrewsbury. Before its reputation as a resort, Eagles Mere was noted for its sands used in glassmaking (around 1810) and lumbering (late 1800s and early 1900s).

The borough was organized in 1899 as Lewis Lake, and the name later changed to Eagles Mere, meaning lake of the eagles. As Eagles Mere became more popular as a resort, numerous hotels were built with modern conveniences, including electric lights and sewage systems. The chautauqua and rentable cottages added to its appeal. A narrow-gauge railroad was built from Eagles Mere to Hillsgrove.

One half mile long and half a mile wide, Eagles Mere Lake (Lewis Lake) is located at 2,000 feet on the spur of the Allegheny Mountains. The lake averages 40 feet in depth and is fed by numerous springs. White sand still covers the bottom and forms a beach at one end. On early maps, Lewis Lake was often confused with nearby Hunters Lake.

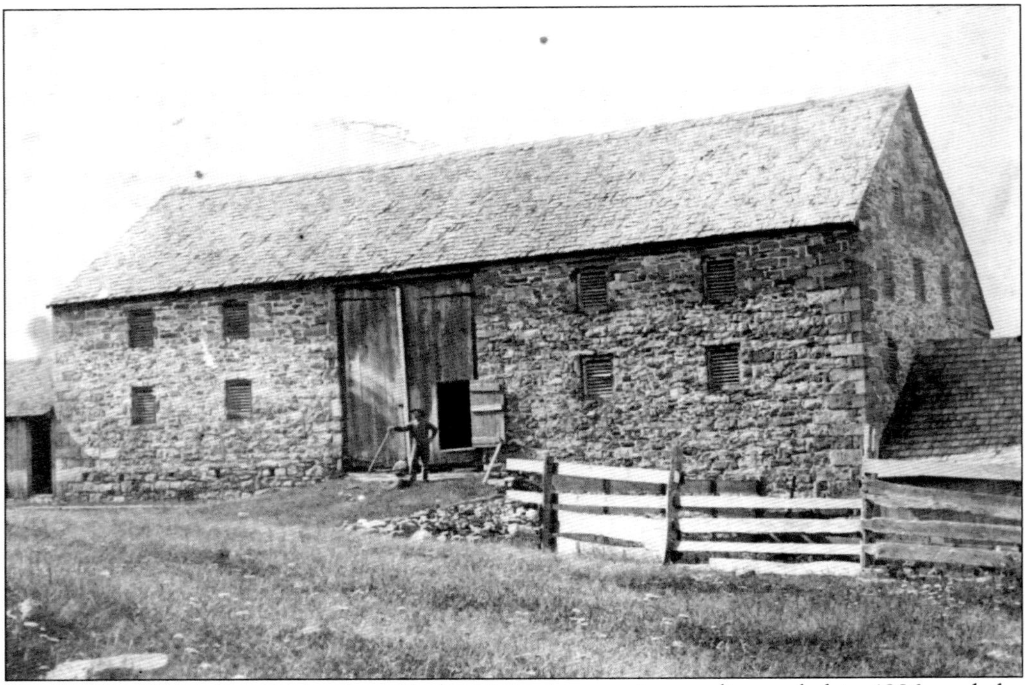

George Lewis's barn once stood on Eagles Mere Avenue. It was dismantled in 1886, and the stone was used to build the Presbyterian church in 1887. The baptismal font in the Episcopal church (below) was two grinding wheels from Lewis's glass factory. There are pieces of colored glass from the glass factory embedded in the communion rail.

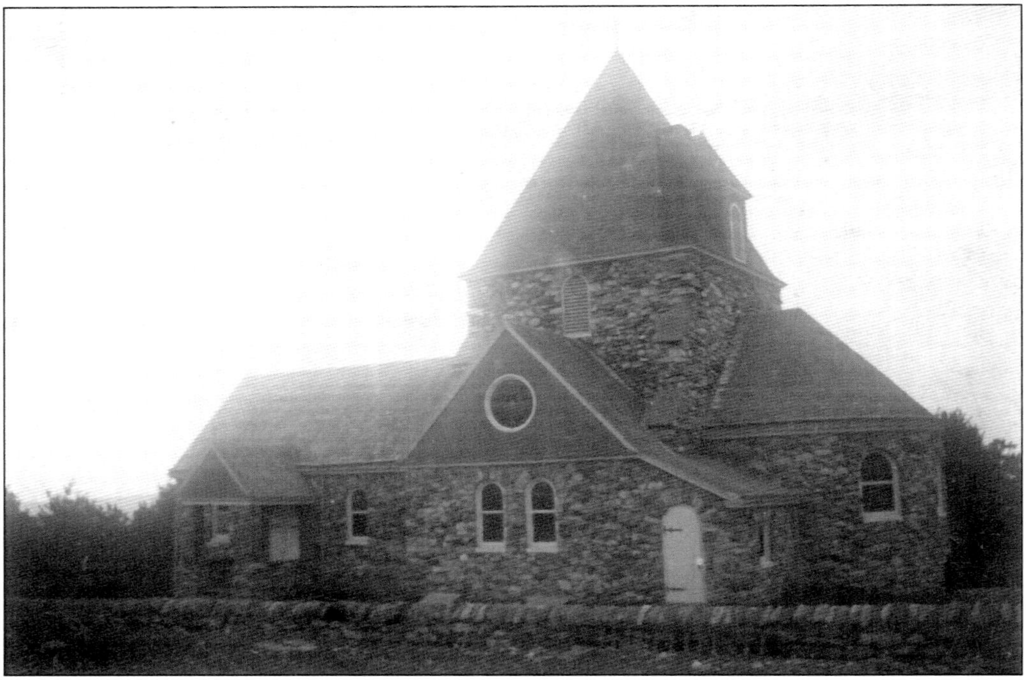

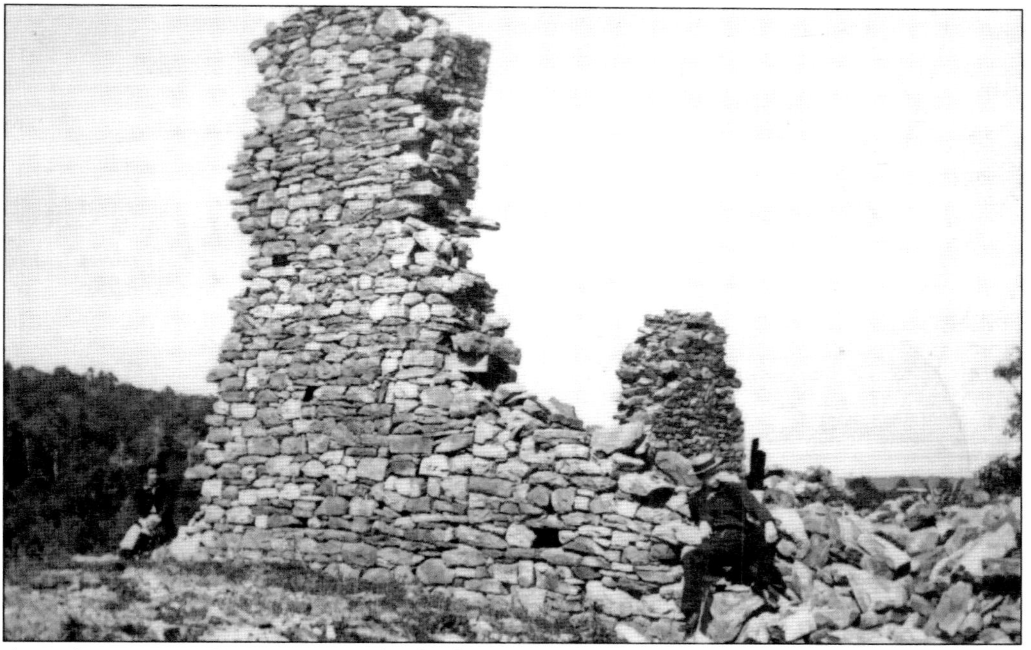

According to an 1868 interview with Charles Shoemaker, the glassworks at Lewis Lake had been abandoned and were partly in ruins by 1820. Charles Howlet, who kept a store at the lake, was probably left in charge of the property and was said to remain there until 1832.

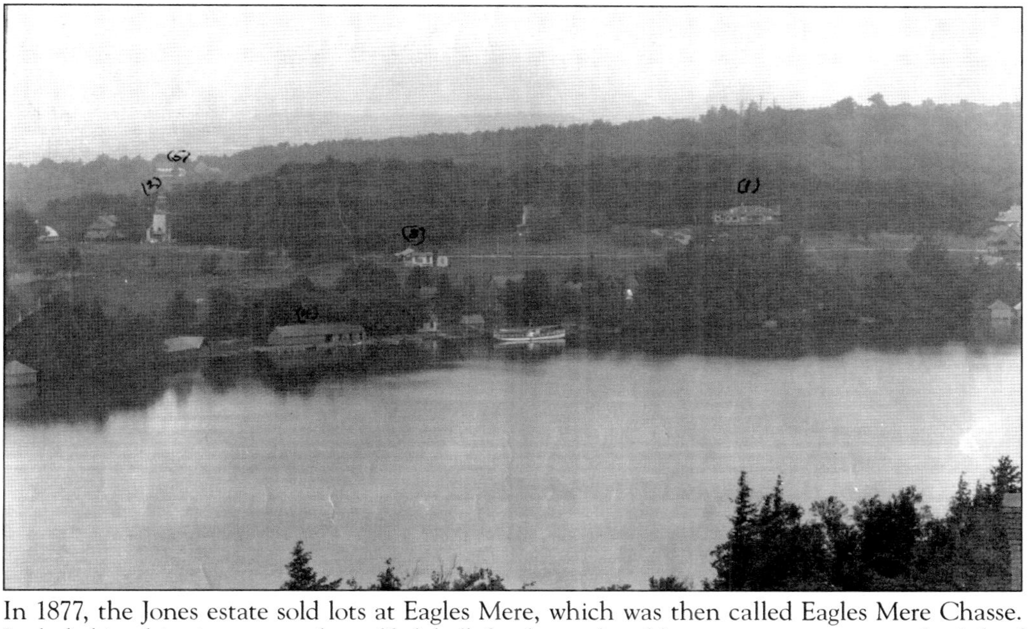

In 1877, the Jones estate sold lots at Eagles Mere, which was then called Eagles Mere Chasse. Included in this picture are the golf club (left, above church), a summer cottage to the left of the Presbyterian church, Ralph Philip's studio (white building left of center), a summer cottage (last building on right), and the Eagles Mere Landing (foreground, left center). The Raymond Hotel was to the right out of the picture. By 1881, the lake boasted a steamboat and hundreds of rowboats.

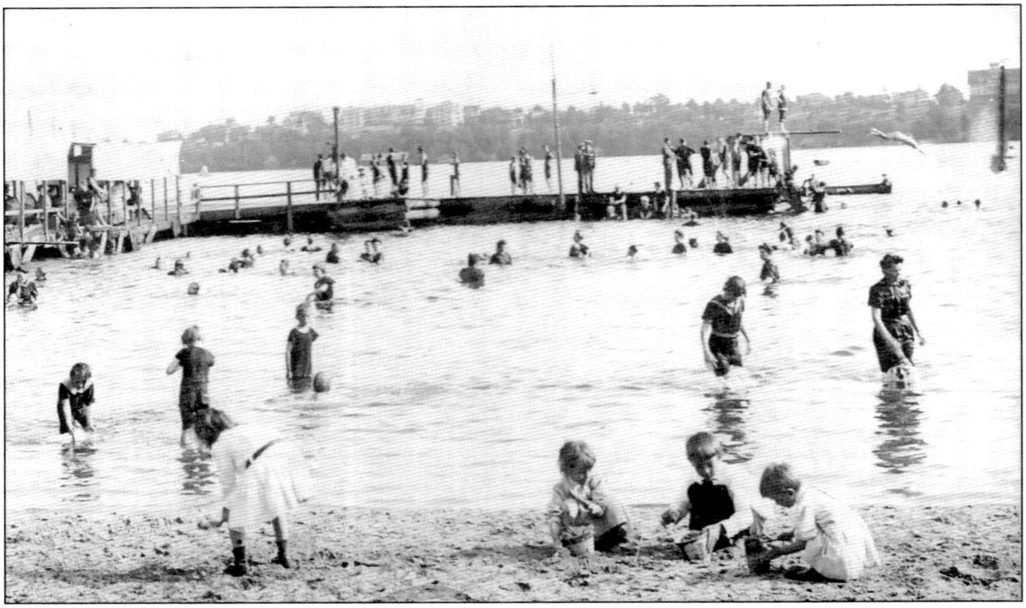

On early maps, the settlement at what became Eagles Mere was called Lewis Glass Works or A Lake, named for George Lewis (1756–1830), an English businessman who purchased 10,217 acres from Charles Walstoncraft of New York State in 1794. Lewis visited his property for the first time in 1803, where he discovered an extensive quantity of white sand. Upon his return to New York City, he learned that many of his friends had died from yellow fever during his absence. Believing that he was spared for a purpose, he returned to Lewis Lake the following year and began his plans for a village and a glass-manufacturing operation.

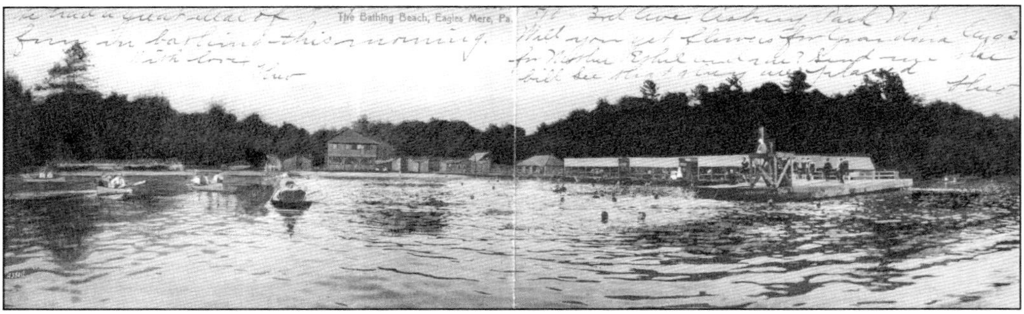

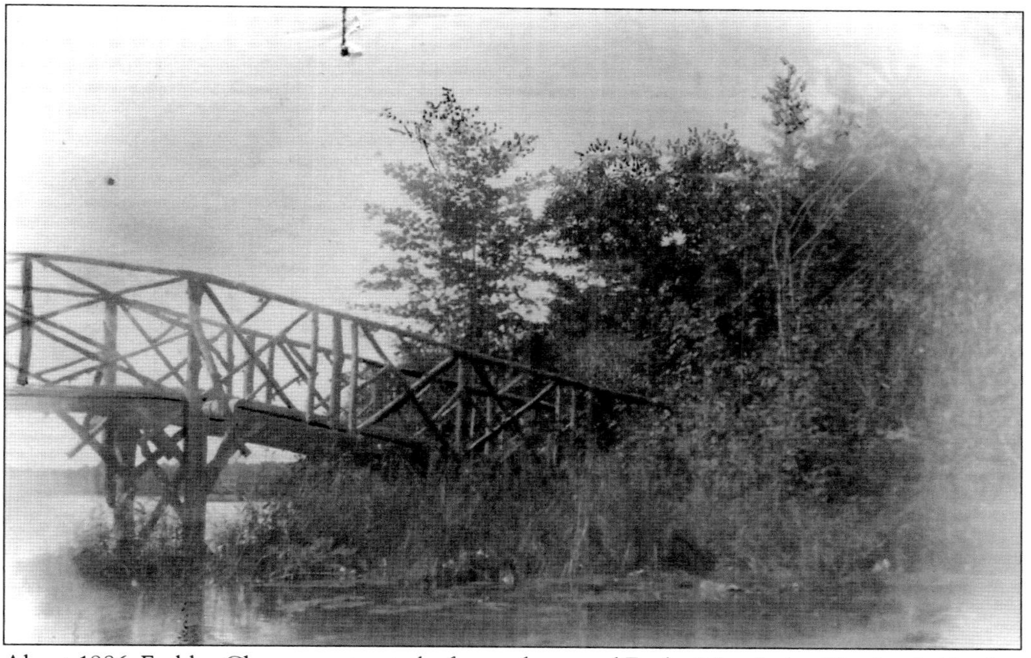

About 1886, Embley Chase constructed a footpath around Eagles Mere Lake. The footbridge has been replaced many times, but one still crosses the outlet.

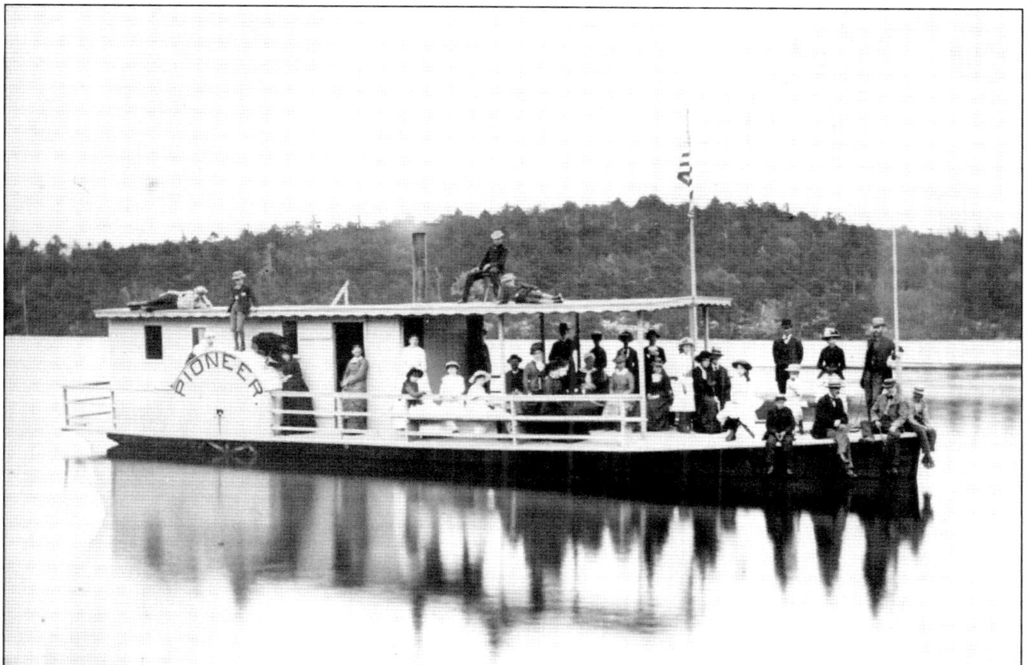

The *Pioneer*, a side-wheeler launched in 1881, was built and captained by H. D. Myers. At 40 feet long, it included an enclosed salon and was powered by an eight-horsepower steam engine. A tour of the lake usually took 30 minutes. In 1888, the steamer was beached at the foot of Lake Avenue and dismantled. The steamer has since been replaced by other boats.

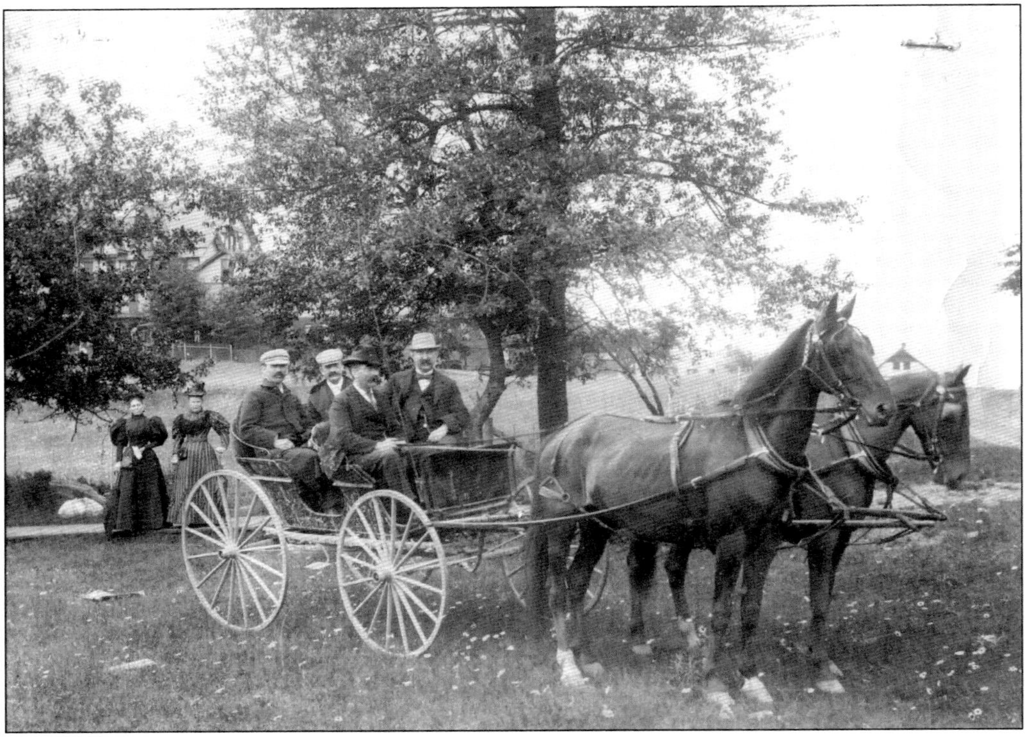

When this picture was taken in 1895, Will Laird (above, holding reigns) was the proprietor of the Raymond Hotel (below), built in 1886. Beside Laird is John Boloker, and in the rear are James Z. Holt and a Mr. Mayhow. The women are identified only as Mrs. Bowka and Mrs. Holt. The Raymond Hotel was named for Laird's son. After Laird's death, the Eagles Mere Hotels Company purchased it and operated it until 1941, when it was destroyed by fire.

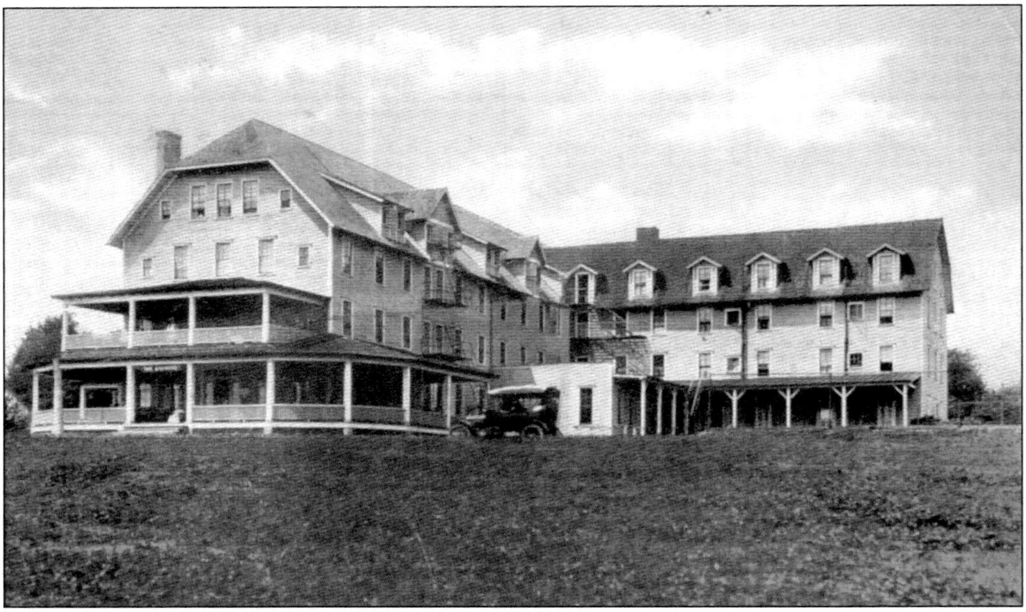

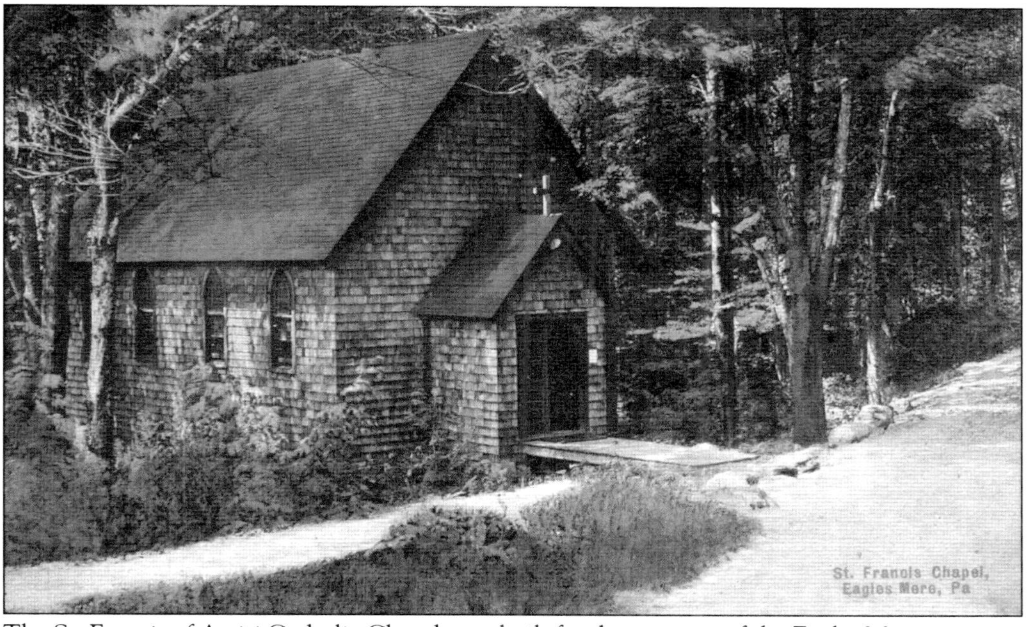

The St. Francis of Assisi Catholic Church was built for the servants of the Eagles Mere cottagers in 1905. Most of the servants were indentured Irish. The chapel was enlarged in 1916, and a rectory was constructed in 1923.

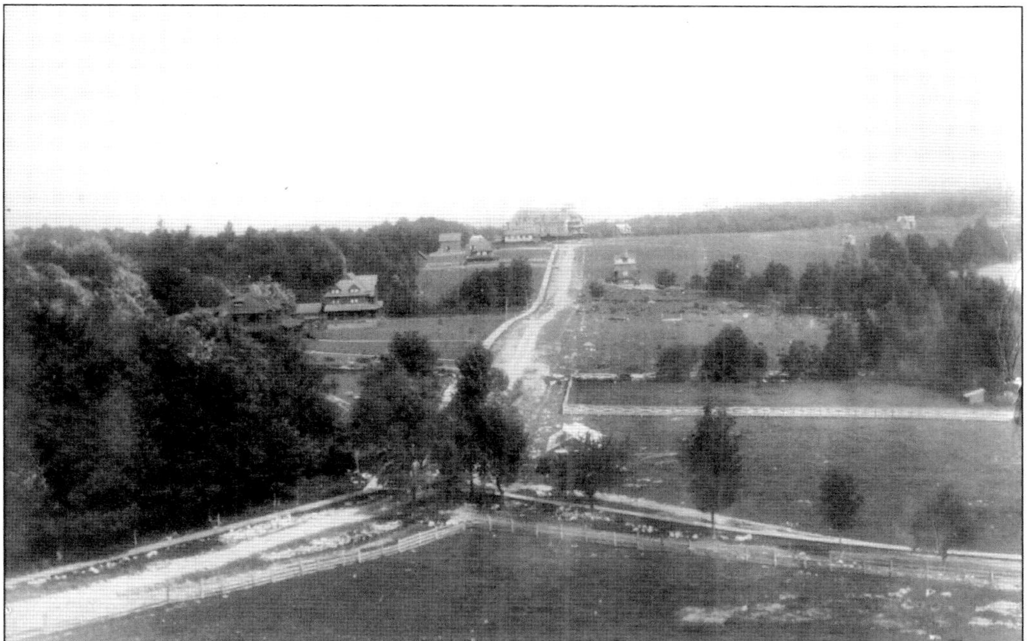

Eagles Mere's Pennsylvania Avenue led up to the Raymond Hotel in the late 1800s. The building in the foreground the behind trees was the photographer's shop. The roof was raised for light. This was first used by Edmond Draper, then by Harrison Krips, and later by a Mr. Phillips of Bloomsburg. The sidewalk is made of boards. The lake is to the right out of the picture.

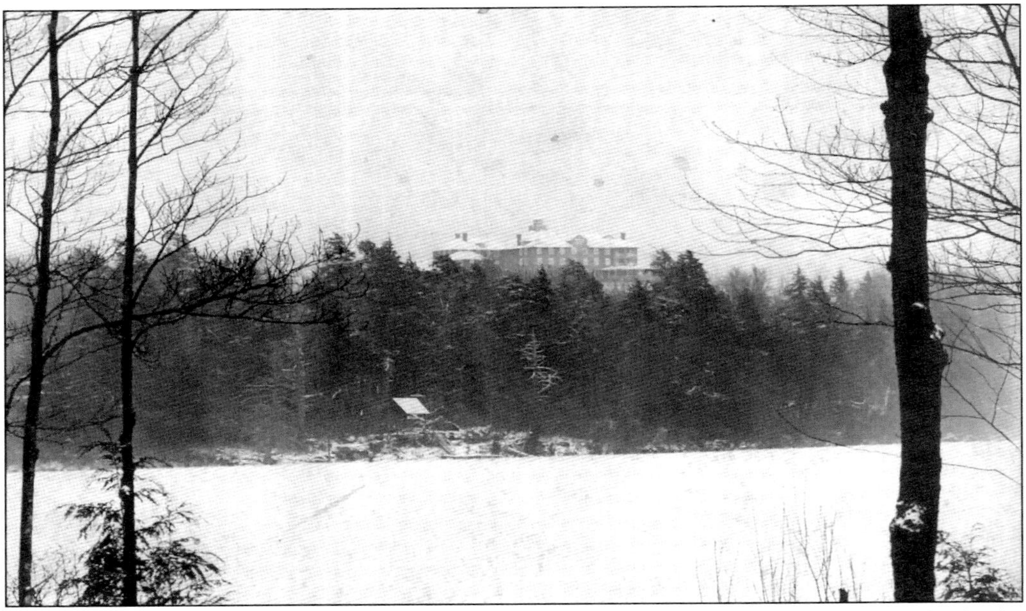

As the result of a visit to Eagles Mere in 1899, William Warner of Germantown built the Crestmont on 22 acres he purchased on Cyclone Hill. It was named due to a tornado clearing off the trees. Subsequent owners were William Woods, Warner's son-in-law, and W. Tingle Dickerson, Woods's son-in-law.

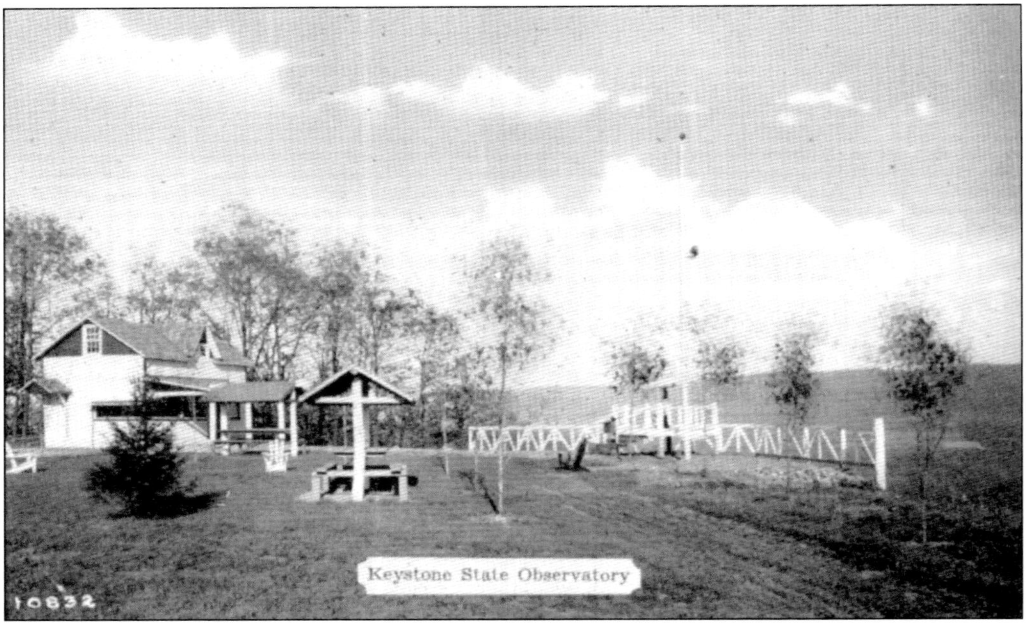

Lorenzo Albertson operated the Keystone Observatory during the 1940s. It was located near Route 42 on Edkin Hill Road and is now Keystone Park. The mountain has a panoramic view of 90 miles and a radius of 450 miles. It was formerly known as Fulmer's View after the family who owned the mountain farm.

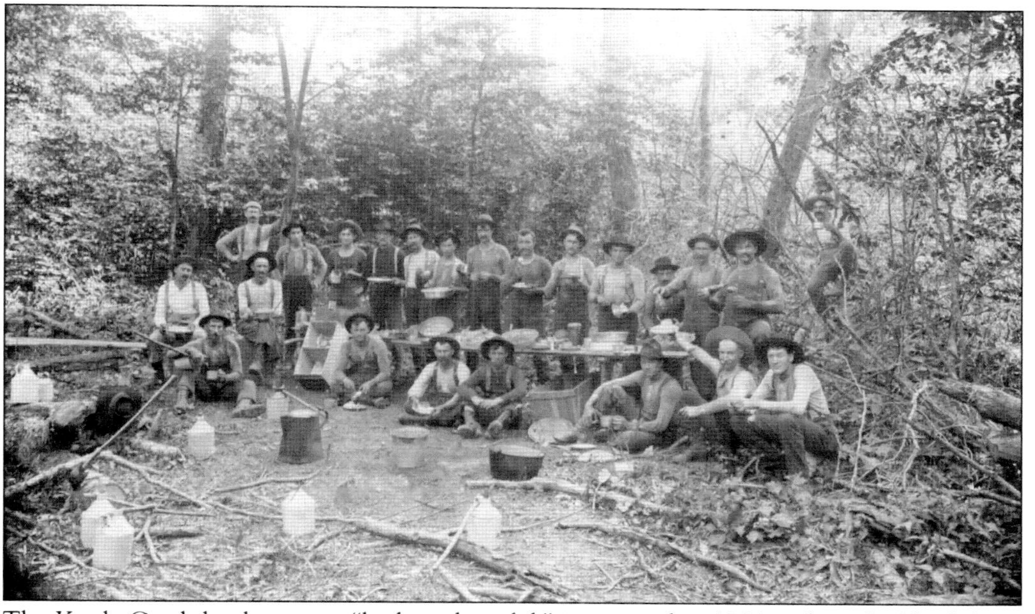

The Kettle Creek lumber camp "bark peelers club" is pictured in 1904 with pushed-back hats, long-sleeve flannel shirts, and high laced-up boots over trousers to deter snakes. Jugs with sticks through the handle contained water or cider and were carried over the shoulder. The big pots held coffee strong enough to peel bark off a tree. The No. 4 camp cut 40,000 feet of hardwood and 50,000 feet of hemlock a day.

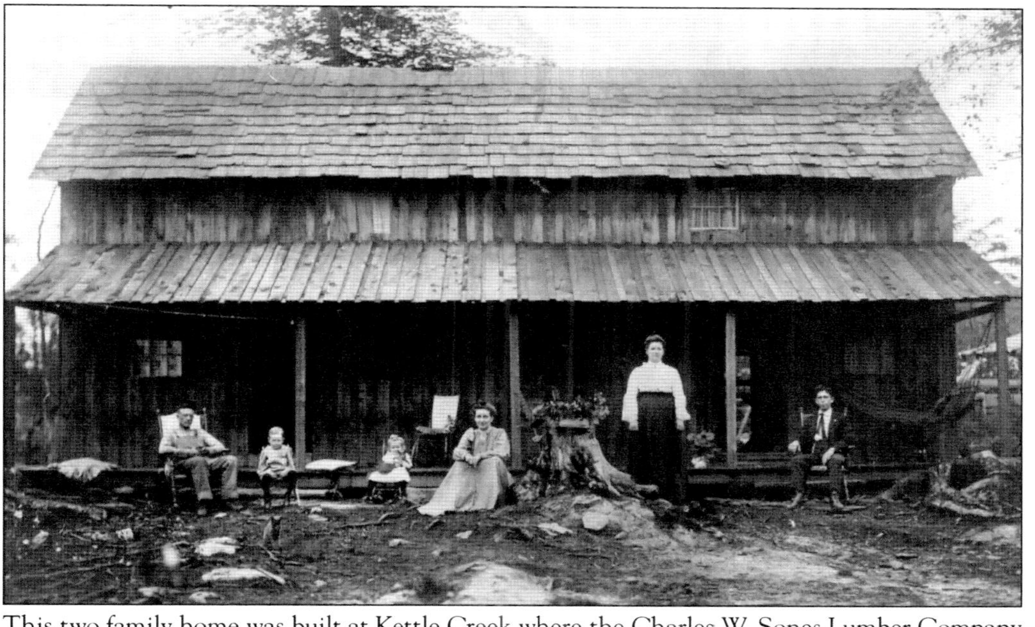

This two family home was built at Kettle Creek where the Charles W. Sones Lumber Company operated a mill starting in 1901. About ten years later, the company was sold to the Central Pennsylvania Lumber Company (Bradford County) that worked this area for another ten years. Pictured are (L to R) Henry Bates, his children (not identified), Mrs Bates, Mrs. George Fraley, and George Fraley.

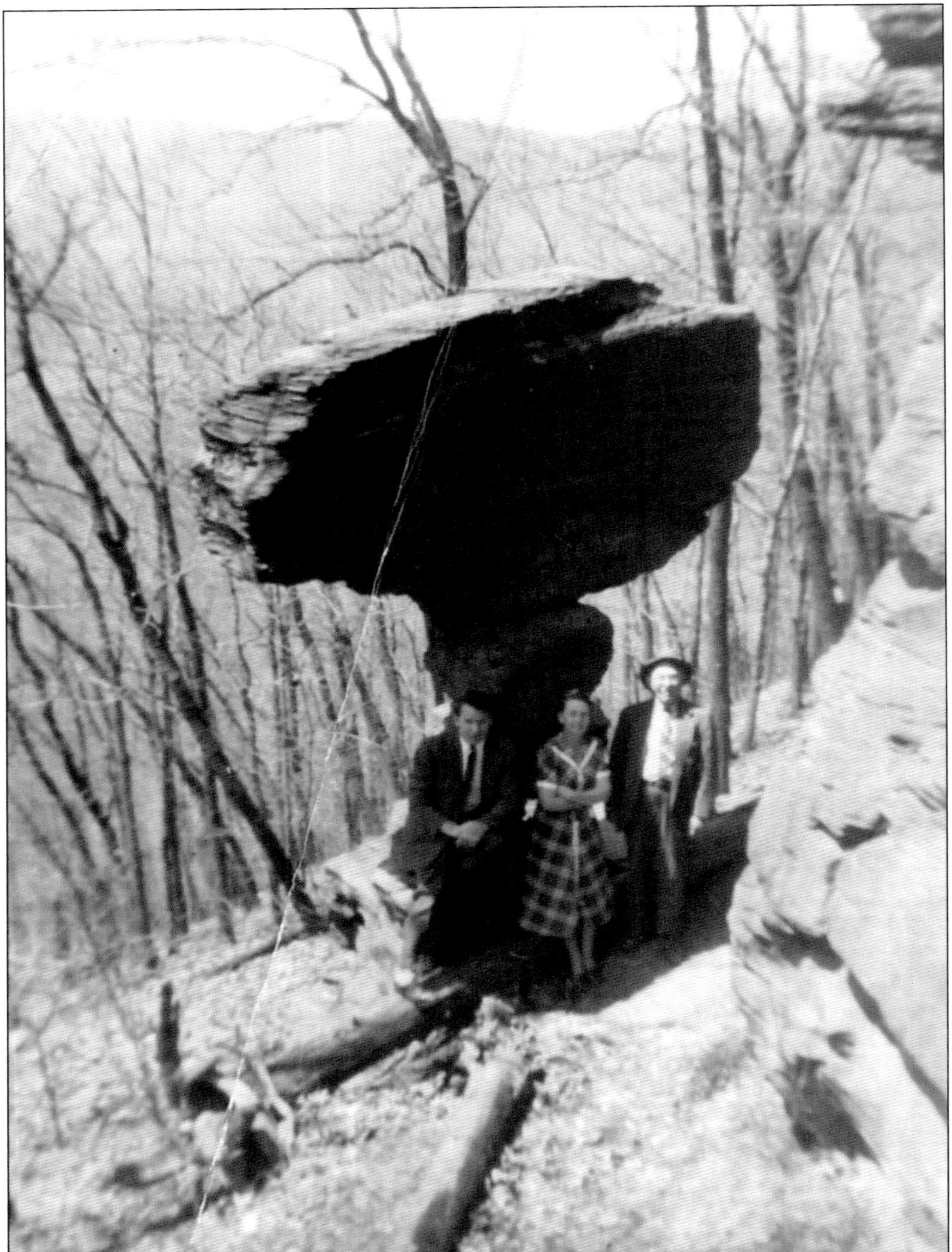

Ticklish Rock is a flat-lying, three-by-eight-foot brown and green sandstone block that is six feet thick. It is "roughly the size of a Volkswagen," wrote one visitor in the 1950s. The 10-foot-tall pedestal is a mere 18 by 30 inches. The whole formation clings to a weathered outcrop on the rim of the Allegheny Ridge. The visitors are unidentified.

BIBLIOGRAPHY

Egle, William Henry. *Illustrated History of the Commonwealth of Pennsylvania*. Harrisburg, PA: De Witt C. Goodrich and Company, 1876.

———. *Notes and Queries: Historical Biographical and Genealogical*. 1879. Reprint, 2006.

Ingham, Thomas J. *History of Sullivan County, Pennsylvania*. Chicago: Lewis Publishing Company, 1899.

James, Barbara C. and D. Bushrod. *'Mere Reflections: A Unique Journey through Historic Eagles Mere*. Montoursville, PA: Paulhamus Litho, 2001.

Rogers, Fred M. and Charles Lose. *Loyalsock*. Lycoming County, PA: Lycoming Historical Society Publications, 1933.

Sick, Adona R. *History of the Churches of Sullivan County*. Self-published, 1965.

Streby, George. *History of Sullivan County, Pennsylvania*. Dushore, PA: Sullivan Gazette Print, 1903.

Historic Hodge-Podge: Past and Present Pioneer Makers of Sullivan County History. Owego, NY: Tioga Publishing Company, 1955.

Sullivan County Industries: Then and Now (1954). Endicott Printing Company, 1954.